Pieced By Mother

Symposium Papers

Jeannette Lasansky
with
Tandy Hersh
Patricia T. Herr
Alan G. Keyser
Sally Peterson
Geraldine N. Johnson
Annette Gero
Virginia Gunn
Ricky Clark
Dorothy Cozart
Barbara Brackman

An Oral Traditions Project

Published by the Oral Traditions Project of the Union County Historical Society, Court House, Lewisburg, Pennsylvania 17837.

Editor, production and finances: Jeannette Lasansky
Design: C. Timm Associates
Photography: Terry Wild
Typography: Batsch Spectracomp, Inc.
Printing: Paulhamus Litho, Inc.

Library of Congress Cataloging-in-Publication Data

Pieced by Mother.

Bibliography: p.
Includes Index.
1. Quilting—United States—Congresses. 2. Quilts—United States—Congresses. I. Lasansky, Jeannette, 1943-. II. Oral Traditions Project (Union County Historical Society)
TT835.P54
1988 746.46′0973 87-31272

ISBN 0-917127-03-X

Cover: Detail of a sampler quilt made by Rebecca Graham, Northumberland, Northumberland County, Pennsylvania, c. 1890.

Inside cover: A page from the Ladies Art Company catalog, St. Louis, Missouri, 1920s.

ACKNOWLEDGMENTS

In 1985 and 1987 three-day-long quilt symposia were held at Bucknell University in Lewisburg, in conjunction with major quilt exhibitions based on original research in central Pennsylvania by the Oral Traditions Project. The results of those exhibitions and symposia have now been published with grant support from a variety of groups, including the Pennsylvania Council on the Arts and the National Endowment for the Arts.

The Oral Traditions Project will next focus its research efforts on the evolution of the dowry in Pennsylvania. The goal is another exhibition and publication held in conjunction with a quilt symposium in the spring of 1990. This time the symposium will be at Franklin and Marshall College in Lancaster, Pennsylvania. At the same time the Heritage Center of Lancaster County is concentrating on Lancaster dowry quilts. Their findings will be the result of quilt search days and documentation. As in the past, when the next symposium is held, there will be simultaneous related exhibitions at area museums and historical societies.

To bring such multi-faceted efforts as the past two quilt symposia to fruition necessitates contributions from many talented and dedicated people, each individual searching through new and familiar materials, assessing their findings and formulating often new ideas—a job sometimes mind-expanding, never dull. We were fortunate indeed, to have had so many fine collaborators on this last symposium. Their material is in this volume. Most of the papers follow in the order in which they were presented: focussing first on different ethnic groups in Pennsylvania and their traditions (the Anglo-Saxons, the Quakers, the Pennsylvania Germans, the Hmong) followed by the issue of "plain" versus "fancy" quiltmaking, and then the plainest of the plain, the "hap," and its cousin the Australian "wagga." The second day dealt with quilt types as they evolved over time and in relation to each other: quilts made of hexagonal pieces—first in template construction, then pieced, friendship or album quilts, fundraisers of all sorts, the Crazy phenomenon, and finally the colonial revival movement. Concluding the conference were papers on the source of pattern names, the latest thoughts on care and conservation, as well as on quilt documentation efforts. The film *Hearts and Hands,* a social history of women and quilts in the nineteenth century, was previewed with Pat Ferrero and Julie Silber, co-producers present.

Allan Keyser's article on Pennsylvania German bedding is reprinted here in a slightly abbreviated form with the permission of the Pennsylvania German Society, which first published it in October 1978. That printing is no longer available. Geraldine N. Johnson's findings also appeared first in *Appalachian Journal* (Autumn 1982) and then in *North Carolina Folklore Journal* (Fall/Winter 1982) and their permission allows us to make it available again in its entirety. By truly serendipitous coincidence Annette Gero, an Australian quilt scholar, was able to extend her visit to the United States and to attend the symposium and share with us some of her research on historical Australian quilts.

The papers represent just part of the excitement of bringing together quilt owners, dealers, makers, collectors, magazine writers and editors, researchers, museum personnel, and the curious for three days of lectures and discussion. Each group was challenged and moved by the presentations. Such was our intent—that quilts not be isolated from the circumstances of their creation, but rather be placed within their social, technical, and cultural contexts. We think we succeeded and we welcome your responses. Ideas of additional research which might be undertaken or refined are not lacking since the public and the scholars in this field are constantly urging each other to explore deeper and further.

I especially want to thank the following individuals for their dedication in making the 1987 symposium such a tremendous success: the speakers Tandy Hersh, Patricia Herr, Alan Keyser, Sally Peterson, Geraldine Johnson, Annette Gero, Virginia Gunn, Ricky Clark, Dorothy Cozart, Penny McMorris, and Barbara Brackman, whose papers and visual materials were uniformly excellent; the audience which responded with thoughtful concerns and questions added dynamism; and Oral Traditions staff members: Emily Blair, Diana Lasansky, Martha Root, Elsbeth Steffensen, and Sue Taylor as well as the Center Gallery staff coordinated by its assistant director, Cynthia Peltier. All were responsible for meeting the needs of over three hundred people and making the event memorable.

Jeannette Lasansky
April 1988

CONTENTS

Quilted Petticoats

Tandy Hersh

When we read or hear the word *quilt,* most of us visualize a bed cover with our favorite pieced or appliquéd design done in contrasting colors. Often, this everyday meaning of the word *quilt* does not call attention to the needlework which secures the decorative top to the interlining and lining. Structurally, these stitches distinguish a quilted item from other textiles, even though we usually relegate the pattern of these stitches to a secondary status as a design element in pieced or appliquéd bed covers.

There was a period in quilting history, however, when the quilting stitches were both the design and the securing device for a particular type quilt that we now call "whole cloth." That name is literal. The cloth was not cut and reassembled. Instead, sufficient lengths to cover a bed were sewn together as they came from the loom, and a design was quilted into this uniform surface. If the cloth had its own pattern, the quilting design was obscured, but if the cloth were one solid color, the quilting design became the only design, often a dramatic one. A general period for this solid color whole cloth quilt is the 18th and early 19th centuries. During this same time, women's petticoats made of one solid color cloth were quilted in a way similar to the whole cloth quilt.

In interior design the solid color quilt was the foil for multiple yards of figured curtains which draped some 18th-century high post beds. The curtains broke up the mass of the whole cloth when they were pulled to the corner posts during the day. In dress fashion the solid color quilted petticoat was the foil for multiple yards of figured gown fabric draped over hoops (fig. 1). Glimpses of the petticoat were caught from the front, sides or back, depending on the drape of the generous gown. The quilt is the size and shape of the bed plus its overhang. The petticoat is the distance from a woman's waist to the floor, with enough material to cover large hoops, approximately 33 by 100 inches. The subject of this study is that rectangle which was quilted for a petticoat that would be partly exposed, fully exposed or completely hidden under a skirt, as styles changed over two centuries. Throughout the paper there will be explicit or implicit comparisons with quilted bed covers.

One feature of a piece of quilted cloth is insulation against the cold, and over many centuries quilted garments have been constructed to meet this need. We are especially aware of this insulating quality in the 1980s. Most of us have synthetic material or down anchored in our outer winter garments by utilitarian machine quilting stitches. The quilted petticoat was first worn as a warm undergarment, but in the 18th century when fashion centers of Europe and England created gowns that opened at the front from the waist to the floor line, exposing part of the petticoat, it became a high style garment, as well as a warm one. For the less affluent, the utilitarian petticoat continued to be worn as a warm garment with other styles.

The silk industry in France, England and Italy gave the fashion world elegant pattern woven materials, and the solid color petticoat complemented or contrasted with the gown material. Varying styles of hoops exposing different amounts of the petticoat produced unusual silhouettes. Some were so exaggerated that the lady's escort had to accompany her at a distance of four feet and she had to collapse the hoops or paniers in order to walk through doorways. Cartoonists saw the humor and poked fun at the impractical fashion.

Men wore embroidered and brocaded clothes trimmed in gold, silver and lace, and an evening party at a nobleman's house in England, on the continent or in the home of a rep-

Plate 1. *Detail of nineteenth century Quaker silk petticoat shown in fig. 7.*

Figure 1. Eighteenth century divided front, brocaded silk gown with exposed quilted silk petticoat dated 1750 in the quilting. The name Abigail Trowbridge, British heraldry symbols, lady in quilted petticoat, man in tricorn hat and motifs typical of the period are quilted with a variant of the backstitch. Attributed to Connecticut. Collection of Colonial Williamsburg. Acc. No. 1951-50 and 1952-19. Photo. No. 075-658.

resentative of the King in colonial America must have been dazzling. The clothes worn by wealthy Americans copied those worn abroad in countries where we conducted trade, and anything available in those markets was available here. People living in America who could afford imported clothes were of the same families, in the same culture, and with the same interest in style as those in their parent countries. An ocean separated the trend-setters and the American consumer, but Boston, New York, Philadelphia, Charleston and other ports had direct access to these fashions by ship. Trade between the old and new countries was active. It was customary for a dress maker in America to interpret imported printed fashion plates and design a gown for a client. Petticoats were frequently ordered ready-made from abroad, while others were made here. By 1763 stores in Cumberland County, Pennsylvania, where I live, sold a variety of imported fabrics used to make clothing. I have seen no ladies' garment in our area associated with the 18th century, but according to inventories the fabrics were available and gowns and quilted petticoats were owned by some of the leading citizens. Quality fabrics and a modish style of dress existed far from a major city.

Men and women are vain and enjoy wearing beautifully made garments, so some of the finest quilting is found on clothing. Examples of 17th- and 18th-century English cord quilted christening robes, hats, caps, vests, frock coats, stomachers, petticoats and entire ensembles of gown and coordinating petticoat are filled with complex designs of infinitely small stitches. There were professional quilters in 18th-century England and America, so even though women were accomplished in needle skills and could have created the quilted fabrics for their families' clothing, it is probable that professional quilters quilted fashion articles because of the amount of time that work took. In 1717 when an English lady was visiting in London, she bought five different professionally quilted yardages to be used for herself and her two daughters. In 1720 one group of professional English quiltmakers claimed to produce 23,000 quilts annually. American newspapers advertised professional quilters during the 18th century also. Nevertheless the line between a highly skilled needle person and a professional quilter is debatable and results in a research problem. For example, an expertly crafted needlecase was embroidered by an English-born Quaker woman, Ann Marsh, who came to Philadelphia in the 1730s. She did not marry and it is thought she taught needlework in the Philadelphia area. She owned a quilted petticoat which she certainly could have made since she had demonstrated with the needlecase the skill to be a professional quilter. However, since she could have bought the petticoat, it is not clear who made it. Among the affluent, many women developed exquisite needlework items, but did this socially accepted work extend to quilting petticoats?

The decorative, exposed, quilted petticoat was popular in England in the mid-18th century, with some examples as early as 1710 and as late as 1780. In America there is a silk quilted petticoat fragment associated with Priscilla and John Alden's daughter before 1720. Two petticoats worn in Connecticut are dated 1750 and 1758 in the quilting, and many undated examples have 18th-century provenance. Pennsylvania inventories taken in Chester and Cumberland counties between 1750 and 1800 mention 28 and 27 petticoats respectively. Around 1780 the Pennsylvania-German folk artist Johann Adam Eyer painted a watercolor of four women wearing quilted petticoats while members of a wedding party. A lady in a quilted petticoat is one of the designs on a 1750 Connecticut quilted petticoat. Apparently the fashionable quilted petticoat was popular in the American colonies in about the same period as in England.

Before we examine how the petticoats were made, we should note how they were worn by listing, in dressing sequence, the clothes of a 1770s French doll in the Colonial Williamsburg collection (fig. 2). The garment worn next to the skin is a cotton shift. On top of the shift are stays into which a lady was laced to achieve the posture needed for the dress style. Next is a cotton petticoat and then a separate quilted pocket held on by a tape tied at the waist. On top of the cotton petticoat is a quilted cotton under-petticoat. The exposed quilted silk petticoat is next with a panel at the front matching the detail of the gown which is open from the waist to the floor. The rest of the petticoat is quilted in squares set on point. There is a pocket slit where the wearer could reach through the petticoat to the pocket. The gown is added. At the side, part of the gown could be pulled up to reveal the petticoat at the side as well as the front. This is adjusted by a cord permitting more or less of the petticoat to show. The last article is a stomacher covering the stays. Dolls like this one aided a dressmaker in copying the styles of a period. This doll shows there were two quilted petticoats, one under and one exposed, which complicates the analysis of inventory material when the term quilted petticoat is given.

Think of yourself as an 18th-century lady wanting a fashionable quilted petticoat and ready to make the decisions of what kind and what color fabric, which quilting technique to use, what design would please you and whether you or a professional would quilt the material. You would need to take time making these decisions because this would be a major clothing investment, to be worn with many different gowns and altered later for other family members, even in another generation perhaps. Many of the petticoats have had waist bands and hem bindings replaced and pocket slits sewn together or relocated to accommodate smaller or larger women.

I examined quilted petticoats in museums and private collections in Rhode Island, Massachusetts, Connecticut, New York, Pennsylvania, Delaware, Washington, D.C. and Virginia. Using that group of petticoats I found this range of choices which would have been available to you. You could choose one of three fabrics for the outer material: solid color plain weave silk, satin weave silk or glazed wool, often called calamanco. The inner lining could be either carded wool or cotton fibers. The lining could be glazed or unglazed wool, and less often linen. Your color selection could include scarlet, rose, pink, cream, gold, apricot, olive-green, blue-green, pale green, various blue tones and white.

You might have chosen 18th-century loom quilted silk yardage made in France and England in a variety of solid colors and quilting patterns which was sold in America. This was called "Marseilles." A few people in the Chester County inventories owned petticoats of this material in the 1780s and 1790s. An 1809 inventory of a Cumberland County tailor listed "one Masall petticoat patron" and several pieces of "Masall quilting." In addition to this loom product, I found four different techniques of hand stitching used in 18th-century decorated petticoats: running stitch, stuffed work, cord quilting and a variant of the back stitch. With all four kinds of quilting, you could have chosen matching or contrasting color thread.

The running stitch was most frequently used. Some petticoats were done completely this way and I found it somewhere on every petticoat I studied. It is still our traditional, or most popu-

Figure 2. *An eighteenth century doll illustrates the items of clothing worn in the 1770s including: a cotton shift, a plain cotton under petticoat, a quilted cotton under petticoat, a quilted cotton pocket, a quilted silk petticoat and a divided front silk gown with stomacher. Collection of Colonial Williamsburg. Acc. No. 1966-169. Photo. No. C66-319.*

Figure 3. Detail of a red glazed wool petticoat dated 1758 in the quilting. The border shows a mermaid, deer, rabbit, flower and close diagonal background all done with variant of backstitch. The body of the petticoat done with running stitch in an overall diamond motif is separated from the border by scalloped bands. Made for or by Sarah Halsey and attributed to Connecticut. Collection of the Connecticut Historical Society in Hartford. Photo: Robert J. Bitondi.

lar, quilting stitch. Some of the running stitch petticoats also had stuffed areas in the border to add a raised, contoured texture. Cotton or wool fibers were carefully stuffed from the lining side into parts of previously outlined designs through pinholes made in the lining. Such holes are observable today on an 1846 quilt which has never been washed. Cord quilting designs were created by stitching two parallel lines of running stitches which formed a small casing through which a cord was threaded. The elevated cord gave a precise outline to the designs. All of the corded examples I saw were in silk. In some petticoats these three stitching techniques are combined.

I have labeled the fourth hand stitching technique a variant of the back stitch. It is the most time-consuming of all the techniques and the most tedious, in an already time-consuming and tedious medium. You have to question why anyone, professional or amateur, would choose to spend this amount of time on a single petticoat. The answer lies in the type of design desired. The dragon on a gold silk petticoat worn in Connecticut measures eight inches from tip of the barbed tongue to tip of the barbed tail (fig. 3). Each curved scale is a series of stitches, and it is obvious that in such a small tight curve the up, down, up, down rhythm of running stitch cannot be used. Even a tiny cord could not outline the scale, so the only way to quilt this type figure was to make one stitch at a time and to draw the thread completely through on each stitch. The regular back stitch is made by drawing the thread through on each stitch, but there is a common hole between stitches making a solid line of thread on front and back. The variant stitches are spaced to look like running stitches on the front cloth but are made as back stitches. This is revealed by inspection of the lining side of the petticoat which does not look at all like a simple back stitch (fig. 4). This variation makes the quilter lose the rhythm of running stitch by having to pull the thread through on each stitch. It sacrifices the guide of the common hole between back stitches and forces a decision on every needle entry into the cloth. In a way it is a form of embroidery, which also develops one stitch at a time. This type petticoat has been found in New England and one has a New Jersey provenance.

The gown that opened from the waist to the floor created a larger area at the bottom. Picture an inverted V. In non-quilted petticoats this larger lower area was accented by some special treatment near the hem line. Fringes, multiple flounces, embroidered bands and applied pleated ruching all emphasized weight of the design at the bottom of the petticoat. The quilted petticoat achieved that emphasis of weight of design with more elaborate quilting in a band around the entire petticoat near the floor. This border was roughly one-third to one-half of the petticoat. The area above the border was filled with overall repeated designs such as squares set on point, interlocking ovals, shells and parallel curving lines. Sometimes the two areas were separated or defined by a smaller decorative band. The machine quilted Marseilles followed the same proportions and had the same kinds of repeated designs. The top overall quilting designs on all of the hand quilted petticoats, including variant stitch type, were done in running stitch (fig. 5).

The inspiration for the designs on the petticoats probably came from horticulture, animal and bird books and from earlier textiles in Europe and England (fig. 6). Fourteenth and 15th century books contain woodcuts of natural and mythical animal and bird forms. A 17th-century needlework picture of Orpheus charming beasts with music includes a camel, an elephant, a unicorn, a peacock, a stag, a monkey, a tiger, a lion, a frog, a leopard, a snail, a cow, a dog, a fox, a squirrel and a wild boar. Later embroiderers and quilters copied these designs. All of these "beasts" were used in quilting the 18th-century variant-stitch petticoats.

Embroidered vines which form a pattern of curves on 17th-century English ladies' jackets are like vines found in art of the Middle Ages. Flowers placed in the curves appear to be framed by the vines. This relationship is also found in quilting. In other embroidered pieces fruit trees, bunches of grapes and flowering plants are stitched in a fanciful way with little or no attention to scale. Again there are early quilted examples of these designs. Leaves, flowers, fruit, curving vines and plumes are found on petticoats with running stitch, stuffed work and cord quilting. These designs are also quilted on the variant type petticoats, but in addition there are the exotic motifs of peacocks, snakes, lions, turtles, fish, mermaids, sailing ships, people in period dress, heraldry symbols and confronting animals made possible by the method of stitching. The animals on the variant stitch petticoats seem more exotic with their skeletal rib cages. Designs in the borders of these petticoats stand out against the close, compacted diagonal quilting that surrounds them providing a contrasting background.

After your choices of kind of material, color, stitch technique, size border, design and quilter resulted in a quilted rectangle, there was still the actual sewing to be done. A piece of unquilted material was sewn across the 100-inch top edge to be pleated or gathered at the waist. Two pocket slits were cut into the quilting and bound with silk tape matching the petticoat. The 33-inch sides of the rectangle were sewn together to make a cylinder. A waist band was added to the front and to the back between the pocket slits. Tapes for tying the petticoat on were sewn on each side of the pocket slits. The material was too heavy to turn up a bottom hem, so a matching silk tape was applied as hem binding.

Concurrent with the floor-length gown with its divided skirt and decorated petticoat, there were other styles worn in the 18th century appearing more like jackets, with fully exposed petticoats. One was the short gown. It had a low cut neck, long sleeves, a front opening, draw strings at the neck and waist and ended slightly below the waist. It corresponds somewhat to our over-blouse and the petticoat to our long skirt. When described in 18th-century sources the two pieces are usually of contrasting colors or fabrics. Ellen Gehret's book, *Rural Pennsylvania Clothing* (York, PA: Liberty Cap Books 1976), gives historical material, pictures of short gowns and detailed instructions for making one. Claudia Kidwell's article in *Dress* (Vol. IV, 1978) has period paintings of the gowns, and adds an analysis of 28 which she studied. Miss Kidwell suggests that the majority of women in colonial America wore the short gown because they could not afford the fabric for the more fashionable gown and because they needed a comfortable garment for daily living.

In my Cumberland County inventory study, I found 104 short gowns between 1772-1800. In 1784 a Scots-Irish woman had three quilted petticoats, eight long gowns and no short gowns. In 1794 a German woman had eleven short gowns, fourteen petticoats and no long gowns or quilted petticoats. Long and short gowns and quilted and nonquilted petticoats were sometimes in the same inventory, so it is difficult to be precise about how these garments were worn. In any event, whenever the short gown was worn, the petticoat was exposed and a utilitarian quilted petticoat could have been worn with it as an outer garment. This style had a popularity that bridged the 18th and 19th centuries and may account for quilted petticoats found in some collections.

I did not find the quilted petticoat documented as a popular style in 19th-century America. *Godey's Lady's Magazine* fashion plates, fashion notes and needlework sections make only two references to quilted petticoats from the late 1830s-1900. In a search for a specific early 19th-century dress style that included a quilted petticoat, I found one dress and quilted petticoat combination worn by Mrs. Daniel Hake, a Quaker, around 1828. The Historical Society of York County owns the matched ensemble. The interest for us is that the petticoat is completely hidden and yet is not a utilitarian undergarment. The material is a three-over-one twill weave, iridescent, grey-green silk. The running stitch quilting pattern is three-quarter-inch diamonds for the border and two-inch diamonds for the overall top pattern. It is 78 inches around the bottom and 37 inches long. It is lined with brown glazed cotton and interlined with cotton fibers. It has a six-inch placket but has no pocket slits. The material is pleated to the waist band. The quilting lines are not always parallel, nor do they keep the same angle from beginning to end, so the patterns do not match at the seam. Neither the petticoat nor the dress appear to have been made by a professional seamstress.

Since there are more than 30 silk quilted petticoats from the 19th century in the collections of Chester and Montgomery county historical societies, most of which are associated with Quaker families, it is possible that they are the remaining parts of similar gown and hidden petticoat ensembles. Underarm perspiration and stains on the dresses have caused sufficient damage for many dresses to be discarded. The predominant colors of the surviving petticoats are brown, tan, grey and black, although other brighter colors were also found, grey-green, blue, rose, mauve, white and ecru. The proportion of border to overall pattern found in the 18th-century examples is preserved in these, but the patterns are less complex (fig. 7). All the ones examined are in running stitch. Single cable, double cable, large plumes with graceful curves, leaves, shells, small squares and diamonds were favorite designs (plate 1).

According to *Godey's,* even though the full length divided skirt was in vogue again and that style was pictured over thirty to forty years, it was combined with a quilted petticoat only in the November 1874 issue. However, large numbers of quilted petticoats that fit no obvious style are evidence that many American women made and wore quilted petticoats throughout the 19th century for warmth and fashion. The materials, methods of construction, amount of quilting and use vary from one petticoat to the next. Some are work petticoats with only straight lines of machine quilting. Others, in black satin and ones with velvet piping as the hem binding, were worn for dress occasions. Two white cotton ones are decorated with nineteen machine-sewn pineapple motifs around the bottom. Another white petticoat has expertly handmade stroke gathers but no ornate quilting designs.

Many different materials were used for the outer cloth: striped silk, satin, wool brocade,

***Figure** 4. Detail of the lining side of a fragment of an eighteenth century gold silk quilted petticoat. The mermaid and diagonal background are quilted with a variant of the backstitch. These longer, sometimes parallel, stitches on the back are characteristic of this technique. Dark blue glazed wool lining provides contrast with gold silk thread to make stitches visible. Attributed to New Jersey. Collection of the DAR Museum, donor Mrs. Robert M. Weber. Acc. No. 3622.*

printed wool, printed calico, white muslin and brown ribbed cotton for example. Indeed one maker used five different scraps of material to construct her quilted petticoat, apparently not for high style. Linings included printed chintz and calico as well as solid color cambric and muslin. The width at the bottom ranged from 76 inches to 143 inches. One was decorated with a hand-knit wool fringe at the bottom hem, but for some reason two quite different colors were used. This group of petticoats, with all of its variety, reminds us of the similar variety of materials, skills, motifs and colors found in quilted bed covers during the same time. One observation about these 19th-century quilted petticoats is that the quilting patterns were often the same ones used on quilts.

Whatever the original use of the petticoat, when the style was out of fashion or the garment was worn out, there was a way to reuse it. For the silk or glazed wool petticoat, the waist band was removed, the pocket slits sewn together and the petticoat was incorporated into a quilt with sufficient material added to cover a bed. One 1800-1825 whole cloth quilt contains a mid-18th-century red glazed wool petticoat. The striped wool petticoat lining stands out in contrast with the solid lining of the quilt. Another quilted petticoat was used to make a doll's petticoat around 1825. A practical person who had patched her printed wool petticoat in four places while it was still in use, removed the waist band and used the rectangle as part of the inner lining of a tied bed cover.

To summarize, the 18th-century quilted petticoats illustrate how the social standard of ornate dress demanded superior craftsmanship to satisfy the need for a woman to own clothes that fit a prescribed style. The style kept driving the quilter to more difficult needlework. Eventually the complexity of designs forced use of a variant of the back stitch, with all of its tedious and time-consuming qualities. Running stitch, stuffed work, corded and loom-quilted Marseilles petticoats had their parallels in English and American bed quilts of the same period. The variant stitch with its irregular appearance on the lining side was not used as far as I know in quilts. Taken together the designs and quilting on the variant-stitch petticoats represent a technical high point in quilting.

Many of the 18th-century high style petticoats were saved and placed in museum collections making it possible to study them. Not so for the other 18th-century style which required an exposed petticoat. Everyday work clothes designed to be serviceable lacked the value at-

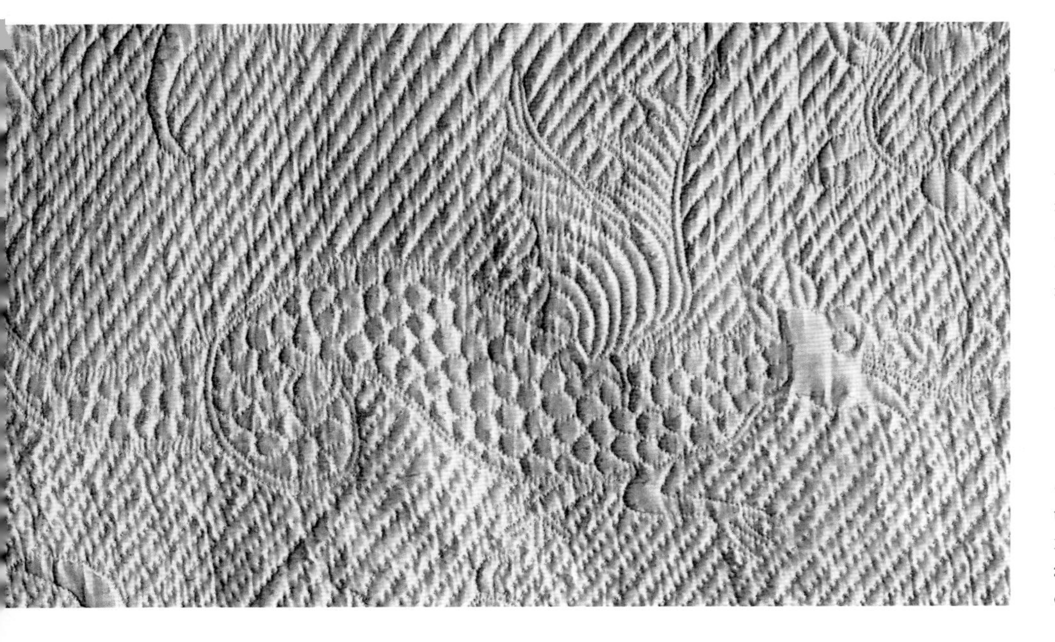

Figure 5. A detail of an eighteenth century gold silk petticoat showing a dragon with barbed tongue and tail quilted with a variant of the backstitch. The dragon is eight inches long. Attributed to Connecticut. Collection of the Smithsonian Institution. Acc. No. 323525. Photo. No. 76-7986.

Figure 6. Detail of a seventeenth century English embroidered bed hanging with exotic plants and animals including dragons with barbed tongues and tails. Collection of Victoria and Albert Museum. Photo. No. GF6473.

tached to the high style garments and were more likely to have been completely used. Some short gowns have been preserved but their quilted petticoats have not been found or clearly linked to them. Quilted petticoats of this period are listed in inventories but none, to my knowledge, is available for study. We may conjecture that the quilting was more utilitarian than ornamental.

In the early 19th century some quilting for petticoats seems to have followed the general style of the exquisite 18th-century quilting. However, the petticoats were worn under dresses. Similarly the utilitarian quilted petticoats were also worn as under-petticoats. For these a wide variety of material was used but the quilting patterns were simple by comparison. Generally the techniques and the materials used in petticoats were similar to those employed in bed quilts of the times. In the earlier period when cording, stuffing and ornamentation by quilting stitches were popular for bed covers, they were also popular for petticoats and other items of clothing. Later when piecing and appliquéing dominated design in bed quilts, simpler quilting stitches and designs were used in them and in petticoats and fewer other garments were quilted, very few if any for ornamentation.

From time to time in the 19th century fashions in gowns, now called dresses, and petticoats, now called underskirts, resembled the 18th-century style. The quilted petticoat, however, was not revived as a foil in design, rather the same material as the dress was used unquilted for the underskirt and ornamented with bows, swags, fringes, pleats, braid and tassels.

***Figure** 7. Nineteenth century quilted silk petticoat. Quilted in running stitch. The body of the petticoat is decorated with an overall shell pattern and the border is an undulating plume motif. Attributed to the Quaker community of Pennsdale, Lycoming County, Pennsylvania. Collection of the Lycoming County Historical Society.*

Suggested Reading:

Baumgarten, Linda. *Eighteenth Century Clothing at Williamsburg,* Williamsburg, Virginia: Colonial Williamsburg Foundation, 1986.

Bradfield, Nancy. *Costume in Detail, Women's Dress 1730-1930, Boston: Barnes and Noble, Inc., 1971.*

Cavallo, Adolph S. "The Kimberly Gown", Metropolitan Museum Journal, 3-1970 pp. 199-217.

Colby, Averil. *Quilting,* London: Batsford, 1972.

Coleman, Dorothy Smith. "Fashion Dolls/Fashionable Dolls", *Dress,* Vol. 3/1977 pp. 1-8.

Ettesvold, Paul M. *The Eighteenth Century Woman (Exhibit Catalog),* New York: Metropolitan Museum of Art, 1981.

Garoutte, Sally. "Marseilles Quilts and Their Woven Offspring", *Uncoverings 1982,* Mill Valley, California: American Quilt Study Group, 1983, pp. 115-134.

Gehert, Ellen J. *Rural Pennsylvania Clothing,* York, Pa.: Liberty Cap Books, 1976.

Hersh, Tandy. "Eighteenth Century Quilted Silk Petticoats Worn In America", *Uncoverings 1984,* Mill Valley, California: American Quilt Study Group, 1985, pp. 83-98.

Kidwell, Claudia. "Short Gowns", *Dress,* Vol IV/1978, pp. 30-65.

Klingender, Francis Donald. *Animals In Art And Thought To The End Of The Middle Ages,* London: Routledge and Kegan Paul, 1971.

Maeder, Edward. *An Elegant Art: Fashion and Fantasy in the Eighteenth Century,* New York: Los Angeles County Museum of Art in Association With Harry N. Abrams, Inc., 1983.

Rowe, Ann Pollard, "American Quilted Petticoats", *Irene Emery Round Table on Museum Textiles, 1975 Proceedings* pp. 161-171, LC76-56646.

Warwick, Edward, Henry C. Pitz and Alexander Wyckoff. *Early American Dress,* New York: Benjamin Blom, 1965.

Tandy Hersh is an avid collector and student of Pennsylvania textiles. Her in-depth work on decorated hand towels was evidenced in Ellen J. Gehret's definitive book on the subject, This Is the Way I Pass My Time *(1985), and in her guest curating, along with Frederick Weiser, an exhibition of decorated hand towels at the Heritage Center in Lancaster that year. Tandy also wrote "Pennsylvania German Decorated Handkerchiefs" for the Pennsylvania German Society in their* Reggeboge *(1986). She has also published three papers on a wide variety of quilt subjects, all for the American Quilt Study Group: "Some Aspects of an 1809 Quilt,"* Uncoverings 1982, *"18th Century Quilted Silk Petticoats Worn in America,"* Uncoverings 1984, *and "1842 Primitive Hall Pieced Album Quilt Top: The Art of Transforming Printed Fabric Designs Through Geometry,"* Uncoverings 1986. *Tandy has also lectured on Pennsylvania textiles at New York University as part of Dr. Judith R. Weissman's graduate course on "Folk Art: Textiles and Needlework," and more recently for the Cumberland County Historical Society and the Questers of Pennsylvania.*

We whose names are here recorded, have paſsed many pleasant
hours, may we humbly look forward with an eye of faith, to a reunion,
in those bleſsed abodes where praise & thanksgiving, are the sweet
strains of the Redeemed of the Lord,
Ann Burns
will please accept this Block as a small token of
regard from her sincere friend S. Wistar who is sensible of
her valuable services bestow'd at the House of Industry. —

Quaker Quilts And Their Makers

Patricia T. Herr

The Quakers, more properly known as the Religious Society of Friends, were meticulous record keepers. Because of this, quilts made by members of this sect often can be well documented. As a body, these Quaker quilts have much to tell us, not only about their makers, as a specific group of people apart from other religious organizations, but also about the art, craft and social history of quiltmaking during an early period of our American history.

In order to put the Quakers and their quilts in the proper context within our colonial and early Republic period, a brief history of the Friends, as they are sometimes called, would be helpful.

The Quaker movement was founded in England in the mid-1600s by George Fox, and the first Quakers came to the American colonies in 1692. These early settlements were in Rhode Island, Massachusetts and Maryland, and by 1681 the first Yearly Meeting of East and West Jersey was held in Burlington, New Jersey.

The Yearly Meeting was the apex of a pyramidal lay organization that had no paid clergy. Within these regional Yearly Meetings were small county-wide Quarterly gatherings, and under these, the Monthly ones, on down to basic weekly or twice weekly Preparative Meetings.

Important to those researching Quaker history and artifacts is the occurrence of the Schism within the sect in 1827. At this time, Hicksites, the followers of Elias Hicks, broke away from the Orthodox Meetings and set up Meetings of their own within the same communities. Generally speaking the Hicksites represented the more rural population. But the result of this break was the establishment of two separate sets of records for Quakers in any given area, and a loss of continuity as far as present day researchers are concerned. Nevertheless, Quaker records, whether they be minutes of Meetings, birth and death lists, or records of other Quaker organizations, are usually well written and complete.

When thinking of the Friends in their context as quiltmakers, we must remember that they were not a separatist religious group as were the Amish and Mennonites. As a result the Quakers and their decorative arts responded to changes that occurred in the society around them more quickly than their isolated separatist neighbors. Thus, it will be valuable to look at Quaker quilts in at least rough chronological order, as the various forms developed. It should become evident to the reader that there were trends in the development of bedcoverings that were quite distinctive, and yet mirrored changes occurring in quiltmaking within the rest of the American tradition.

The earliest documented Quaker quilt, presently known, is a whole cloth silk quilt bearing the inscription in the quilting, "Drawn by Sarah Smith Stiched [sic] by Hannah Callender and Catherine Smith in Testimony of their Friendship 10 mo 5th 1761." It is interesting to note that the date on this piece is written in the typical Quaker manner, listing the month numerically, followed by the day and the year. This quilt, which is owned by Independence National Historical Park, Philadelphia, is illustrated on page 11 of *Forget Me Not: A Gallery of Friendship and Album Quilts* by Jane Bentley Kolter, (Pittstown, NJ: The Main Street Press, 1985). It closely resembles other silk bedcoverings, which appear to be contemporary and have histories of Philadelphia/Burlington County, New Jersey, Quaker ownership. The makers of this particular piece, two of whom were sisters, had ties with both the Burlington and Philadelphia Meetings.

The top is a light blue silk, backed by a natural cotton, which is block-printed with a brown

Plate 2. *Details of a number of squares, large central block and border of Ann Burns's quilt. See fig. 5. Names of 76 of the Society members are inscribed on this quilt. Collection of the Philadelphia Yearly Meeting, Arch Street Meeting. Photos by Donald M. Herr.*

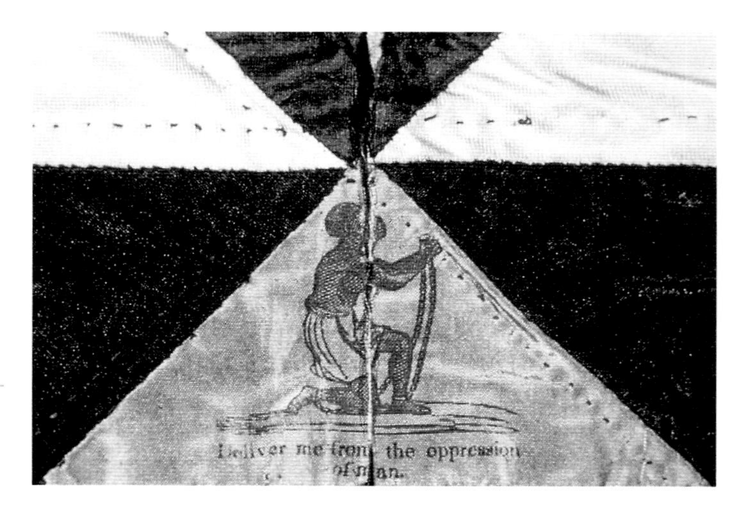
Deliver me from the oppression
of man.

floral design. The interlining is of undyed unwoven wool. The whole piece, which is surprisingly light in weight, is finely quilted together with blue silk thread.

The quilting designs are beautifully executed in a central medallion with a pastoral scene containing houses, trees, animals, rock and flowers. This is surrounded by meandering vines laden with large stylized flowers and leaves. The edges are then bound with silk tape. The technique is similar to that used in the petticoat illustrated in Tandy Hersh's article in this same volume (plate 1).

Silk continued to be a popular fabric choice of Quaker quiltmakers throughout the late 18th and into the 19th centuries. By the early 1800s pieced tops began replacing the whole cloth silk technique in popularity. An example of such a pieced quilt dating sometime prior to 1850, is pictured in figure 1. This quilt and its history as an abolitionist Quaker statement is illustrated on pp. 70 and 71 of *Hearts and Hands: The Influence of Women and Quilts on American Society* (San Francisco: Quilt Digest Press, 1987).

As can be seen in the detail view of a central triangular block, figure 2, this quilt has an unusual theme. Imprinted on a white cotton triangle is the abolition stamp picturing a slave kneeling in chains, with the message beneath, "Deliver me from the oppression of man." The rest of the quilt is composed of small scale printed and patterned dress silks, and appears to have been pieced together using the English template technique.

Fortunately a caring family has preserved the history of this heirloom, and although the quilt was cut through the center at one point in its history, and probably one half given to each of two sisters, the two pieces are now in the permanent collection of The Heritage Center of Lancaster County Inc., a gift of descendant Marjorie Ayars Laidman.

This lovely silk cover accurately portrays the strong convictions of its maker, Deborah Simmons Coates, and her prominent abolitionist husband, Lindley Coates. Deborah, a Chester County resident, married and moved to Sadsbury Township, Lancaster County in 1819. Here in 1833, Lindley Coates was one of the organizers of the Anti-Slavery Society. The Coates's home became a stop on the Underground Railway. In 1840 Deborah's husband attained national prominence, when he was elected president of the American Anti-Slavery Society. It is likely that Deborah created the quilt during this period.

This information was gleaned from a booklet titled, *The Pilgrim's Pathway: The Underground Railroad in Lancaster County* by Charles D. Spotts (as part of a series, *Community History, Vol. 5 No. 6,* published by Franklin and Marshall College Library, Lancaster, PA in December of 1966). Mr. Spotts, while describing in detail the stations and personalities involved in the Lancaster County portion of the Underground Railroad, makes the reader aware of the important part Quakers played in the Anti-Slavery movement in southeastern Pennsylvania.

By the mid-19th century quiltmakers throughout America were producing Signature quilts in large numbers. With a strong sense of community and close religious bond, it is not surprising that the Quaker women were caught up in this trend. Signature quilts could have consisted of repetitious pattern blocks, each bearing a different individual's or couple's name, or a piece in which each signed block was of a different configuration. This latter type are often referred to as Album quilts.

Sophia Pyle's 1848 bedcovering (fig. 3) is one such piece. This quilt also tells us about families who had strong Quaker connections, but for one reason or another were no longer members of the Friends meeting.

The daughter of Joseph and Milcah Churchman Lesslie Pyle, Sophia was 17 when this was made for her by her mother, in Cecil County, Maryland. As can be seen by the legend, "Sophia Pyle's Quilt/pieced by her/ Mother in/ 1848," in the center block of this appliquéd quilt (fig. 4). Milcah Pyle was an accomplished needlewoman. Besides immediate family members, names of other relatives and friends from neighboring areas of Maryland and also Pennsylvania and Ohio appear inked by various hands on a number of the quilt blocks.

Family genealogy and a search of Quaker Meeting Minutes in the Friends Historical Library of Swarthmore College, Swarthmore, Pennsylvania reveal the story of a family that faced difficulties in a time of changing values and more mobile society; a story that might have similar variations in other Quaker families of the period.

The maker, Milcah Pyle, was the daughter of a Quaker mother and a father who had left the Friends. At the time of their marriage, her husband, Joseph, was still officially a member of the Hicksite Nottingham Monthly Meeting in Maryland. Previously he had been a member of the Deer Creek Meeting in Maryland and earlier the Little Britain Meeting in Pennsylvania, where his family originated.

At the time of their marriage and birth of their first child, Sophia, the couple must have faced difficult times, as Joseph's name was continually being mentioned in Meeting notes as taking "strong drink in excess," "apologizes in writing," "drinking again," and meeting with the committee appointed to deal with the situation. Finally on the 14th day of the 1st month 1831, Joseph Pyle was disowned.

Members were disowned from Meeting for many reasons during this period of time. Some examples taken from an article by Willard Heiss, entitled "Guide to Research in Quaker Records in the Midwest," published in *Indiana History Bulletin,* Vol. 39, pp. 51-53 (March-April, 1962), other than "drinking spiritous liquors and keeping ale drink and giving it to oth-

Figure 1. *Quilt made by Deborah Simmons Coates, born in Chester County, Pennsylvania, and married to prominent anti-slavery leader Lindley Coates in 1819. They lived in Sadsbury Township, Lancaster County, Pennsylvania. Pieced (probably by English template method), silks and cottons, c. 1840. This quilt had been cut through the middle to be divided between relatives, 96" × 89". Collection of the Heritage Center of Lancaster County Inc. Photo: This quilt first appeared in* Hearts and Hands: The Influence of Women & Quilts on American Society, *published by The Quilt Digest Press, San Francisco. Courtesy of the publisher.*

Figure 2. *Detail of Deborah Coates's quilt, white cotton triangle on which is stamped the abolitionist motif of a black slave in chains. The Coateses' home was used as a stop on the Underground Railroad. Collection of the Heritage Center of Lancaster County Inc. Courtesy of Quilt Digest Press.*

Figure 3. Signature quilt made by Milcah Churchman Lesslie Pyle, Cecil County, Maryland in 1848. 95½" × 93". Pieced and appliquéd cottons with reverse appliqué and needlework techniques. At the time this quilt was made the immediate members of this Pyle family were not members of a Quaker meeting. Collection of Dr. and Mrs. Donald M. Herr. This quilt first appeared in The Quilt Digest 4, *published by Quilt Digest Press, San Francisco. Courtesy of the publisher.*

ers," were: "deviating from plainness in dress and address, neglect of debts, asking more than 25% on loans, profane language, marrying contrary to discipline (not in Meeting) and marrying out of unity (to a non-Quaker)."

Joseph and Milcah went on to have seven more children, all of whom are named on their sister's quilt. At least one of them, S. John, was a Quaker, and it was in his family that this quilt was passed down. No record has come to light as to the fate of Sophia, for whom the lovely needlework was made. But it does survive as a testimony to a network of caring friends and relatives of this family and their daughter, Sophia.

The final quilt to be considered here is another Signature quilt which belongs to the Philadelphia Yearly Meeting, Religious Society of Friends (fig. 5 and plate 2). This lovely piece, the only example in this paper associated with the Orthodox Friends, is on view at the Arch Street Meeting House in Philadelphia. Made for Ann Burns, a retiring matron at the House of Industry, run by the Female Society of Philadelphia for the Relief and Employment of the Poor, this quilt bears 76 names, all members of this Female Society. The complete records of this Society are in The Quaker Collection, Haverford College Library, Haverford, Pennsylvania. Credit must be given to Kathy Pokstefl for making this author aware of the information and sharing her extensive knowledge of these papers.

The large central block of this quilt, a detail of which can be seen in plate 2 bears this inscription:

Figure 4. Detail of center square of the Pyle quilt, bearing the inscription, "Sophia Pyles's Quilt/ pieced by her/ Mother in/ 1848." Sophia was 17 at the time this quilt was made. Collection of Dr. and Mrs. Donald M. Herr. Photo by Lyn Wagner.

We whose names are here recorded have passed many pleasant/ hours, may we humbly look forward with an eye of faith, to a reunion/ in these blessed abodes where praise and thanksgiving are sweet/ strains of the Redeemed of the Lord./ Ann Burns/ will please accept this Block as a small token of/ regard, from her sincere friends S. Wister, who is sensible of/ her valuable services bestowed at the House of Industry—/ May the sweet reward of peace be abundantly shed abroad in her heart./ The approbation of a clear conscience is more desirable than gold, that/ perisheth—. Mayest thou when retiring from thy useful labours/ reflect with satisfaction on the time devoted to this useful Institution./ 4th mo 20th 1844

The Female Society of Philadelphia for the Relief and Employment of the Poor was founded in 1795 by Ann Parish and 23 other single Quaker women who, at their early meetings, called themselves the "Friendly Circle." By 1811 they had adopted the longer "Female Society" name. The original purpose of this organization (the first charity founded by women in Pennsylvania) was to relieve the suffering following the yellow fever epidemic of 1793, when so many families lost their breadwinners and women and young children were left in poverty.

At the beginning, members of the Society visited poor families in their homes and gave them food, clothing and money. Entries such as this one, written in "1796, 5th mos 24th," on pp. 73-74 of the first book of minutes of the Society, were common: "Blods Wildgoose, an industrious tradesman, far gone in a consumption and quite unable to work, his wife has supported the family by her needle and a small shop, but finding it difficult to get work . . . reduced to distress—handed her 3 dollars to furnish her shop and at several times Coffee, sugar, Chocolate, rice, sago, and wine."

They felt, however, that their efforts and money might be better used in a central location. The Minutes of the Society, Book 2 (1798) pp. 5-6 report setting up rooms with flax, wool

Figure 5. Signature quilt presented to Ann O. Burns in 1844, on the occasion of her retirement as "matron" [supervisor] of the House of Industry, a refuge for poor women operated by Orthodox Quakers, The Female Society of Philadelphia for the Relief and Employment of the Poor. The quilt was made for Ann Burns by fellow inmates under the supervision of the Quaker "managers." Pieced and appliquéd cottons, 108" square. Collection of the Philadelphia Yearly Meeting, Arch Street Meeting House. Photo by Theodore Brinton Hetzel.

and large wheels and other utensils for spinning. There women could be warmed by the fire and given food, all of which would cost less there than if sent to individual families.

The plan, at this particular meeting, was to: "distinguish between the industrious and those who are not." They also remarked that, "Elderly women who are not capable of laborious employment to have care of the children the days their mothers are employed in spinning, to prepare food for both parents and children, and whatever business may be found necessary. There are under our care a number of ancient women whose infirmities disable them from almost every other kind of work except knitting, who might also have the comfort of a warm room during the day."

By the end of that year, industrious women were being sheltered from the winter cold and given employment to "spin shoe thread and stocking yarn [which] will answer better than linen as we have reason to believe there will be ready sale for them (Minutes Book 1798, p. 34)."

Generally this activity continued each winter until the advent of spring and warmer weather. At this time entries, such as one, written on p. 163 in book 2 of the Minutes, would appear: "3rd mos 9th 1811/As the number of Spinners decline at the House of Industry and the materials are nearly all manufactured, it is concluded to leave it at the discretion of the ensuing attending committee to close it, the last of next week or the middle of the week after."

By 1816 the Society purchased a property of their own, a house in Philadelphia on Ranstead Court and Fourth Street below Market Street. The minutes are filled with the discussion of plans for the use of this house, and on December 21 the first mention of quilting as an occupation for the women is recorded. Figure 6 pictures p. 110 of Book 3 of the Society's minutes where this is recorded. The passage in its entirety reads:

The Acting Committee taking into view, the added risponsibility [sic] that the members of the Society must feel attached to their situation, in consequence of the trust reposed in them, by many of their friends, either in the bequeathment of legacies, or increasing their funds by donations, agree to propose to the Society, the practacability [sic] of extending their sphere of usefulness, by introducing some other mode of Employment as well as continueing [sic] that of Spinning; also feeling in a peculiar manner, for women who have small children, who find difficulty in procuring work, either at, or from their own home, and, securing to the original object of this institution, which was to cherish and employ such,—submit the following plan for consideration.

1st. To employ a few deserving women at the house of Industry, such as have small children, or those who are unable, either by advanced age, or some infirmity to obtain work in any other way.

2nd. That the children be taken care of in a nursery, by a suitable woman, during the hours their mothers are employed, she being allowed a reasonable compensation for having charge of them.

3rd. That each member of the Society, use every exertion to obtain work from their friends (as the preference will be given to work taken into the house) where that cannot be had, the Society to furnish sewing, knitting etc. It is proposed to make into garments, some of the Society's linen which shall be sold for the benefit of the Poor, and to have quilts made and disposed of in the same manner.

4th. That two of the members be appointed, for one week, to superintend the sewing department, keep regular accounts of all work taken in, furnish bills to customers for work done, pay the women, and see that the work be executed according to the directions given, and to render to the Society a statement of their transactions at the end of the week.

5th. Each member is priviledged [sic], to give work to one deserving woman—as spinning or other employment. If the poor woman be employed at the house she must come well recommended. If any of the members should prefer giving them sewing at their own houses, it is expected that the member will recommend them, and be their security for the returns, (and responsibility for the neatness) of the work.

6th. The managers [Society members] attending at the house of Industry shall endeavour to be there at nine oclock [sic] in the morning.

7th. The managers shall if possible, have all the articles returned during their terms of service and give a correct list of those not returned to their successors, with whom one shall remain at least one day, to initiate them in the duties of their office.

8th. This plan may be altered, and amended, as the experience of the Society, or the future circumstances of the Society may render advisable.

Rules for the Women employed.

The women employed at the house shall begin to work at eight oclock [sic] in the morning. They shall be satisfied with the work allotted them, and the price paid them—they shall come to work, in decent apparal [sic], the strictest attention to cleanliness of person, required—no improper language to be used, talking, laughing, and singing during their stay at the house—no smoking admitted in the working rooms.- - - - -

Should the above plan meet the approbation of the Society, no doubt, its members will sympathise [sic] with the poor women, thus employed when they reflect, that there is no provision in it, to furnish them with food;—but as the design is, to introduce this in a very limited scale, the employment of them in the house of Industry and the saving of their fuel, we feel a hope, that if we commence on this contracted plan, we shall be enabled to meet in future the more benevolent views of the Society—and that a way will open for realizing what we conceive would be the wish of all.

Signed by the Acting Committee
Sarah Bacon etc.

The society approves of the proposed plan, and resolves to adopt it.

The minutes offer interesting reading as the Society implemented this, their plan of 1816. Thirteen years later, quilting is mentioned (p. 10): "muslin calicos to be made into quilt sheets in the house." With the introduction of machine spun yarns it is not surprising to note that in 1831 spinning activities were discontinued in the House of Industry and that quilting then became the frequently mentioned activity: "The wages at present fixed upon, are for quilters and best sources, 15 cents a day and 12 1/2 c for most others, as there are those among our women who from inability or wont of application perform very little work, the committee used the discretionary power visited in them of reducing the wages of such to 10 cents to be raised should an improvment be observable." (January 6, 1844) The managers cut, prepared and also inspected the work.

Over the years other entries on quiltmaking appeared: "Wages for quilters from 27-30c per day the coarse quilters receiving 27c and the fine quilters 30c." (February 19, 1887). "The quilters are unruly and too rapid in their work, they missed of doing sections of Sewing and then waiting for each other. This must be stopped and better work enforced." (December 12, 1890); [of Bridgette Hagen's death] was 98 years old and a fine quilter." (March 30, 1896); "Wages of all quilters 60c day regardless of quality of work." (October 7, 1912); and finally, "Quilting temporarily discontinued for lack of personnel and materials." (January 8, 1946)

So ended a 130-year history of quilting in the Female Society of Philadelphia for the Relief and Employment of the Poor's House of Industry. It may, however, be interestng for other quilt historians to note that Friends in other areas set up similiar institutions, patterned after this one. Some of these organizations were: 1. Whittier at 11th and Cherry Street, Philadelphia, 2. Five Points House of Industry in New York state, 3. Hicksite "The Female Association of Philadelphia for Relief of the Sick and the Infirm and Poor, founded 1828, incorporated in 1837, and 4. Philadelphia Society for the Employment of and Instruction of the Poor, established in 1847.

The "Miscellaneous Papers" of the Female Society of Philadelphia from the 1930s and 1940s, located in the Haverford Quaker Collection, indicate that about 25-30 women were employed annually in this sheltered workroom. Each year they produced thousands of garments, hundreds of pounds of carpet balls, which were sold to the Pennsylvania Working Home for the Blind, and 15 to 20 quilts.

Also included in this "Miscellaneous" file are letters such as this one (written sometime in the 1930s) from satisfied quilt customers:

My dear Miss Cranmer
10th March

I am enclosing check for $5.24. I am delighted with my quilt and please tell the women who sewed at it how much I appreciate their work.

Very Sincerely
B. Lamb

Along with these letters, survives a newspaper clipping, 1914, titled, "Making Quilts for 119 Years." The article gives a brief history of the House of Industry.

Also, on the occasion of the centennial celebration of the Female Society in 1895, a pamphlet *Sketch of the House of Industry,* was published. This mention of quilting activities for that year was made:

During the winter months from eighty to one hundred women are employed five days in the week from 9 A.M. to 5 P.M. They do coarse and fine sewing, quilt silk afghans and cotton comfortables, under the direction of a seamstress and a quilter employed for the purpose. Part of this work is sold in the store attached to the house; the rest is made to order for outside customers.

The quilt pictured in a detail in the color plate and fully in fig. 1 is important as material evidence of some of this quiltmaking activity and specifically because of its connection with Ann Burns.

In looking back to the entry in the Minutes on the date "3rd mos 6th 1844," one can note that of the 11 women being presented with new dresses, inmate Ann Burns is the only one mentioned by name. This hints of the special place that she held as Matron in the House of Industry and in the hearts of the Quaker women who were the Managers of the Society.

This is further underscored by a letter (also in this collection) written by one of the Society members 38 years after the quilt had been presented to Ann Burns:

Went to the House of Industry this morning to see Ann Burns—found her lying on the bed apparently asleep—& I was about to leave the room without speaking, when she opened her eyes, and then we had quite a nice talk together.—In the course of it she said 'I do not think you will have me long. And I think you will miss me a little too—Have for so long a time been a part of the place.—And I am very grateful for the many kindnesses I have received—I know that I did try to do my duty faithfully.—I came in the autumn of 1826 & was the first matron in the new house in Ransteads Court——I do not feel any doubt or apprehension in regard to the future. I am in the Lord's hands—& I hope to pass a joyful Eternity above.——She also said 'While this is here I want again to say what I have already told Miss Coates, regarding my Album bed quilt.—There is not a name there that did not belong to a member of the Society—and I want the quilt to remain at the House of Industry, as a rememberence of your old matron, It is carefully wrapped up. I had meant to have had a box to keep it in, but never got one——I would like it kept nice & clean, so that it need not be washed.—My grandchildren have never seen it—& if they had it would not make any difference—I told her we would be glad to procure a box & place a memorandum in it along with the quilt—& she seemed gratified at the suggestion.——Susan Anadown, Ann's old friend & associate, did most of the quilting.
Mary Randolph
[February 22, 1882]

Ann Burns died shortly after Mary Randolph's visit for, as noted in the "Extract from the Annual Report 1883":

To many of our Subscribers, the name and Christian character of Ann O. Burns, who deceased the first of third mo, 1882, are very familiar. For 56 years she was an honored inmate of the House of Industry. Its Matron for forty years, during which time her her[sic] fidelity so endeared her to the Managers, that when her failing sight, and advanced age made it needful for them to release her from active service, they thought it right to ensure her a home for the remainder of her days.—

Since that time many changes have occurred in the Society—but her presence continued to be a valued link with the past.—Cheerful & patient in her blindness, she for years seemed only waiting a Heavenward summons; and after one week's illness, the summons did arrive, there was apparently nothing for her to do, -but calmly to fall asleep, trusting in her Saviour.——We doubt not that after her ninety-two years of probation, she has now received the Master's Verdict of Well done.

So ended, one lady's life. A life intimately connected with one aspect of Quaker quiltmaking in Pennsylvania.

Suggested Reading:

Betterton, Sheila. *Quilts and Coverlets from the American Museum in Britain.* The American Museum in Britain, 1978.

Colby, Averil. *Patchwork.* London: B.T. Batsford, Ltd., 1958.

____. *Quilting.* New York: Charles Scribner's Sons, 1971.

Herr, Patricia T. "All in Modesty and Plainness." *The Quilt Digest 3.* San Francisco: The Quilt Digest Press, 1985, pp. 22-35.

Kolter, Jane Bentley. *Forget Me Not/A Gallery of Friendship and Album Quilts.* Pittstown, New Jersey: The Main Street Press, 1985.

Lee-Whitman, Leanna, "The Silk Trade/Chinese Silks and the British East India Company." *Winterthur Portfolio,* 17, No.1, 28. Winterthur, Delaware: The Henry Francis Dupont Winterthur Museum, 1982, pp. 21-41.

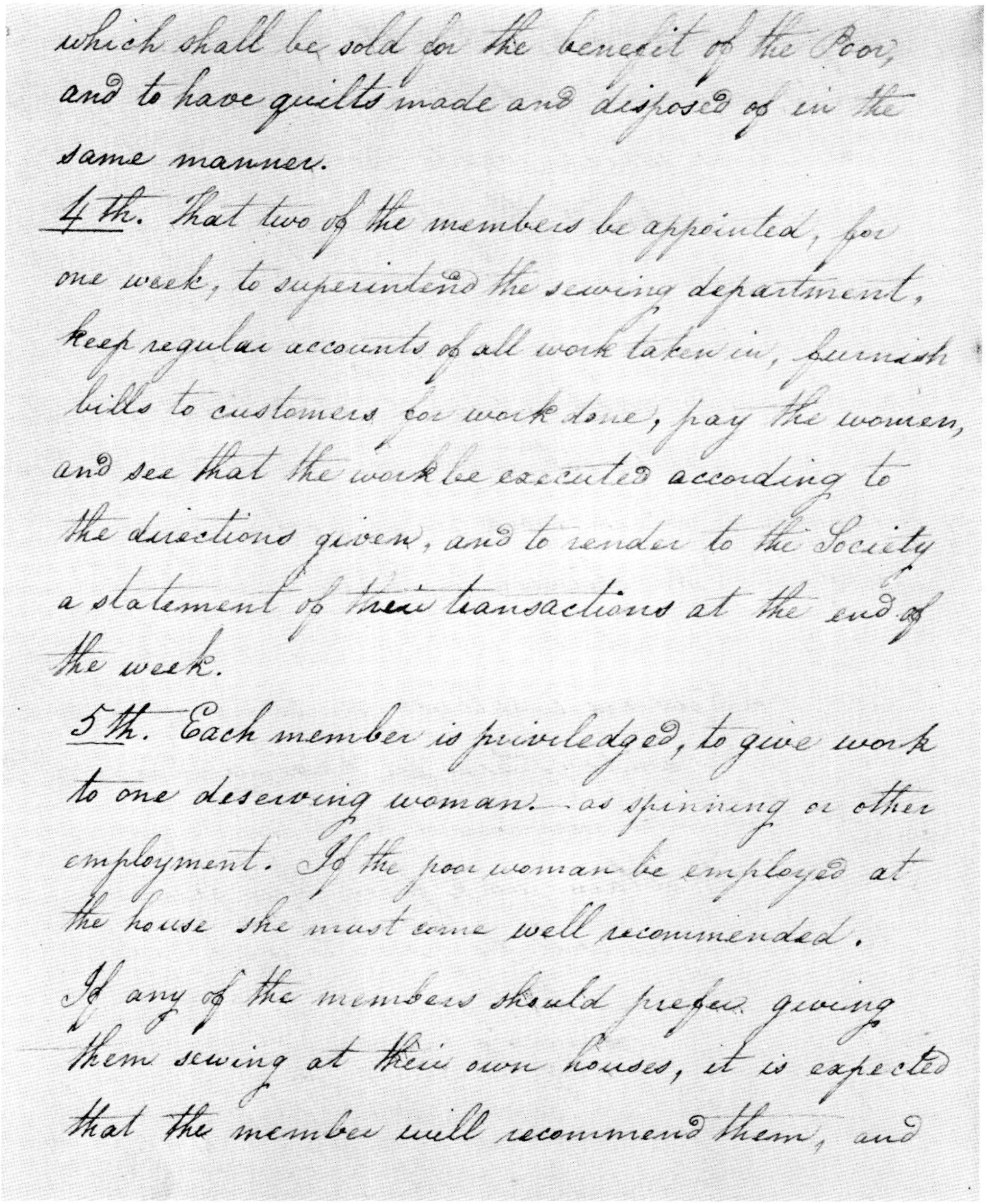

which shall be sold for the benefit of the Poor, and to have quilts made and disposed of in the same manner.

4th. That two of the members be appointed, for one week, to superintend the sewing department, keep regular accounts of all work taken in, furnish bills to customers for work done, pay the women, and see that the work be executed according to the directions given, and to render to the Society a statement of their transactions at the end of the week.

5th. Each member is priviledged, to give work to one deserving woman: as spinning or other employment. If the poor woman be employed at the house she must come well recommended. If any of the members should prefer giving them sewing at their own houses, it is expected that the member will recommend them, and

Figure 6. *Page 110 of Minute Book 3 (1813-1817) of The Female Society of Philadelphia for the Relief and Employment of the Poor dated "21st of 12th mo: 1816." At the top of this page is the first mention of quilting as an occupation for the inmates of the House of Industry, "and to have quilts made and disposed of in the same manner." The Quaker Collection, Haverford College Library.*

Montgomery, Florence. *Printed Textiles/English and American Cottons and Linens.* New York: The Viking Press, 1970.

____. *Textiles in American 1650-1870.* New York: W. W. Norton & Co., 1984.

Nicoll, Jessica F. *Quilted for Friends/Delaware Valley Signature Quilts, 1840-1855.* Winterthur, Delaware: The Henry Francis Du Pont Winterthur Museum, 1986.

Orlorsky, Patsy and Myron. *Quilts in America.* New York: McGraw-Hill Book Co., 1974.

Patricia Herr in one of Pennsylvania's leading collectors and authorities on historical needlework and weaving traditions. She has written "Jacquard Coverlets" and "Handwoven Masterpieces" for Early American Life *(1982), an article on Pennsylvania Quaker quilt traditions for* The Quilt Digest *(1985), and "What Distinguishes a Pennsylvania Quilt" in* In the Heart of Pennsylvania/Symposium Papers *(1985). She has served as the guest curator for textiles in the major tercentenary exhibition called* The Pennsylvania Germans *which was organized jointly by the Philadelphia Museum of Art and Winterthur Museum. Trish Herr has lectured widely on Pennsylvania's textile traditions at the Philadelphia College of Textiles, the Pennsylvania Farm Museum, the Hershey Museum of American Life, the York County Historical Society, the Lititz Historical Foundation, Winterthur Museum, and the 1985 Bucknell quilt symposium. She has served on the board of the Pennsylvania Farm Museum at Landis Valley and the Acquisitions and Museum Committees of the Heritage Center of Lancaster County, where she has been guest curator for a show on Lancaster Amish quilts, another on Lancaster coverlets, one on Lancaster schoolgirl needlework and a fourth which contrasted Pennsylvania-German material culture of Lancaster with that of Ontario, Canada. Trish practices veterinary medicine in Lancaster and is currently President of the Pennsylvania Veterinary Medical Association.*

Early Pennsylvania-German Traditions

BEDS, BEDDING, BEDSTEADS, AND SLEEP

ALAN G. KEYSER

Over the years the sleeping equipment and practices of the Pennsylvania Germans have changed. The old methods which were brought from the continent of Europe to America are now all but a memory in most segments of the surviving Pennsylvania German culture. Hopefully we will be able to examine, if only in passing, the major points of the ancient art of sleeping. Several areas which will be left for future students are nocturnal marital and extra-marital conduct, bundling and sick and death bed practices.

The Kammer

In a Pennsylvania German farmhouse during the 17th, 18th and 19th centuries generally the head of the household, his wife and small children slept in *die Kammer* located on the first floor. This *Kammer* was a long narrow bedroom usually with one long side as an exterior wall with either a northwestern, northern or northeastern exposure. The *Kammer* had two or perhaps three windows and one interior door which opened into the *Kammer* from the *Schtub* or living room.

In some 18th century houses one of the *Kammer* windows was a small casement window. In log houses it was merely a hole cut out of two logs with a wooden plug to close it. This window or hole was probably used as a "soul window" at the time of death of anyone in the *Kammer.*[2] This window was opened just after death to allow the soul free exit from the house.[3]

The exterior walls of the *Kammer* were either whitewashed plaster in the stone houses or smoothed, chinked logs in log houses. The interior walls were either inch-thick vertical board paneling or a four-inch-thick plastered wall. One of the exterior walls had a row of turned wooden pegs six feet or more from the floor on which to hang clothing. In some homes a mirror hung on the *Kammer* wall,[4] but until the last one hundred and fifty years there were no framed pictures. Traditionally one item of decorative needlework was displayed on the *Kammer* door of some houses. This was the embroidered hand towel known popularly today as the door panel or show towel.[5] One exterior wall in some stone houses contained a small built-in cabinet about four feet from the floor.

The contents of the *Kammer* varied from house to house and depended on the economic standing and age of the occupants. Fairly typical, though, is the inventory of George Trumbour of Lower Salford Township, Montgomery County taken in 1811.[6] No bed or bedstead is listed probably because these items belonged to the woman of the house and were not part of the husband's estate. So if one were to add a bed, bedstead, bedding and curtains to Trumbour's "bedroom" list, a typical picture of the *Kammer* furnishings would come into focus.

The Bedroom [Bed, Bedstead, bedding and curtains]	
2 checked Bed casings & Linen stripe	6.00
Chaff Bag Bolster case wallets	2.50
83 yds Flaxen Linen	41.50
21 yds Tow Linen	7.00
6 sheets	6.00
9 table cloaths	4.00
a cloath press	4.00
a looking glass	.75

The only pieces of wooden furniture in this room would have been the mirror on the wall, the bedstead, and the clothes press. Many houses would also have a painted chest as part of the *Kammer* furniture.[7]

Since the farmer and his wife slept in the *Kammer,* it was here that the children were born and slept until they were old enough to graduate to colder sleeping quarters. Sallie Landis told us that her parents had a trundle bed under their bed which they pulled out at night.[8] The second youngest child slept on this. They also had a cradle in their room in which the baby slept. Next to the *Kammer* they had a *glee Kammer*—small chamber—and it was here that the small girls slept. Once they reached about eight years of age they were thought to be old enough to sleep in the cold rooms on the second floor. The boys were considered a little tougher and by-passed the *glee Kammer.*

The *glee Kammer* was entered through a door leading from the *Kammer,* and like the Kammer was along the northeast wall. Within a mile of Sallie Landis's childhood, central-chimney, log home today stands the Dielman Kolb house built in the 1730's. The northwestern corner of Kolb's house contains evidence of having once had a *glee Kammer.* There is no window on the northwest side of this room and only one window on the southwest side. This

Plate 3. This fully dressed bed appears as it would have c. 1850 in the spare room of many Pennsylvania-German homes. The drawn-work edge of the top sheet is folded over the bed case just below the pillows. This dressed bed was photographed while on exhibit at the Lancaster Heritage Center in 1980. Collection of the Lancaster Heritage Center, Dr. and Mrs. Donald Herr, Joan Johnson, and other private collections.

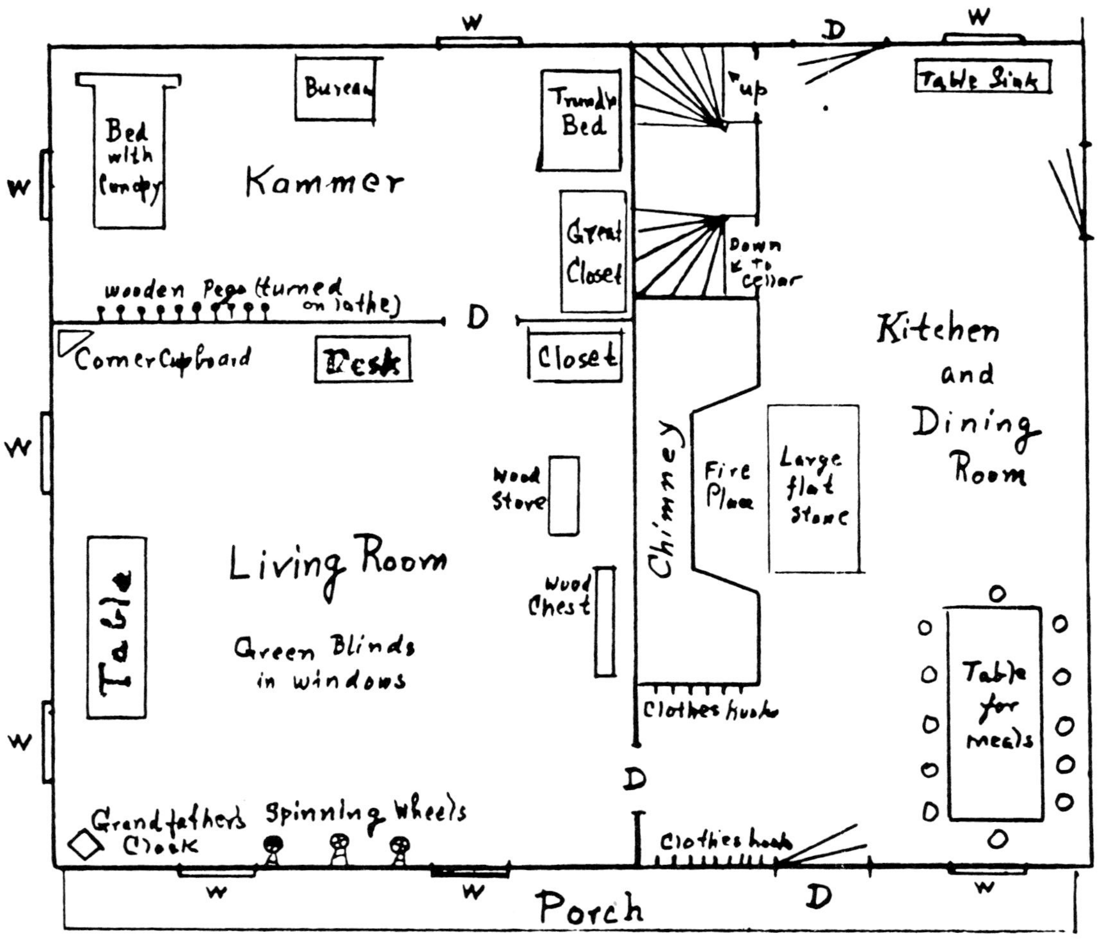

Figures 1 and 2. These floor plans show the placement of sleeping and bedding storage furniture in the Amos Schultz house in Douglas Township, Montgomery County ca.1850. This was researched by Dr. Elmer E. S. Johnson from his aunt Sarah Schultz c. 1920. He made the drawings in 1950. Courtesy of the Schwenkfelder Library, Pennsburg, Pennsylvania.

lack of windows would tend to conserve heat and cut down on the drafts.

The bedstead and bed in the *Kammer* came into most families as an important part of the bride's dowry at the time of her marriage. This equipment was very similar from one family to the next, and its ownership was retained by the wife. Moses Bender of New Hanover Township, Montgomery County in his will stated that his "wife Anna . . . shall keep her marriage bed and bedstead, curtain and what is thereunto belonging in advance . . . "[9] In the estate inventory of Dietrich Boocher of the same township in 1789 the widow kept "her bedstead with curtain."[10] From these and many similar accounts we see that the marriage bedstead was a high posted one with a curtain and belonged to the widow.

Esther Clemens married William Ziegler of Skippack in 1751, and at that time her father Jacob Clemens gave her the following sleeping equipment typical of that given in many moderately well off farm families in the mid-eighteenth century: four linen bed sheets, one bedstead, 14 yards of bed curtain, one linsey-woolsey under bed tick, one linsey-woolsey bolster tick, one fustian upper bed tick and two fustian pillow ticks.[11] She was given two checked cases for the bed, two checked cases for the bolster and four pillow cases. This was one set for the bed and one for the wash. To fill the fustian upper bed and two pillow ticks she was given 3½ pounds of feathers. When William Ziegler died in 1797 he left his wife Esther "one bed and bedstead with pillows sheets and everything to make a good complete bed."[12] Esther Clemens Ziegler died in 1798[13] and from her inventory we learn what she thought necessary "to make a good complete bed": "10 bedsheets, 4 piller cases, 6 bed cases, 1 coverlid, 1 feather bed, 1 under featherbed, 2 pillows, 2 large pillows, 1 bed, 1 bedstead." Esther slept on a chaff bed, and an underfeatherbed, two bolsters, two pillows and a bedsheet and slept under a featherbed and a coverlet. In her lifetime she made one major addition, the coverlet, and for comfort several minor additions, a second bolster and an underbed of feathers.

The master of the house and his wife slept in the *Kammer* in most Pennsylvania German families until about 1850. After this date the number decreased rapidly and today it is only the conservative religious sects such as the Old Order Amish and the Old Order Mennonites whose heads of household still sleep in the *Kammer.* Kaschbar Hufnagel (Pierce Swope) tells of how his family used the *Kammer* in the late 19th century.[14] He states that their two young hired men occupied the once honored place in the *Kammer* while the rest of the family slept in rooms on the second floor. At least people slept in that *Kammer.* Today the *Kammer* in some houses has been remodeled for use as either the modern kitchen or the pantry or, in still other houses, relegated to junk storage. Some people even used the *Kammer* to store apples and potatoes.

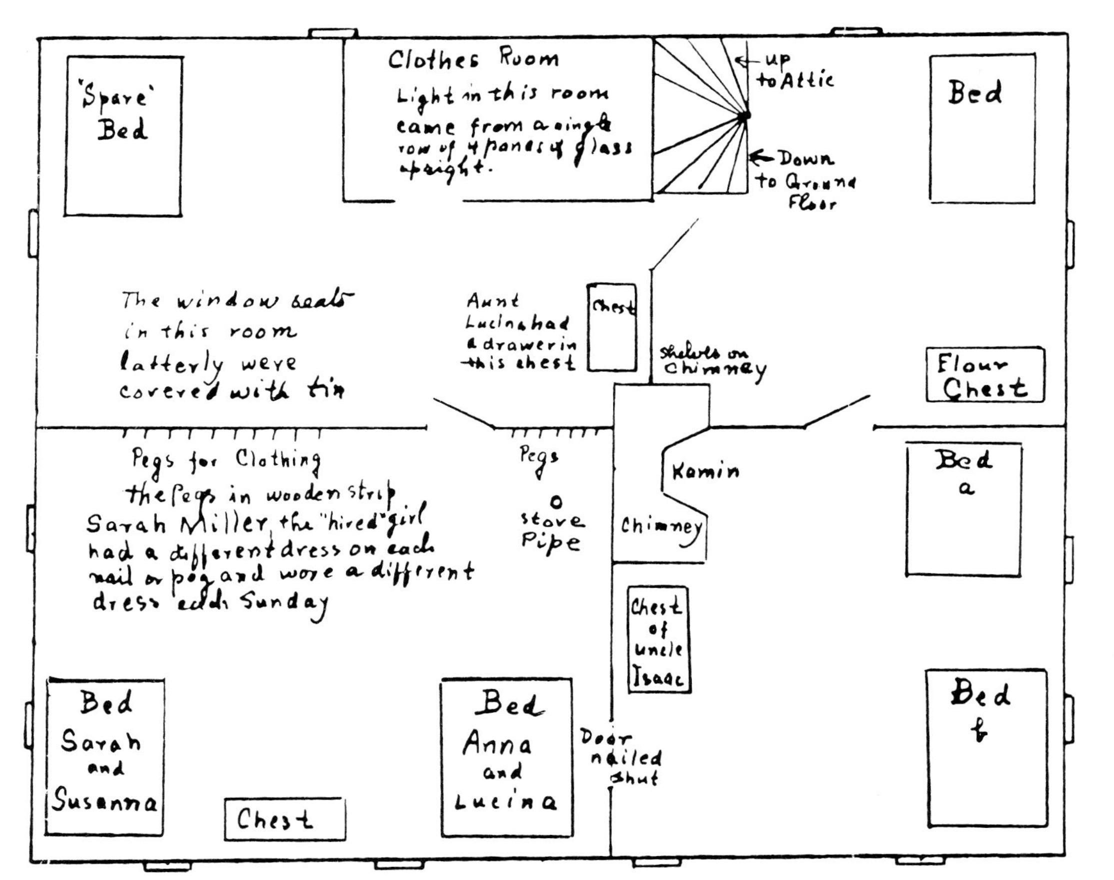

The Schtub-Kammer

Some 18th and 19th century houses had no *Kammer,* but followed the old European custom of having one end of the *Schtub* or living room serve as the master bedroom. Architectural historians tell us that the *Kammer* evolved by partitioning off the end of the *Schtub* where the bed was built into the wall or stood.

Theophile Cazenove in 1794[15] describes one of these *Schtub-Kammer* combinations after he "visited several farms in the famous Lancaster County belonging to farmers known to be worth 10 to 15 thousand pounds . . . [They have in their houses] for down-stairs rooms a kitchen and a large room with the farmer's bed and the cradle, where the whole family stays all the time; apples and pears drying on the stove, a bad little mirror, a walnut bureau, sometimes a clock. . . . " Either he forgot the table and benches and chairs or the family was so large that they covered them completely, for there was surely furniture to sit on, if, as he says, they stayed there "all the time."

Henry Been of Skippack and Perkiomen Township in Montgomery County died in 1803 at about 50 years of age. His estate inventory taken at that time gives some idea of what a typical well-equipped *Kammer-Schtub* combination would have contained.[16] The inventory is listed by the room and since no living room is mentioned it is safe to assume that what is called the "bedroom" was this large combination living room-master bedroom on the first floor.

Item	Value
To all his wearing apparel	31.85
a 30 hr clock and case	32.00
a walnut clothes press	5.00
a walnut chest	4.00
a ten plate stove and coal rake	24.50
a dough trough & milk cupboard	1.20
a walnut dining table and bench	3.50
6 rush bottom chairs (good)	4.50
6 rush bottom chairs (inferior)	1.50
2 setts enamelled cups and saucers bowl, teapot & sugar bowl	1.25
1 sett white cups & saucers & 6 teaspoons	.35
10 knifes & forks	.75
to all his books	4.30
2 pr. wool cards	.50
a pewter teapot, oil can and 3 lamps	.75
To Bedstead Bedding and curtains	24.00

Had this room been just a bedroom as the inventory says, it would have been an unusually well furnished bedroom, but it is probably not too far from what many farm families might have had in the two rooms which here were combined into one.

The Schtub as Sleeping Quarters

In houses that had both the *Kammer* and the living room, at times the living room was used as a bedroom. This occurred in families where the grandparents lived under the same roof with the younger generation. The younger farmer and his wife slept in the *Kammer* while the retired older people slept in the stove room or *Schtub.* The stove provided heat for the thin-blooded old folks, and eliminated the need for climbing stairs to one of the bedrooms on the second floor. John Jacob Long of Marlborough Township, Montgomery County, in 1789 willed his wife "that bedstead and bed with the curtain which is in the stove room together with the blew chest with all her clothes in it."[17] Here he was very likely giving his wife the things which were actually hers. Her clothing was certainly hers and the bed, bedstead and "blew" chest she had probably brought to him as part of the dowry when they were married. Such generosity!

John Custer[18] of Skippack Township in Montgomery County also had a "Bed, bedstead and bedding in the Stove room" in addition to the bedding in the *Kammer* which in his inventory is called "the lower room next to the pump."

Sleeping in the Kitchen

The third room on the first floor of the traditional Pennsylvania Dutch house was the kitchen. Thus far no evidence has come to light which would indicate that the Dutchman ever kept a bed in his kitchen. However, that is not to say that he never slept there. He certainly slept sitting in his *Daadischtuhl* after having read an especially inspiring story in the almanac, but he also slept on the lid of the woodchest. With the advent of wood stoves for cooking, if not before, the woodchest became a necessary item of kitchen furniture. Many a farmer took his after dinner nap lying on the woodchest behind the stove. It is related of one farmer that "er waar so faul ass er zwee Holskischdedeckel darrich gewore hot in seim lebszeit." (He was so lazy that he wore through two woodchest lids in his lifetime.)[19] Beyond these regular naps, probably the only other sleeping in the kitchen was done by small children who fell asleep on the floor or bench before bedtime, and by the house cat or dog.

Bedrooms Upstairs

Many of the farmhouses were two and a half stories high, and the second floor was used almost exclusively for sleeping. The floor plan of the second floor was usually a carbon copy of the first. The room at the top of the stairs was the shape of the long narrow kitchen below, and was considered *die Gangschtub,* the hall room, by some. This was used as a sleeping room for the children or the hired help of either sex. Since it was frequently on the north side and well travelled, it was not a choice room. The room just above the *Kammer* was, as the room below, long and narrow. The room above the stove room was the same shape and size as its counterpart on the first floor. This large, square, well-lighted room with a southern exposure was the guest bedroom or spare room.

The guest bedroom was the best room in most houses. This room had the finest panelling, the best weather conditions and no through traffic. Some guest rooms in stone houses have built-in wall cabinets and clothes closets. Others had a jambstove and still others had a fireplace. Almost nothing was too good for a guest. No matter how large the family, a room was kept ready for guests even at the expense of those family members who regularly slept three to a bed on the freezing cold or blistering hot attic.

The guest bedroom was used regularly by the family for one purpose. It was here that all the Sunday clothes were hung on the pegs or hooks on the wall.

The spare room bed was always made, and on it were the best bed linens. In the chest in the room were the coverlets which have come down into the last quarter of the twentieth century looking as if never a warm body lay under them. The bedstead was usually a good piece of furniture but probably not as good as the marriage bed and bedstead. John Custer's 1794 guest bedroom contained several bedsteads—two were high posted and one was a truckle bedstead. The description of one of them in the upper room, southwest corner was the following: "to an high posted bedstead, 2 chaff beds, 2 boulsters, upper bed and case and 1 pillow."[20] Beyond the bedstead and a chest for the unused best linen and coverlets, the spare bedroom probably contained no more than a chair or two and perhaps a small table during most of the 18th and early 19th centuries.[21] By the late 19th century most farm homes had a wash stand with a bowl and a pitcher set on it and a bureau in the spare room.

Not all visitors who stayed overnight at a Pennsylvania Dutch farmhouse were considered candidates for spare room quarters, only visiting dignitaries, relatives and friends and occasional strangers who were travelling through the countryside. Tramps, peddlers and day laborers who may have stayed at the farm were offered the barn and not the guest room.

Not everyone had a spare bedroom or even a spare bed for visitors and Robert Boyd, a Methodist circuit rider, wrote in 1862 of his experiences among the people of the Allegheny Mountains between the years 1815 and 1825. He stated that "some of the poor have no spare bed, and therefore can only furnish the preacher by putting him with another person, or giving him a bed while its regular occupant prepares a sleeping place on the floor."[22]

In houses that had a second floor the two or three rooms besides the spare room were occupied by the older children and the hired help. Children were segregated by sex. Boys did not sleep with girls even if they were brothers and sisters. In 1836 Johannes Z. Gehman of Douglass Township, Montgomery County, turned over the operation and possession of his farm to his son. At that time he made a list of everything on his farm, and among those notes is the only listing we have of the contents of the boys' room on a farm. He says, "ein Bett u Tepig und ein Kist in der Buben Stube," (a bed and coverlet and a chest in the boys' room). Other than the contents of the chest and the individual items on the bed, probably everything in the room is listed in his brief statement. Quite likely the girls' rooms on most farms were just as sparsely furnished.

The typical children's bedstead in the early period was the one described in John Custer's inventory of 1794: "to a short posted bedstead, chaff bed, one sheet, upper bed and case 2 pillows, cases and boulster in upper room N. corner 4-10-0."[23] As time went on, the half-high posted bedstead of midcentury came into use. Near the beginning of the 19th century the "drawer" (chest of drawers) became a piece of bedroom furniture and has now replaced the once common chest. Also most bedrooms of the 19th and 20th centuries had a chair or two and in the latter part of the 19th century the washstand and bowl and pitcher set became part of the farmer's bedroom furnishing. The bowl and pitcher set was never used in most farm bedrooms. Its use was reserved for company in the spare bedroom. In the other bedrooms it was just part of the decor.

Usually two or three children slept in a bed. If four small children slept in one bed, three lay the conventional way and one lay across the bed below the feet of the other three. This was not quite as bad as the proverbial "so voll ass siwwe imme Bett." (as full as seven in a bed) that was used to indicate packed quarters.

The hired help slept with the family. If the farm was large enough to employ a *gross un glee Gnecht*—a hired man and a hired boy—they slept in the same bed. However, if only one hired man was required he slept with one of the boys. The maid at times had a bed of her own and at other times slept with one of the girls.[24]

Some houses during the 19th century contained a *Kischdeschtub*—a chest room. The room usually had no other furniture than several blanket chests full of bedding. The walls of this room and not the spare room were then hung with the family's Sunday clothes.[25]

After the *Kammer* fell into disuse as the farmer's bedroom, the *Rohrschtub,* or pipe room, on the second floor became the master bedroom. The stove pipe from the kitchen stove below served to take the chill off the room through which it passed before entering the chimney. The room was not warm, but in the winter it was not as cold as the rest of the upstairs rooms. If the head of the household did not sleep in the *Rohrschtub,* usually it was used as the girls' room. In addition to the usual bedroom items, the sweet potatoes were sometimes wrapped in newspaper and kept in a covered barrel or box in this room. They would not keep if the conditions were too cold or too hot. This room had the proper climate for sweet potato storage.

For the last hundred years each bedroom had a chamber pot under the bed for night use. These pots were apparently either seldom used during the 18th and early 19th centuries, or they were of only minor value, for they seldom appear on estate inventories. John Biwighouse's 1811 inventory from central Bucks County lists "2 chamber pots, 1 shilling 9 pence." Some people kept the chamber pot on the attic stairs just inside the door rather than under the bed. This was done only in the room from which the attic stairs led to the third floor. One woman observed that that location was fine in all seasons but summer. It was at that time that one ran the risk of encountering wasps on the dark attic stairs.

The Attic

All houses with and without a second floor had a loft or attic for storage of unused or seldom used items. This area, depending on the family size, was also used for sleeping. In most cases after 1850, it was the bigger boys who slept here through heat and cold. Many older men who once slept on the attic tell of their experiences with snow on the covers, ice on the chamber pot under the bed and of *hochbeenich laafe* (high legged walking) through the snow on the floor in the morning. They also tell of shoveling snow from the attic floor out the attic window. An old Berks countian from Centerport recalled, "I slept in the attic . . . The bed . . . was the usual kind with high posts, a rope stretched side to side over wooden pegs then crosswise head to foot as the foundation spring. On top of that was a chaff bag and for a top cover a feather bed . . . The snow would sift in between the shingles and cover the bed. I put my shoes or boots at the foot of the bed post, hang my clothes on the post and wrap my scarf around it. On top my hat."[26]

Charlie Sittler told his experiences sleeping in the attic of his parents' old Germanic central fireplace log house. The attic was a single room with no partitions. In the middle of the floor was the four foot by eight foot stone chimney which tapered to the peak of the roof. At the north end was the stairs leading up from the first floor. He told us that he and his new bride slept on the south side of the chimney, the hired man slept on the north side and the maid slept to the west, all within four or five feet of each other. He remarked that this was probably not the ideal situation for a new wife.[27]

The attic in at least one family contained a somewhat unusual sleeping room. Hannah Rittenhouse Clemens born in Towamencin Township, Montgomery County, about 1880 said that her parents had a *Bettelmannschtub*—beggar's room—on their attic. It contained the *Bettelmannsbett,* the beggar's bed, a chair and a night stand. The reason she gave for having tramps sleeping in the house rather than the more customary barn, was that her father did not trust tramps in his barn.[28]

In one Lancaster County house the family had a similar room called *die Yuddeschtub*—the Jew's room.[29] This was reserved for the ped-

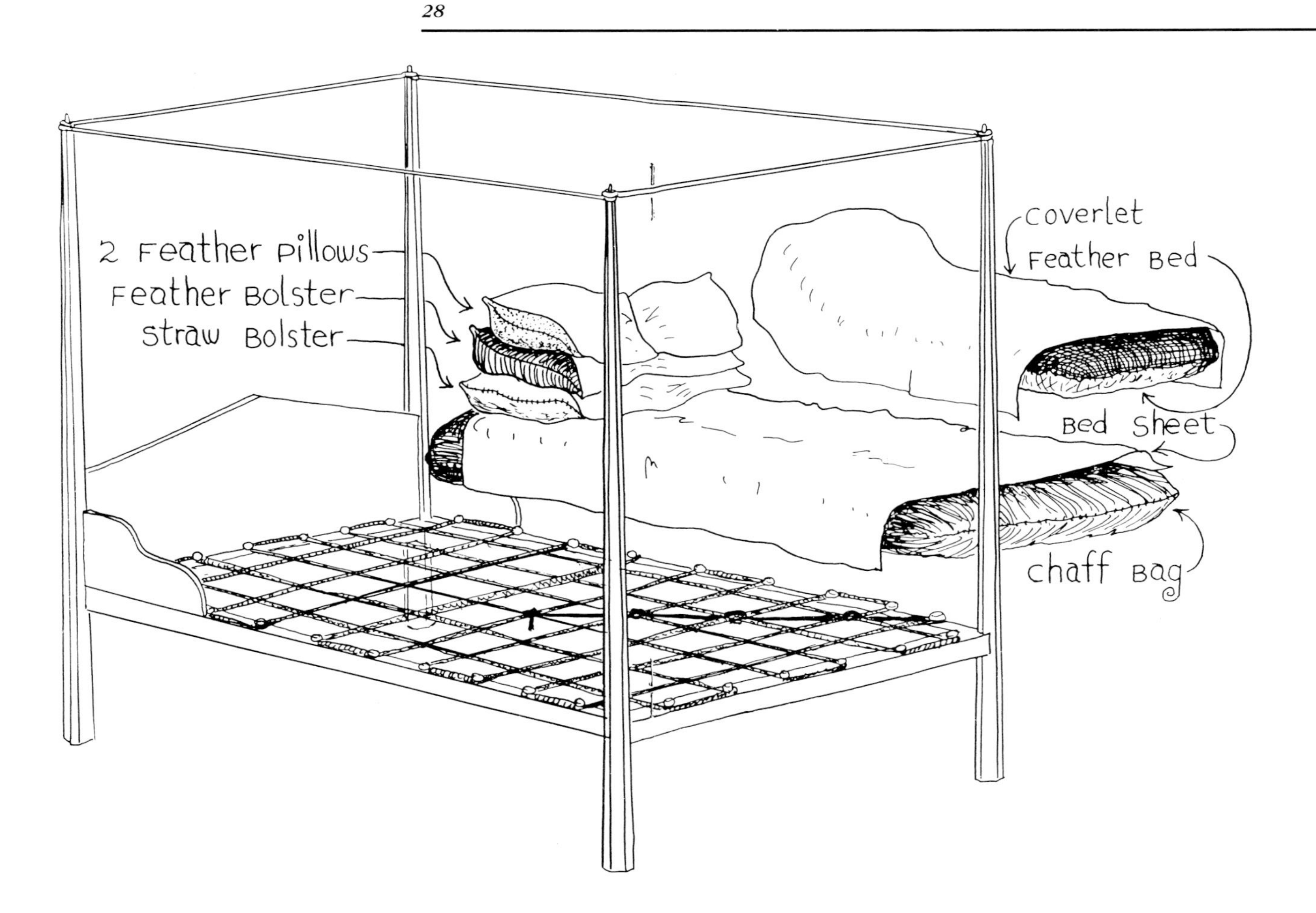

Figure 3. *A Pennsylvania-German four posted bed dressed as it might have been about 1800.*

dlers who wandered over the countryside selling all sorts of wares. They did not have to sleep in the barn, but the tramps did.

Most farmers were minded just the opposite of Rittenhouse. They did not want these dirty shiftless characters under the same roof with their family. But almost no farmer ever refused the shelter of their barn to any traveler. However, several conditions had to be met. All farmers required that all tramps turn over all their matches until morning. Others, fearing that the tramps turned over only part of their fire-starting equipment, asked to hold the contents of all their pockets until morning.

Tramps and peddlers preferred to sleep in the cow stable mow, because it contained the soft *Schwammhoi*—meadow hay—while the horse stable mow contained the coarse timothy. Most tramps stayed only one night, but some stayed longer during hay making and harvest to earn a little money.[30]

People slept in a number of places throughout the countryside, but since this is primarily an examination of the farm family those areas will not be covered.

The Bed and Its Furnishings

Now that we have seen where people slept, a detailed look at the bedstead and bedding might be in order. The entire bed, bedstead, bedding and curtain are mentioned in several of the examples given in the discussion of the *Kammer,* but the 1734 estate inventory of Johannes Schneider of New Hanover Township, Philadelphia County, lists the components of the full bed of the immigrant generation: "four fether beds with the civirings and 3 boulsters and 2 loose civirings and 5 sheets all belonging too two bedsteads."[31] Another immigrant, "Johann George Muller arrived here several weeks ago on August 13, 1750 on the Edinburgh from Germany, and on his trip from Philadelphia to Goschenhoppen two packs with beds fell off the wagon and until now he has not been able to learn anything about them. The one is a new fustian upper bed and a bolster. The other is of twill and has a case of plaid linen. They were both packed in cloth. He needs them for winter . . ."[32]

By 1871, Phoebe E. Gibbons described the bed in a Lancaster County farm home. "I turned down the woolen coverlet to find no sheets on the feather bed. I lifted this light downy bed that was neatly covered with white and found one sheet, a straw bed and bed cord in place of a sacking bottom. The pillow cases were trimmed with edging and marked in black silk in a large running hand—Henry G. Kreider, 1864,"[33] In the one hundred and twenty or more years from the immigrant generation to the 1870s several changes had taken place in the traditional equipage. The under bed exchanged its feathers for straw and chaff, one sheet was removed, the bedcase changed from plaid to white and a coverlet was added to the top of the pile.

Bedsteads

The old bedsteads were most frequently made of tulip poplar wood and were painted. From account books and estate inventories it becomes clear that the bedsteads were painted only a few colors. Abraham Overholt names the color for twenty-two of the bedsteads he made between 1790 and 1806 in his account book. Of that number thirteen were brown, four were blue, four were green and one was red.[34] White was the only other color for a bedstead mentioned in a primary source.[35] Several yellow beds have survived, but this was not a common color.

The bedsteads were made by local furniture makers in their shops all over the Pennsylvania countryside. The bedposts of the high-posted bedsteads were frequently turned on a lathe, but some were octagonal pencil posts. The bed rails were shaped with a moulding plane to form a recess for the rope pegs. This made the top of the rail even with the rope. Most of the Pennsylvania German bedsteads had pegs for stringing the bed rope rather than holes through the rails seen on some early beds from other cultures. The top of the bed rail was about two feet off the floor and by the time a chaff bag was put on the rope the sleeping level was at least three feet from the floor.[36] The bedsteads were nearly always about 49 to 53 inches wide. In modern terminology they are referred to as three-quarter size beds but they were originally built as full-sized double beds. The lengths of the old beds vary from five-and-a-half feet to a little over six feet. By today's standards these are quite short, but when they were new they were quite long enough. First, the original owner was probably not much over 5 feet 6 inches tall and second, he nearly sat to sleep.

The head board was ten to fourteen inches higher than the foot board. This was to hold the pile of bolsters and pillows. To help hold the bolsters and pillows old Pennsylvania German bedsteads had an additional twelve to eighteen-inch long side board eight inches high fitted into the top of the side rails and the head board on both sides. Four bedstead screws[37] were used to hold the bed together. They passed through the head and foot bed posts into an iron nut set into the bedrail about 1 to 1½ inches from each end. These screws were actually bolts which the furniture maker bought from the blacksmith.

The bed posts on the high posted bedstead varied in length, but most were about six and a half to seven feet high, topped by a pin or peg to hold the curtain rods or wooden cornice.

The curtain rods, as the bedstead screws, were made by the blacksmith.[38] Henry Roshong made curtain rods in sets of two and four rods. This would tend to indicate that the curtain on some beds moved on only the two sides and was fastened to a wooden member at the foot. On the bedsteads that had four curtain rods the curtains could be pulled open and closed on all four sides.

The bed curtain was a necessary part of the high posted bedstead furniture. It provided privacy for the head of the household and his wife and also cut down on some of the drafts in the none-too-tight old houses. Some bed curtains were of red and white cotton cloth[39] (probably printed copper engraving), some were striped[40] others were resist dyed indigo, and still others were of chintz. Some sets of curtains were made of eleven yards of fabric while others required fourteen yards. It is probable that the eleven yard curtain hung on only three sides of the bed with the head board against the wall. The fourteen yard curtain surrounded the bed. One of the Samuel Rex store ledgers from Schaefferstown[41] records the sale of curtain rings in two dozen and two-and-a-half dozen lots. The two dozen would have been enough for one ring every eight inches on three sides of the bed and the two and a half dozen would have supplied all four sides every eight inches.

The spring in the traditional Pennsylvania Dutch bed was a bed cord or bed rope. This was of hemp, frequently raised, spun and plied on the farm where it was to be used. Many estate inventories list the *Schtrickgeschirr*—rope machine—necessary to make the 120 feet long rope. The bed was roped by tying one end to a peg at one of the top corners of the bed. The cord was then stretched to the peg in the same position on the foot rail. The rope was then taken to the next peg on the foot rail, and from there to the head rail and across to the next peg on the head rail. This was continued until the rope was stretched lengthwise to each peg on the top and bottom rails. The rope was taken from the last peg on the foot rail on a 45° angle to the nearest peg on the side rail and the same process used in stringing the bed lengthwise was continued until the cord was stretched between all the pegs on the side rails. The crosswise cord was not woven basket fashion, but merely lay on the lengthwise ropes. Once the rope was stretched to the last peg at the top, the rope was kept taut and turned on a 45° angle toward the middle of the bed and taken diagonally to the first intersection of lengthwise and crosswise ropes. It was then looped around this intersection and taken to the next diagonal intersection until it was passed around at least four such intersections. The rope is then tied to secure the end. The rope is now drawn tight enough to pluck it and have it vibrate like a string on a bass violin.

The Bed (Chaff Bag)

On the rope lay the bed. This in the early period was filled with goose feathers, and in later years with straw chaff or cornhusk. The bed was made of three lengths of coarse tow fabric 39 or 40 inches wide. The finished unfilled size, of course, depended on the size of the bedstead for which it was made, but the average size was about three to four inches longer and wider than its bedstead. The chaff bags ranged from 53 to 59 inches wide and 70 to 80 inches long.

The chaff was replaced at least once and usually twice a year at housecleaning time.[42] The one end was opened and the old straw was emptied on the manure pile in the barnyard. The tow tick was washed and refilled. This emptying and washing led to the old riddle: "Was geht noch der Grick un losst sei Bauch daheem?" "En Schprausack." (What goes to the creek and leaves its belly at home? A chaff bag.)

The fill was most often rye straw cut into 1½ to 2 inch lengths on the threshing floor of the barn using the straw bench. Some farms had no straw bench and one family used a plank laid on the threshing floor and the broad axe to cut the bed straw.[43] Rye was raised for its straw to tie corn fodder and fill beds long after it was used for rye bread.

Other families collected the corn husk, broke off the hard stems and saved the soft part of the husk. Then sitting at the kitchen table with scissors, they cut the husk into strips one and half inches wide, and stuffed beds and bolsters. Sleeping on a newly stuffed bed was considered great fun by children. The bed was then two to two-and-a-half feet high in the middle, but after one slept on it a while "hot mer en Graawe neigewore" (one wore a ditch into it).

Sheets

The bed was covered with a single homespun bed sheet which reached from head board to foot board and was tucked under the chaff bag on both sides. Charles West Thompson's diary records a trip in 1823 on which he travelled from Philadelphia to Lehigh County. One night he slept at a tavern in Fogelsville, "Here the dumb Dutchman did not know how to make a bed. There was just one sheet on the bed—no upper sheet." The tavern keeper stated that he had never heard of putting *two* sheets on *one* bed. That tavern keeper was not alone in the Dutch country. By 1823 many people had probably never heard of two sheets on anything less than two beds.

Some few did continue the early eighteenth century practice of sleeping on a sheet and under a sheet, because perhaps a half dozen or more sheets survive that have a decorative border along one edge. This border appears to have been folded down so the decoration showed on top of the feather bed.[44]

Bed sheets were made of fine linen and of tow. The linen ones were always sun bleached but the tow sheets were bleached only occasionally. The tow sheets when new had a surface akin to coarse sand paper but once they were washed several times they were no longer so abrasive.

Cotton bed sheets were in later years made of yard-wide fabric bought at the store, cut and sewn together. The older homespun yardage was custom woven for the client by a local weaver and made into bedding by the women of the family who had spun the yarn.

Many bed sheets were embroidered in one corner with initials and a number. These enabled the housewife to keep track of the rotation of the sheets and proper ownership.

Bolsters

Two bolsters were required on some beds while only one was needed for others. The determinant was probably personal or family preference. If two were used the bottom one was of tow of the same weave as the chaff bag or bed. The tow bolster was filled with straw or corn husk cut the same as the bed.

Clarence Kulp, Jr. has in his possession a homespun tow bolster from Bedminster Township, Bucks County, which still retains the old straw filling. Since the bolster is sewn shut with two-ply homespun linen thread, it is safe to assume that the filling has been in the bolster tick since some time in the last quarter of the last century. The bolster measures 55½ inches by 20 inches, weighs 8 pounds and 10 ounces and is filled with straw from one-and-a-half to two inches in length.

Resting on the straw bolster in the old beds was a feather bolster. The ticking for this bolster, the featherbed and the pillows was blue and white striped fustian—a fabric with a linen warp and a cotton fill. This ticking was tightly woven and held the goose feathers which were either home plucked or city bought. John Newton Culbertson[45] born in Franklin County, Pennsylvania, in 1841 said, "I often watched my mother holding a flapping, squawking goose with one hand and with the other hand plucked the soft white feathers." This practice bothered Julian Ursyn Niemcewicz as he observed, "Geese plucked alive drag themselves about pitiful and naked. The owners pluck their down two or three times a year. This terrible practice is the result of need or rather greed. For a pound of down one pays 5 shillings."[46]

The bolster case was of checked linen from the earliest days and woven in either two, three or four colors. The two most frequently found colors are blue and white but there is almost no end to the pattern variations in which these two colors were woven. The bolster case, pillow cases and bed case were made as a matching set, but today only a few of these sets are still together. During the eighteenth century the cases were sometimes made of printed indigo resist and at other times were made of sixteen- and twenty-harness pattern-weave fabric in blue and white.

Pillows

The pillow tick was of fustian and the pillow case was part of the matching set. The bolster case, pillow cases and bed case all had homespun tape ties to keep the cases on the items inside. There was no danger that the pillow case would slide off the pillow.

Margaret Van Horn Dwight stayed overnight at Rikers' tavern in Hanover Township a few miles from Bethlehem on her way to Warren, Ohio in the fall of 1810. She describes the bed in this way: "I never laughed so heartily in my life—Our bed to sleep on was straw—the pillows contained nearly a single handful of feathers and were covered with the most curious and dirty patch work I ever saw—we had one bed quilt and one sheet—I did not undress at all . . . "[47] Certainly not all farmers had as few feathers in their pillows as Watt Riker, but many pillow cases were probably no cleaner nor did they contain fewer patches. Patched bedding was probably commonplace among the thrifty Dutch who repaired everything as long as possible.

Featherbeds

The single bedding item most frequently mentioned by travelers through our region was the featherbed. The Dutchmen loved and defended it; the outsider feared and despised it. A Mr. Kennedy stopped at Nazareth in 1751 and at 10 o'clock was taken to his bed. While he was undressing, "High! says he, here is no bedclothes, I will lay my match coat over me." "No sir," said I, "This is the prettiest bed you ever lay in, it's prepared after the Dutch fasion, with a bed of the finest down to cover you with. It is a vast deal lighter and much warmer than any covering the English use!" "What," said he, "must I get under that bed? No indeed, that I never shall." You must understand the man that tended us in the evening was a very lusty, coarse man very near six foot high . . . Said he, "Shurely five or six of them Nazareen monsters intends to smother us under that bed to-night. Indeed I'll not sleep here! After some time he ventured to feel of it and then try'd if he could bear his head under it; at last he ventured to get in, and in a very short time got fast asleep."[48]

Elkanah Watson, a New Englander in a tour through Pennsylvania in October 1777, says "at Reamstown, [Lancaster Co] Pa. I was placed, between two beds, without sheets or pillows. This as I was told was a prevailing custom, but, which, as far as my experience goes, tends little to promote either sleep or comfort of a stranger."[49] Probably the difference between Kennedy's pleasure and Watson's bad experience was salesmanship. Watson had no good tavern keeper to explain the benefits of the feather bed.

Robert Wilson on the other hand did encounter a good salesman in the Dutch settlement in Maryland in 1807, "Stopping one night at the house of an old Dutchman, who was gone to bed, I was ushered into an extensive room in the middle of which was a large Dutch stove. The family were seated around the fire, and I was desired to sit down with them. Endeavoring to repay their kindness by entertaining them with a revelation of circumstances that had been presented to my notice, I was repeatedly answered by a voice from the farther corner of the room. I looked toward the part whence the sound seemed to arise, where stood a bed, but it was made, and no one on it, nor any person to be seen. I then said to the people seated about me, 'There is a voice comes from that corner, I can perceive nothing but the bed, and that appears to be made; however, there is certainly nobody on it.' Looking more attentively at the bed, I saw the head of the old Dutchman, the master of the house, peep out: 'No' said he, 'there certainly is not anybody *on* this bed—you English people are fools! You lie *on* the bed to keep you warm!—The best way is to have the bed on you.' I solemnly declare, the old Dutchman lay under a feather-bed! What he had between his carcase and the bedstead I do not remember."[50]

The feather bed did not reach from head board to foot board, but filled only the area between the pillows and the foot board. It, as the feather bolster and pillows, was made of wide blue and white striped fustian, and covered with a bedcase to match the bolster and pillow cases. The bedcase was slipped over the bed like a pillow case and was tied closed at the foot of the bed with homespun linen tape ties.

Jacob Mensch of Skippack, Pennsylvania, in his diary of 1888 gave the recipe for making a feather bed: feathers: goose, 19 pounds; weight of ticking, 8 pounds; total weight, 27 pounds.[51] No wonder Elkanah Watson did not think much of the Pennsylvania Dutch bed. He was probably pressed flat by the feather bed, because 16 to 19 pounds was the usual weight of feathers in a feather bed.

Coverlets

With the equipment covered this far, the eighteenth century bed would have been complete, but about 1760 the Pennsylvania Germans began putting a coverlet on top of the feather bed. The earliest ones were plain weave wool or tow in large plaid or check squares, or woolen bird's eye twill. From this humble beginning, the master weavers of Pennsylvania developed patterns to be hand woven on looms with 16, 20 and even 40 harnesses. The complicated looms required much skill to operate and still the patterns were limited to small repeats of geometric designs. With the invention of the Jacquard loom the horizons broadened and weaving became easier. The intricate floral and architectural patterns were now possible with less required of the weaver.[52]

Some coverlets were made in sets of two with one for the large bed and a matching one for the trundle bed. The trundle bed was made up in much the same fashion as the large bed but with only one pillow or bolster.

Laundering Practices

In the early days bed linen was not washed every week or oftener as is the present practice. In the careful households it was washed twice a year, at the time of the Spring and Fall house cleaning. Phoebe E. Gibbons says, "In the Spring there is a great washing of bedclothes, then blankets are washed which during the winter supplied the place of sheets.[53] These blankets were the white homespun blankets with a seam down the middle, which look just like the linen sheet but are of wool. Blankets for cover were not much used among the Pennsylvania Germans in the early period.

At housecleaning time the bedroom walls were whitewashed, the floors were scrubbed, the linens were washed and new chaff was put into all the beds.[54]

However, not everyone kept house the same and Robert Boyd encountered these conditions: " . . . The filthiness of these beds was the greatest hardship. In some places the cover consisted of a small feather bed, and nothing else; and in most cases the tick was too dirty to ascertain whether it was composed of woolen or linen, and very much resembled an oil-maker's apron. When I got warm, the odor was so strong that it reminded me of the description I have had of the middle passage of a slave ship. I have often been under the necessity of using my pocket handkerchief muffled about my mouth and nose, to prevent the covering from touching my face. In some places, other covering besides feathers were quite as filthy, and scarce at that. In some situations I have spent much of the night awake and sometimes got low-spirited and wept as I lay."

Boyd also encountered clean spare room beds which were damp. "A damp bed, though good and clean, is more dangerous than a dirty one, not damp. Such damp beds are more likely to be found among those in good circumstances, than those of the poorer classes. But a bed standing in a room without fire in the winter, or during a long rainy season, will become damp. I have often gotten into these fine clean beds, when in less than five minutes my feet and neck would give notice of the damp state of the sheets. With heavy drawers and flannel shirt, I have sometimes risked a slight degree of damp and lain still. In more extreme cases I have gotten on the top of the covering, lying at one side of the bed, and turning the opposite side of the covering over me."[55]

Benjamin Franklin also encountered the damp sheet syndrome in 1756 on his way to supervise the building of the frontier fort at Gnadenhutten near the Blue Mountain, "As to our lodging, 'tis on deal feather-beds, in warm blankets and much more comfortable than when we lodged at our inn the first night after we left home; for the woman being about to put very damp sheets on the bed, we desired to have her air them first; half an hour afterward she told us the bed was ready and the sheets were well aired. I got into bed, but jumped out immediately, finding them as cold as death and partly frozen. She had aired them indeed, but it was out upon the hedge. I was forced to wrap myself up in my great coat and woolen trousers. Everything else about the bed was shockingly dirty."[56]

The Pennsylvania Dutch were great believers in purification by air if not by water. The bed linen including the pillows and feather bed were hung out the second floor window by clamping them under the closed sash. This method of cleaning can still be seen in the Dutch country. Guy Reinert says that coverlets were cleaned by airing. "During Spring and Fall house-cleaning time a trip into the rural areas pays big dividends to him, or her, interested in seeing coverlets, as it is then that many can be found suspended from wash-lines and gaily waving in the breeze."[57] Quilts and coverlets can still be seen airing on the wash line at house cleaning time.

After airing, the coverlets were folded and returned to the chests where they were kept. The homespun bedcases and bed sheets were also kept in the chest folded in sixteenths to form a rectangle 18 inches by 20 inches.

Alan Keyser is a student of and author on many phases of Pennsylvania-German folklife. He is director of the Goschenhoppen Historians' Museum and Library at Green Lane, Pennsylvania and served as a consultant for the Philadelphia Museum of Art and the Winterthur Museum in their tercentenary exhibit The Pennsylvania Germans *in 1983. He has researched and authored "Beds, Bedding, Bedsteads and Sleep" that appeared as the entire quarterly for the Pennsylvania German Society (October 1978) and he co-authored with Ellen J. Gehret* The Homespun Textile Tradition of the Pennsylvania Germans *(1976). He was the editor for* The Account Book of The Clemens Family 1749-1857 *and co-editor of* The Accounts of Two Pennsylvania German Furniture Makers, *both books published as part of the sources and documents series of The Pennsylvania German Society, and Alan worked with Ellen J. Gehret on her book* This is The Way I Pass My Time/A Book About Pennsylvania German Decorated Hand Towels *(1985). His other articles on Pennsylvania-German gardens and log constructed buildings have appeared in* Pennsylvania Folklife *among others. Alan has lectured on these subjects for the Goschenhoppen Historians, the Schwenkfelder Library and the Pennsylvania Farm Museum. He can also be found pump boring each year at the Goschenhoppen Folk Festival in East Greenville.*

---

[1] I would like to thank Ellen J. Gehret for graciously allowing me the use of her research notes for this paper. Without them much of the information would not have been included here. Also, I would like to acknowledge the assistance of Clarence Kulp, Jr., who provided the information from " 'S Pennsylvaanisch Deitsch Eck" and from his notes on interviews with folk informants.

[2] Richard Weiss, *Häuser und Landschaften der Schweiz,* (Erlenbach-Zürich, 1959), p. 141.

[3] P. S. Hurst of Bowmansville, Pa. on June 23, 1977 stated that the window was opened just after his father's death in the 1950's. From Harry F. Stauffer of Farmersville, Pa. we have this account of his grandmother's death: "The family was in the room and grandmother was sitting on a chair when my aunt noticed that she was dying and said, "ich glaab ass die Alt schtarrebt. Duh sie ins Bett." ("I think she is dying. Put her in bed.") They put her into bed and after she died I was standing in the open doorway onto the porch—it was in the summer. My aunt then said, "sie is gschtarrewe. Mach's Fenschder uff." (She is dead. Open the window.) We did but the door was already open. This was to let the soul out the window."

[4] Inventory of George Trumbour, Lower Salford Township, Montgomery County, Pa. March 1811 un-

der the section "Bedroom"—"a looking glass. 75."

[5] Near the top of the *Kammer* side of the door from the *Schtub* to the *Kammer* in a one-and-a-half story half-timbered house on Market Street in Schaefferstown two turned pegs are to be found. The pegs, turned of walnut wood, are about 2½ inches from the top edge of the door and are about 20 inches apart. It is likely that these pegs once held an embroidered hand towel. These towels were decorated with flowers, birds, animals and people and other designs in various stitches with silk, linen and cotton thread.

[6] Inventory of George Trumbour, 1811.

[7] Monroe H. Fabian, *The Pennsylvania-German Decorated Chest,* (New York, 1978), p. 33.

[8] Interview with Sallie Landis of Lower Salford Township by Isaac Clarence Kulp, Jr. and A.G.K. in 1961.

[9] Register of Wills file #586, Norristown, Pa.

[10] Register of Wills file #352, Norristown, Pa.

[11] Raymond E. Hollenbach and Alan G. Keyser, eds., *The Account Book of the Clemens Family,* (Breiningsville, Pa., 1975).

[12] Register of Wills file #7633, Norristown, Pa.

[13] Register of Wills file #7599, Norristown, Pa.

[14] "Der Kaschbar Verzehlt" in 'S Pennsylvaanisch Deitsch Eck, Dec. 12, 1959, *Allentown Morning Call.*

[15] Quoted in Ira D. Landis, "Mennonite Agriculture in Colonial Lancaster County, Pennsylvania," 'S Pennsylvaanisch Deitsch Eck, Sept. 7, 1946, *Allentown Morning Call.*

[16] Estate Inventory of Henry Been, Skippach and Perkiomen Township, Montgomery County, Norristown, Pa.

[17] Register of Wills file #3921, Norristown, Pa.

[18] Register of Wills file #966, Norristown, Pa.

[19] Story collected from Herb Miller of Lenhartsville, Pa. in 1964.

[20] Register of Wills file #966, Norristown, Pa.

[21] Estate inventories which indicate room and area location of items on the farm are rare in the Pennsylvania Dutch area and to date no inventory has come to light which identifies entire room contents on the second floor of the house. Only partial listings have been found and it is from these that the upstairs room contents have been assembled.

[22] Robert Boyd, "Hardships of Circuit Rider Life on the Pennsylvania-Ohio Frontier," *Pennsylvania Folklife,* XVIII, No. 1 (Autumn 1961) 31.

[23] Register of Wills file #966, Norristown, Pa.

[24] Interview with Samuel R. Heller of Farmersville, Pa., June 11, 1978.

[25] Interview with Samuel R. Heller in August, 1963 in the *Kischde Schtub* in John Lentz's house between Frystown and Bethel in Berks County.

[26] Lewis Edgar Riegel, "Reminiscences of Centerport [Berks County] 1876-1885," *Pennsylvania Folklife,* XIV, No. 2 (December 1964), 34.

[27] Interview with Charles Sittler, New Tripoli, Pa., in November 1961.

[28] Interview of Hannah Clemens by Clarence Kulp, Jr. and A.G.K. July 14, 1961.

[29] Interview by Robert C. Bucher of Elam Becker of near Lititz, Pennsylvania during the Schaefferstown Folk Festival in 1976.

[30] A manuscript list kept by Susan Landis of Lower Salford Township, Montgomery County during the last quarter of the 19th century names all the tramps, peddlers and Fraktur artists who stayed on their farm and gives the dates of their stay. Owned by Robert C. Bucher.

[31] *Perkiomen Region,* Old Series, II, 9, p. 143.

[32] Pennsylvanische Berichte Nov. 1, 1750. Original in the Schwenkfelder Library, Pennsburg, Pa. Strassburger-Hinke, *Pennsylvania German Pioneers,* I, 430.

[33] Phoebe E. Gibbons, *Pennsylvania Dutch and Other Essays* (Philadephia, 1882), p. 115.

[34] Alan G. Keyser, Larry M. Neff and Frederick S. Weiser, *The Accounts of Two Pennsylvania German Furniture Makers,* (Breinigsville, Pa., 1978).

[35] Register of Wills file #352, Norristown, Pa.

[36] Old, short-legged and stiff people needed help getting into bed and to remedy this problem Joseph Overholt of Franconia Township, Montgomery County had "1 bedstead bench" listed in his inventory. Register of Wills file #14597, Norristown, Pa.

[37] Manuscript book entitled "Henry Roshong Black Smith of Summerytown" 1796 to 1804 owned by Clarence Kulp, Jr. Under the date April 10, 1800: "Ein zwey sett betlat Schrauben 0-3-9." This "zwey sett" meant a set of eight bolts and eight nuts. Here all four posts were bolted to the four rails. On a high-posted bedstead this allowed the otherwise large head and foot sections to be disassembled when the bedstead was moved.

[38] *Ibid.,* January 4, 1798 "2 umhanck stangen gemacht 0-6-6." December 12, 1803 "4 umhanck Stangen Gemacht 0-11-3."

[39] "Bill of Sale Womelsdorf May 9, 1787 bought by Joseph Fischbach from the firm of Friederich Ehrenfield and Henrich Hirsch." 12 yards red and white cotton cloth for curtains. 2 doz curtain rings. Raymond E. Hollenbach translated this in 1964.

[40] *The Account Book of the Clemens Family.* Three of Jacob Clemens's daughters were given 11 yards of stripe for a bed curtain. Other daughters were given 14 yards for a curtain.

[41] Samuel Rex Ledger No. 18 from Schaefferstown owned by Robert C. Bucher. January 19, 1802 "2½ doz curtain rings to Joseph Kratzer."

[42] Martha S. Best, "The Folk Festival Seminars: Crafts and Customs of the Year," *Pennsylvania Folklife,* XVIII, No. 4 (Summer 1969), p. 9.

[43] Interview with John K. Kerr of Harleysville, Pa. in March 1970.

[44] Ellen J. Gehret and Alan G. Keyser, *The Homespun Textile Tradition of the Pennsylvania Germans,* (Landis Valley, 1976), plates 15-17 show these decorated bedsheets, one with cross stitch, one with drawn work and one with knotted fringe.

[45] John Newton Culbertson, "A Pennsylvania Boyhood," *American Heritage,* XVIII, No. 1, (Dec. 1966) p. 80.

[46] Julian Ursyn Niemcewicz, *Under Their Vine and Fig Tree, Travels Through America 1797-1799, 1805* (New Jersey Historical Society, 1965) p. 111.

[47] Mahlon Hellerich, "A Journey through Pennsylvania in 1810," from 'S Pennsylvaanisch Deitsch Eck" *Allentown Morning Call,* 1944.

[48] "Travel account of 1751," *Mountain Echo* (Wind Gap, Pa.) Nov. 20, 1879. Copied from the notes of Alfred L. Shoemaker at the Myrin Library, Ursinus College, Collegeville, Pa.

[49] *An Account of the Manners of the German Inhabitants of Pennsylvania Written in 1789 by Benjamin Rush, M.D.,* Notes added by Prof. I. D. Rupp (Philadelphia, 1875) p. 22.

[50] Robert Wilson, *The Travels of that Well-known pedestrian Robert Wilson of March in the Isle of Ely Cambridgeshire . . . Written by himself. London Printed for the Author: 1807,* from " 'S Pennsylvaanisch Deitsch Eck", *Allentown Morning Call,* Jan. 14, 1950.

[51] Jacob B. Mensch manuscript Diary in the Mennonite archives of Eastern Pennsylvania at Kulpsville, Pa., edited and translated by Raymond E. Hollenbach, 1966.

[52] For a more detailed discussion of the Jacquard Coverlet see: Guy F. Reinert, *Coverlets of the Pennsylvania Germans,* Vol. XIII of the Pennsylvania German Folklore Society 1948. Also see Gehret, Keyser, *The Homespun Textile Tradition of the Pennsylvania Germans,* plates 69 through 88.

[53] P. E. Gibbons, p. 44.

[54] Diary of Mary Cassel copied by Herbert Harley 1944 at the Historical Society of Montgomery County. This diary covers the period January 1858 to September 1863. She mentions bedroom cleaning and whitewashing. "Sept. 16, 1858 Been busy in the bedroom puting Chafe [chaff] in and cleaning. . . . May 10, 1859 Tuesday Cleaned the best room. May 25, 1859 Whitewashed my room." Mary Cassel was born in 1828 in Lower Salford Township, Montgomery County.

[55] Robert Boyd, 31

[56] Benjamin Franklin, *The Autobiography of Benjamin Franklin, Poor Richard's Almanac and Other Papers.* (The Spencer Press) p. 290.

[57] Guy F. Reinert, p. 52.

A Cool Heart And A Watchful Mind

Creating Hmong Paj Ntaub in the Context of Community

Sally Peterson

The Hmong community in Philadelphia hosts a celebration of the New Year during Thanksgiving weekend. In the highlands of their Laotian homeland, harvest's end and the fullness of the moon determines the proper days to celebrate. But here, people calculate that a four-day work and school holiday will enable kinsmen from North Carolina, Rhode Island, Ohio, New Jersey, Michigan and even California to attend the festivities.

The New Year is more than a reunion, more than a celebration. It is an affirmation of community, an enactment of history, a time to measure the year's successes and a time to plan for the future. Tradition and innovation merge as the generations unite. It is a time to express what it means to be Hmong.

The New Year continues to be an occasion for the display of traditional styles of clothing, decorated with intricately-worked paj ntaub (pronounced "pa ndau"). Translated literally as "flower cloth," paj ntaub refers to the geometrically designed, symmetrically arranged embroidery, appliqué and batik work practiced by generations of Hmong women. The cultural significance of paj ntaub is as richly textured and thickly layered as the aprons, skirts, jackets, sashes and silver that constitute festive dress. Paj ntaub can be seen as a visual metaphor for both social organization and community interaction, incorporating a culture's principles of identity, creativity and responsibility.

Clan legends and sporadic documentation in ancient Sinitic texts distinguish the Hmong as an independent people migrating ever southwards from the northernmost reaches of Mongolia. Struggles with the Han and their dynasties propelled the Hmong through the valleys of China and on into the highland provinces of the southern border. Though frequently regarded as dangerous rebels in the annals of ancient China, historians took note of the brilliance of Hmong needlework (Yih-Fu 1967).

The Hmong retain a strong sense of history, and oral accounts speak of lost battles and kingdoms, of lost alphabets and literature, of conflicts with the increasingly imperialistic Chinese. Approximately a century and a half ago, thousands of Hmong resisting assimilation began to leave China, migrating through the mountainous terrain of Southeastern Asia. They settled in the north of Vietnam and Laos; some later continued westward to Thailand and Burma. Most preferred to live in the mountains, practicing swidden agriculture and maintaining traditional customs. They remained relatively distant from the lowland political strife of weakened kingdoms, European colonialism and awakening nationalist fervor, yet they were keenly aware of their lack of educational opportunity and political influence in the governments serving the Lao majority.

The mountainous highlands of Southeast Asia host a diverse number of both indigenous and immigrant ethnic populations, and the lowland-based Lao government counted the Hmong as one of the largest ethnic minorities in Laos. The Hmong established villages throughout the northern provinces, and continued to institute and practice the customs and traditions which characterize their culture. Extensive clan networks facilitated communication and contact between isolated communities. The annual New Year celebration united distant kin each year, and marriages cemented alliances between clans. Most material wealth was converted to silver bars and jewelry by Hmong silversmiths, and was displayed with the brilliant paj ntaub fabricated by the women.

A Hmong infant first encounters the world sheltered and supported by paj ntaub. Gifts from mothers to daughters and daughters-in-law, baby carriers literally bond children to pre-

Plate 4. *Detail of Green Hmong funeral piece (Hmoob Ntsuab Noob Ncoos) made by Yeu Chang, in Philadelphia, c. 1984. Cotton broadcloth. 18" square. Collection of Sally Peterson.*

The style of appliqué is called "dab tsos dhos," which requires the seamstress to plot her design upon a grid scratched onto the fabric. Several different interpretations of symbolic meaning have been attributed to this design. Some say it represents family unity, others believe that it stands for a man's wealth on earth, or the pathway to heaven. This funeral pillow was displayed with other, modified traditional pieces, and sold to an American.

Figure 1. *(left) Green Hmong Baby Carrier (Hmoob Ntsuab mooj peej). Made by Yer Yang, c. 1984. Cotton, nylon, wool yarn. 16¼" w. × 24" l. Collection of Pang Xiong Sirirathasuk.*

The smaller upper rectangle is referred to as the head, and the larger rectangle is called the body. Pang Xiong explains that this head design is named for the difficulty of the technique used to produce it. A rough translation might be: "straight-edged perfection." The batik and appliquéd design on the body represents a guardian spirit that protects the child from harm. (right) Funeral pillow also seen in Plate 4. Children try to provide their parents with many such funeral pillows, to make their journey to the next life comfortable, to show their respect, and to make their parents feel well-loved. The designs sewn onto funeral pillows may also be sewn onto the collars and cuffs of funeral jackets.

ceding generations (fig. 1). Reciprocally, funeral pillows and burial clothing are presented by daughters to parents and in-laws, insuring that the elders will leave this world well-respected and loved (fig. 1 and plate 4). Ancestors in the next world will recognize them by the designs of their funerary splendor. Every New Year, feasts and courtship games provide opportunities for young people to meet and to admire each other's new finery; prospective parents-in-law assess character, economic standing and filial devotion by the quality of needlework and silver displayed. The weddings that follow on the heels of the New Year also require newly-made, freshly-embroidered clothing, symbols of the new life to begin for the young couple. Paj ntaub marks the rites of passage in an individual's life, and the passage of time in the life of the community.

Throughout their long mutual history, the Chinese distinguished regional and dialectic Hmong sub-groups according to a prominent color or feature of their traditional dress, and the terms Green Hmong (*Hmoob Ntsuab*), White Hmong (*Hmoob Dawb*), Striped Hmong (*Hmoob Txaij*) and Black Hmong (*Hmoob Dub*) continue to identify differing cultural and dialectical patterns of the Hmong in Laos. All Hmong women, whatever their sub-group, practice embroidery. Accounts of Hmong embroidery grace the pages of missionary treatises, 19th-century travelogues, and French, German, Chinese and English ethnographies. Folktales collected from the Hmong in early 20th-century China relate stories of heroines abducted by tigers, who rescue their erstwhile rescuers through resourceful manipulation of their embroidered sashes (Graham 1956). Strips of cross-stitch embroidery continue to embellish hats, turbans, sleeves and hems, and cross-stitched squares form belts, collars, baby carriers, and funeral pillows.

According to traditional practices in Hmong culture, a young girl embarks on her first piece of paj ntaub between the ages of three and six. She first learns the counting techniques of cross-stitch embroidery. Instruction occurs more through modelling than by spoken directions; indeed, one later measure of skill is the ability to analyze and reproduce a design just by looking at it. In the words of one seamstress, "The Hmong little girl, she doesn't need the mother to teach a lot. The mother just shows the design, and the daughter has to figure it out. The mother just shows, and the daughter has to count by herself."

Girls learn early that patterns can be varied through slight changes in counting and alterations of color. The fabric chosen for embroidery has a raised weave which allows the maker to count threads. Older Hmong recall using handwoven hemp cloth, particularly in the more isolated regions of Laos. Most now prefer commercially produced cotton broadcloth, which allows a greater degree of freedom in the choice of background color. Most designs are worked outwards from a central point, in symmetric multiples of two. Often just one color is worked at a time, requiring precisely accurate counting on the part of the maker. Embroidery designs may be named after the natural phenomena they resemble, but many names simply refer to the counting formula required to form the design, such as "Three times three Cross-stitch". Hmong women have also adapted designs practiced by the ethnic Lao and by the Mien, who also inhabit the highland areas known to the Hmong. A girl will learn other embroidery stitches, such as the chain, running, blanket and the satin stitch, as she begins to learn appliqué techniques.

White Hmong and Green Hmong women execute several styles of appliqué. The most difficult, called *dab tshos dhos,* appears on collars, baby carriers and funeral accoutrements. Strips of appliqué form maze-like patterns, guided by a grid which has been scratched freehand onto the fabric with a needle. The maker attaches each side of the strip to the backing fabric with a series of minute stitches, traditionally sewn with a short, inch-long needle, reputedly, and understandably, very difficult to thread. Like the daughters of American quilters, Hmong girls remember being called upon by their elders to " . . . come thread my needle!" Often the appliquéd strips of dab tshos dhos are of the same color as the background fabric; the maker layers smaller fillets onto the base, and additional embroidery, strategically placed, adds depth to the design. A background fabric of a contrasting color also produces the desired textured effect. Some of these complex patterns, magnified to wall hanging sizes, produce striking visual effects and optical illusions.

The White Hmong produce the precise, geometrical symmetry of paj ntaub through a folding and cutting technique reserved for reverse appliqué effects. Fiber arts of many cultures utilize this technique, including the ubiquitous "snowflakes" familiar to American school children. The art of reverse appliqué demands precision cutting, and developing this skill requires much practice; a slip of the scissors will render a design useless. A woman may guide her eye with a thread spool or a coin while making a curved design, but few rely on the use of a straightedge for angular patterns. White Hmong use single squares of reverse appliqué (fig. 2) to form the base of decorative shoulder bags, an essential feature of festive dress for women and men. Doubled squares efficiently form the rectangular collars of women's jackets and funeral pillows, and squares sewn together sequentially function as belts and borders. The Hmong also fold and cut with paper, fabricating spirit money and other necessities for religious ceremonies.

Traditional reverse appliqué designs include the *Snail,* which becomes the *Elephant's Foot* when additional rings are added (fig. 2, upper). Other frequently seen designs are the *Star,* and *Ram's Horn.* Straight-edged designs like *Rooster Tail* and *Snake Running,* once made by the grid technique, were reportedly changed a generation ago, as Hmong women learned to produce these designs with the less time-consuming fold and cut reverse appliqué style.

The maker has several options available to her as she finishes sewing down the appliqué design. She may embellish the focal square with overlaid appliqué, embroidery, or a combination of the two. She may choose to add layers of borders, and apply embroidery or appliqué to them. Unembellished reverse appliqué pieces are not considered to be complete without an embroidery complement.

Hmong Ntsuab women, the Green Hmong, practice the art of wax resist. English speakers often translate Hmong Ntsuab as 'Blue Hmong', because the Hmong concept of 'green' includes

Figure 2. *(upper) "Elephant Foot" paj ntaub. Embroidery and reverse appliqué, fold and cut technique. Artist unknown, c. 1986, Thailand, cotton and polyester blend. 20" square. Collection of Sally Peterson. This design, produced by adding rings to a circle of snails (see central motif) is based on a spirit paper pattern produced by ritual specialists. (lower) "Dream Maze" paj ntaub, reverse appliqué, dab tshos dhos technique. Artist unknown, c. 1985, Thailand, cotton and polyester blend. 22 1/4" × 21". Collection of Sally Peterson. Some say this design is called "Dream" because it never ends. Expanding designs to fit the sizes required by wall hangings sometimes taps a design's potential in ways not previously explored.*

Figure 3. *Detail of appliquéd belt, White Hmong tradition (Hmoob Dawb sev), made by Mrs. Chia Vang Yang, c. 1984, in Thailand. White cotton appliquéd onto alternate squares of acid green and hot pink nylon, 49 1/2" l. × 3 3/4" w. excluding ties. Collection of Mrs. Pang Xiong Sirirathasuk.*

White Hmong women often wind several sashes around their waists when donning traditional garments. Mrs. Yang anchored her appliqué with a miniscule buttonhole stitch. The pattern seen partially is "Snake Running Inside a Cross", and the pattern seen whole is called "Snake Running in a Windmill". The colors are those considered appropriate for young people.

leaves. The contrast between the light and dark many shades of what is described in English as "blue"; the color of the sky, for example, and many hues of indigo, the dye used to produce batik work. Batiked fabric forms the basis for the pleated skirts and baby carriers worn by Hmong Ntsuab women. One oral account attributes the origin of wax resist work to Green Hmong women of long ago. Observing tiny birds living in banana trees, the women saw the birds drip dancing trails of spit on the young leaves, tracing intricate designs over the bright green surface. As the leaves grew older and developed their characteristic dark green color, the Hmong women saw that the patterns traced by the birds remained the light green of young highlighted the intricate, delicate bird designs. According to the story, this inspired Green Hmong women to apply beeswax to cloth before dyeing it with indigo.

The densely pleated Hmong skirts require twelve to eighteen yards of fabric. Wax is applied in a series of rectangles upon the skirt length. Each waxed rectangle may carry a different design. Hmong Ntsuab wax resist patterns demand considerable conceptual skills as well as eye-hand coordination. Following the grain of the weave, the artist scratches a grid onto the cloth. She constructs the pattern by crossing the intersecting grid lines in a diagonal direction, applying short strokes of hot wax in one direction at a time (fig. 4). She then draws lines parallel to the first direction, and finishes the design outline by connecting the parallel lines with perpendicular strokes. The background may be filled in with small crossed dashes, reminiscent of cross-stitch designs. The batik artist then dips the waxed fabric repeatedly into an indigo dye bath. Hemp cloth was well-liked because it easily absorbed the dye. Today, some artists first soak waxed cotton cloth in instant Tofu mix; the soy bean flour helps to absorb the dye. After the cloth dries, the wax is boiled out.

Batik work is not finished until it has been trimmed with appliqué. Wax resist patterns have imbedded designs, channels which guide the application of red fabric strips. This bold embellishment combines with the batik to create a total effect of layered, interacting geometry.

Hmong women may compare learning the principles of paj ntaub making with learning to cook. One doesn't have a fixed recipe, but rather, a repertoire of ingredients (or designs, as the case may be) which may be combined in a variety of ways. Experimentation is approved and encouraged, yet basic, implicit rules govern the emergent styles. Just as pumpkin water or parsley cool hot peppers and salt, a neutral black or white complements bright reds and greens. Women strive to create a sense of balance as they organize their designs on the fabric plane. Mirror image symmetry and even numbers provide a satisfying reciprocity. The number, color and the width of borders is carefully considered. These principles remain consistent whether the piece produced is an impersonal one sold to a stranger or a baby carrier lovingly stitched for a child.

Americans seldom have the opportunity to observe and to understand paj ntaub in its traditional forms and contexts. The paj ntaub offered for sale in the United States appears in guises radically different from the vestments and accoutrements which clothe body and soul in Hmong culture. The transformations which have occurred within this art form owe their existence to the extraordinary conditions of war, exile and resettlement. Hmong women have invested their traditional artistic resource with a new wave of creativity, generating a myriad of innovative expressions based on ancient principles, and producing designs and forms which have proved to be both financially lucrative and culturally meaningful. The roots of these transformations lie imbedded in both ancient and modern history, in the philosophy and the praxis of the Hmong themselves. A brief description of these historical circumstances should prove useful for understanding the context of contemporary paj ntaub making.

Over the years, the Hmong have faced many obstacles in their efforts to maintain their traditional way of life. Living in the midst of other ethnic groups and resisting assimilation by dominant cultures has endowed them with a strong sense of cultural identity. This independence of the Hmong, their ability to organize militarily and their extensive kinship-based political structures have at times brought them to the vortex of political struggle in Southeast Asia. During the Japanese occupation of Laos during World War II, the allied forces enlisted the aid of the Hmong in rescue operations and guerilla warfare, relying on their thorough knowledge of the isolated mountain terrain. Several Hmong leaders emerged who figured prominently as representatives of their people in the years after war's end. Largely through their efforts, educational opportunities became available to an increasing number of young people, modern technology began to penetrate to the mountain villages, and business opportunities in Laotian towns and cities began to draw some Hmong out of the mountains.

Within a decade of the close of World War II, after the decisive battle of Dienbienphu in North Vietnam, the French withdrew from Indochina. The newly independent Laos became embroiled in a civil conflict which did not officially end until 1975, and still continues on a covert level. The rupture within the nation divided loyalties within the Hmong minority as well. According to clan affinity, political conviction or circumstance, such as geographic location, Hmong lineages aligned themselves with either the American-backed Royal Lao Forces or the communist Pathet Lao.

The strategic advantages of the Hmong territory and their already proven effectiveness as a fighting force brought them to the attention of

Figure 4. *Paj ntaub wall hanging, Green Hmong batik tradition. Indigo dyed cotton with appliquéd red embellishments. Artist unknown, Thailand, c. 1986. 16" square. Collection of Glenn Hinson.*

Traditional batik artists plot their design onto a grid, just as dab tsos dhos appliqué is practiced. The artists apply the wax with short strokes, working in one diagonal direction at a time, which requires precision counting, intense concentration, and a thorough knowledge of the pattern. The artist can vary the look of one design from piece to piece by choosing to highlight different patterns within the design.

the CIA during the 1950s. The Americans provided relief supplies, arms and training to the Hmong supporting the Royal Lao forces. This so-called "clandestine" army fought the North Vietnamese through guerilla warfare and in organized military combat.

Throughout the 1960s, control of several districts within Laos passed back and forth between the Royal Lao Army and the Pathet Lao, disrupting traditional life and forcing thousands of Hmong into internal refugee settlements and lowland towns. A cease-fire was declared and a coalition government formed in 1973. But with the total withdrawal of American support in 1975, the Pathet Lao gained control of the government, establishing the Laos People's Democratic Republic. This move spelled disaster for the U.S. - Royal Lao aligned Hmong who remained in Laos. Tens of thousands attempted to escape, and many died trying. Those who survived the trek to the border and the dangerous crossing of the Mekong River sought haven in the rapidly congested refugee camps of Thailand.

Thousands of Hmong remain in Laos, and thousands still reside in Thai refugee camps, either waiting for resettlement in another country or hoping for a change in government which will allow them to repatriate. Over sixty thousand have immigrated to the United States. They maintain contact with their loved ones in Thailand and Laos and other resettlement countries through letters and audio cassette tapes.

Relief workers in the refugee camps immediately began to encourage the Hmong to produce paj ntaub textiles as a means of economic support. Paj ntaub had occasionally been sold to outsiders before, especially during the war years, but never produced on such a scale as occurred in the camps. The size of small cities, refugee camps provided a common meeting ground, allowing Hmong from all parts of Laos to observe and occasionally share each others designs and workmanship styles. In the camps, perhaps for the first time, many craftspeople encountered different versions of their own traditions, such as the wax resist work of the Green Hmong, the miniscule stitching of the White Hmong; or the designs of a distant province. The camps provided an opportunity for Hmong craftspeople, primarily women, to expand their paj ntaub repertoires. Camp workers also suggested ways to adapt paj ntaub to contemporary market forms found successful with other types of ethnic textile arts, including wall hangings, purses, ornaments, coverlets, bookmarks, pillows, belts, coasters and dolls.

The *objets d'art* produced in the camps are

distributed to the buying public through several channels. Relief organizations such as the Christian Allied Missionary Association have developed marketing networks of their own, utilizing their supporting organizations in the United States and other countries. They have instituted a quality control system in the camps, adjudicating work submitted to them by the Hmong, and they provide seamstresses with fabrics reflecting the pastels and earth tones popular in the United States. An ad hoc market has sprung up on the perimeter of the camp, and paj ntaub wares are displayed in small booths, in hopes of attracting the occasional camp visitor. Merchants of ethnic arts from Bangkok and Chiang Mai regularly visit to buy in volume, although access to the camps has become steadily more restricted. As their relatives become established in the States, families also send shipments of paj ntaub to America, to be sold alongside the articles crafted by Hmong in this country. Many prefer this method of selling their paj ntaub, though they must face the hazards of delayed mail deliveries and customs searches. But the American dollar buys more than the Thai baht, and camp residents, with little means of support, are often desperate for money. Relatives in America can also request items, color schemes and designs that they know will sell. Some send back photographs of successful pieces, requesting duplications.

Following the advice of relief administrators, the Hmong also developed a new form of textile art radically different from traditional abstract designs; a pictorial art painted in thread. The name *paj ntaub dab neej,* meaning paj ntaub of people, customs and traditions, is usually translated as *story cloths* (fig. 5 and 6). These pieces depict scenes drawn from recent experience, from daily life, from an extensive corpus of folktales. A number of cloths are modeled on illustrations from biblical stories, Christmas cards, and children's books available in the camp's limited libraries. These topics, chosen for their appeal to American audiences, also reflect recent Christian proselytizing, and concerns with acquiring literacy. Frequently, captions written in English are stitched onto the cloth, providing would-be American purchasers with a cultural translation. Several means of production have been reported for these textiles, but the general pattern indicates that the majority of the cloths are composed and pencilled by a small number of skilled male artists, and painstakingly sewn by mothers, wives, sisters and daughters, who retain color control. Sewing the cloths is not considered very difficult, but it is exhausting, and time-consuming. But time is one resource in the camps that the Hmong can fully exploit. Story cloths are seldom made by Hmong in the United States, but, paradoxically, most are sold here by relatives of camp residents.

The Hmong have established communities throughout the United States, with the majority congregating in the Minneapolis - St. Paul region of Minnesota and in the Central Valley of California. Many families have crossed and recrossed the continent, seeking employment, educational opportunities, and reunification with relatives and clan lineages. The majority of Hmong in Pennsylvania live in Philadelphia, though there are sizeable communities in Reading, Erie and Lancaster County.

Since the majority of those in Pennsylvania have lived in the United States less than a decade, the Hmong communities still experience a certain degree of flux. It would thus be a mistake to draw conclusions about the current role of paj ntaub production. Some generalizations, however, can be offered. Selling paj ntaub has served as a pragmatic activity for many women during their first years in America. But with increased opportunities for job training and improved English skills, many have found more lucrative employment elsewhere, fully appreciating the added advantage of job security and other benefits unavailable in the uncertain, fluctuating world of crafts marketing. Yet others, kept home due to childcare responsibilities or an inability to work because of age, language or health problems, continue to supplement their families' incomes through occasional sales of paj ntaub. These women sell mostly at local crafts fairs or church and community sponsored events, open to all Hmong women of the community. Though there has been talk of it, none of the Pennsylvania Hmong have established a retail outlet such as those in the larger communities of California and Minnesota. Only a few exceptional women have been able to vigorously pursue selling paj ntaub as a viable livelihood. They must continually analyze buying trends and create new items that attract the interests and tastes of the varied audiences who browse through the dozens of crafts fairs they attend each year.

"I usually use old designs to make new things for sale," says Pang Xiong, a successful paj ntaub exhibitor. Most differences between traditional pieces and market items can be attributed to changes in scale. Design motifs can be expanded, contracted, and combined in a variety of ways. Squares and rectangles, the building blocks used to shape traditional clothing, funeral pillows and baby carriers, have become enlarged to serve as wall hangings, purses and other marketable items. Experimentation with these basic shapes has also produced eyeglass cases, Christmas ornaments, pincushions and a variety of fanciful novelty items. Most women continue to use traditional designs, such as *Snake Running, Ghost Hand, Elephant's Foot, Rooster Tail,* and *Buffalo Horn,* but new designs, unique interpretations of American popular motifs, have also emerged, such as the *Heart* and *Butterfly.* In the tradition of paj ntaub, as in any living, vital art, certain designs, motifs and colors can be very much in demand, then fade from popularity, to be revived again at another time.

Contemporary craftswomen also embroider

Figure 5*. Story Cloth, artist unknown, c. 1987, Thailand, cotton polyester blend, 25" × 51¾". Collection of Sally Peterson. This idyllic view of the lush Laotian landscape incorporates imagery from Lao Buddhist lore and Hmong mythology. It also reveals a keen observation of animal anatomy, behavior, and the natural habitat.*

***Figure 6.** (right) Story Cloth, made by Plia Lee, c. 1985, in Thailand. Cotton and polyester blend. 33½" × 34½". Collection of Pang Xiong Sirirathasuk.*

This story cloth describes the process of leaving the refugee camp for immigration to the United States. Officials conduct exit interviews in the upper-lefthand corner, and tearful goodbyes are exchanged as the immigrants board the buses for the airport. (left) Story Cloth, made by Plia Lee, c. 1985, in Thailand. Cotton and polyester blend. 31¾" × 34". Collection of Pang Xiong Sirirathasuk. The makers of this cloth have chosen to depict an esoteric subject not immediately recognizable to outsiders. The scene portrays the visit of a ritual specialist, or shaman, to the home of a sick person. He communicates with the spirits, a sacrifice is made, and a diagnosis read from propitious signs. A ritual meal is shared, then the family sends the shaman off with his due; the jawbone of the sacrificed pig. This piece has no English text accompaniment.

on a larger scale than did previous generations. Women take advantage of larger weave fabrics and thicker threads, perceiving the preference of Western consumers for large pieces. Many do not attempt to recreate the minute work of their younger days because they cannot find the inch-long, whisker-thin needles and finely-spun sewing silk that was commonly available in Laos. As the size of the stitches expands, however, so does the size of the projected piece, which often requires as much labor, if less skill, as the smaller, finer needlework.

The pastels and earth tones adopted to please an American public contrast sharply with the bright color combinations preferred by the Hmong. But the wisdom of this strategy has begun to be questioned. As Pang Xiong explained recently to a group of countrywomen, "I have to sell through history." A growing number of consumers recognize the value of paj ntaub as a collectible folk art, and seek pieces which reflect their perceptions of authenticity. Information about the cultural context of paj ntaub also heightens interest in the history and present situation of the Hmong themselves. Pang Xiong has found that an informative presentation to interested customers primarily improves intercultural communication, but secondarily, it also boosts sales.

Creative manipulation of media and technique also occurs in new forms of needlework. The figurative designs used to produce story cloths have been translated into chain and cross-stitch embroidery, and are made by women in the States as well as those in the refugee camps. Young Hmong Americans particularly have experimented with combining Hmong motifs with traditional American sampler styles. At least one Hmong artist, a camp resident, has included figurative representations in her batik designs, a practice which exemplifies how an innovative idea can be translated from one expressive medium to another.

It would be premature to predict the long-term repercussions of the changes wrought by these modern expressions of an ancient art. The role of paj ntaub as a commodity to be sold in the marketplace is clearly a radical departure from its traditional functions of reciprocal exchange, community identity and display of self. Yet its very economic viability now helps to maintain its vitality as a useful, meaningful, community-based art. The motive for experimenting with new forms, styles and design combinations may lie in the wish to appeal to an unknown public, but the inspiration comes from the mind of the maker, whose interpretations of new ideas are most often tempered by traditional structures. As the various forms of paj ntaub develop and change, new styles continually emerge, and yet traditional features remain, marking the pieces as distinctly Hmong. Craftswomen are responding with an increasing sophistication to American tastes, and creatively using their inherited design principles to a degree perhaps unprecedented in the history of their needlework.

But many do worry about the very real possibility of losing, forgetting, or truncating this art form, as well as other traditional cultural forms. The Hmong in Philadelphia, as in other communities across the nation, are deeply concerned with issues of conserving their culture in the United States, and have begun to take action to preserve traditions for the coming generations. Recently, Hmong women in Pennsylvania have instituted apprenticeship programs, sponsored by the Folklife Programs of the Heritage Commission and the Pennsylvania Council on the Arts. Three master craftswomen in Philadelphia instructed over a dozen Hmong girls in traditional paj ntaub. Already adept at embroidery, the girls created a series of samplers exhibiting techniques in various styles of appliqué and batik. No contemporary pieces were displayed as examples; the purpose was to instruct the girls in the construction of traditional styles and the rules for their making. The series of lessons opened with lectures in the proper conduct of a Hmong lady. Instructions included manners, morals and work habits. The lessons, conducted in the Hmong language, were modeled on the pedagogic styles practiced in Laotian and Thai schools; the students took assiduous notes, memorized the instructions, and stood to recite when called upon. They carefully sewed finished samples to notebook pages. Paj ntaub, however, would not be taught this way in Laos. Learning paj ntaub and its integration with one's social role would have permeated a woman's life and memories for as long as she could remember. Yet for the master teachers of the apprenticeship programs, skill with the needle implies that one has internalized the codes of behavior expected of a Hmong woman. Praiseworthy paj ntaub indicates a cool heart, a patient hand, a watchful mind. Material art and social action are thickly laminated. To teach one without the other would be unthinkable.

But the balance struck between maintaining tradition and responding to economic necessity is a delicate one. Hmong women in the Delaware Valley have begun recently to master the techniques and aesthetic systems of American quilting. Various organizations and individuals in counties near Philadelphia have taught Hmong women the principles of quilting, supplied them with patterns and materials, and hired them to appliqué, piece and occasionally quilt large spreads, which in turn are sold to the tourist market in Lancaster County and Reading. The Hmong women appreciate this new economic direction which enables them to utilize the arduous training required to master the art of paj ntaub. Already highly skilled seamstresses, they consider the rigors of quilting to be less taxing in terms of time and skill requirements than their own Hmong needlework. They focus almost exclusively on reproducing traditional American patterns for their patrons, but some also experiment with combining the two traditions of piecing and paj ntaub.

Although they receive little public credit for their painstaking efforts, quilting offers Hmong women possibilities of economic return without extensive retraining or reliance on a new language, and it pays better than making paj ntaub. Women are painfully aware that they cannot receive adequate compensation for the hours that their traditional needlework demands. Teenagers are learning quilting at the expense of practicing paj ntaub, motivated by the prospect of earning money. Concerned about their children's future, women do not encourage their daughters to try to make a living exclusively through any kind of needlework. They insist that the youth of their communities pursue skills which will allow them to compete successfully in the mainstream of American culture. The need to explore new economic and educational opportunities has not diminished the respect accorded to the making of paj ntaub, but it has severely limited the time—and incentive—necessary for learning. This trend will continue unless paj ntaub is consistently accorded gallery status, a practice that has been initiated by several museums in states with significantly large Hmong populations. Paj ntaub deserves recognition and support as a creative and technically complex art, one richly endowed with its producers' aesthetic philosophy and rooted in an ancient tradition. Commercial paj ntaub itself documents a crucial epoch in the history of an ethnic people. But one cannot command the same price at a flea market as one can at a gallery, and Hmong women have little or no access to other display venues. In the meantime, women will have to choose the path of economic necessity, and sew for their American patrons. The ramifications of adding American quilting traditions to Hmong craft repertoires cannot be fully reckoned at this time. Hmong women, however, clearly categorize quilting as a temporary activity participated in for economic reasons, whereas paj ntaub, even paj ntaub sewn for sale, remains a meaningful link between themselves and their culture, and a link between their community and the American public.

The concerns of Hmong women, particularly those raised in the traditional milieu, regarding the inevitable loss of knowledge caused by radically changing lifestyles is not new. Distinctions had been made, even in Laos, between city and mountain village standards and abilities in the art of paj ntaub. As commercial fabrics and Western styled clothing replaced hand weaving, the Hmong knew the price they paid for progress. There is tremendous interest within Hmong communities to document the older designs and techniques which now live mainly in the memory of a very few. They recognize that new methods for preserving and transmitting knowledge, such as literacy, photography and video can be exploited for the eventual use of generations to come.

Community valuation of paj ntaub has changed, but it has not disappeared. In the Hmong communities of the United States, a woman's abilities are now evaluated by a different set of criteria than had been the case in Laos. Fine needlework is admired but it is not the *ideal* measure of worth. Even in Laos, though most girls did learn to sew, fewer became experts, and, like everywhere, not everybody liked to ply a needle. In the American context, learning paj ntaub is becoming more and more a matter of personal choice; albeit one that requires tremendous concentration and determination. Those who love to sew will continue to do so, and if their will to maintain their Hmong identity is also strong, then they will continue to perpetuate the dynamics of innovation and tradition that characterize paj ntaub.

Memories can easily idealize the past, and too often scholars can romanticize a folk culture; valuable data is at risk when the assumed cohesion of the past is compared with the apparent chaos of the present. How then can the present social impact of paj ntaub be divined? One way to investigate the meaning that paj ntaub has in the lives of contemporary women is to examine the evaluative criteria used to measure the worth of a piece. Paj ntaub made for personal use is judged by different standards than that made for sale. The funeral clothing a woman sews for her parents must reflect the designs common to her sub-group and region; pattern supersedes other concerns. Similarly, gifts given by a woman to her children should be sewn with the same designs as those she received from her parents, for paj ntaub symbolizes continuity. Paj ntaub given to family members is a gift from the heart and the mind. The stitches should be very tiny; very close together, and very even, indicating the maker's control over her craft and herself. Paj ntaub worn at weddings and at the New Year should incorporate bright color combinations; fluorescent pinks, greens and yellows for the youth, more sedate reds, greens and blacks for the elders. In the words of one craftswoman:

"We need white, black, dark red, dark green, dark yellow, dark blue.
Everything has to be very bright colors
It is the Hmong combination of colors.
Sometimes, people order their own colors.
But, our idea, when we make for ourselves,
(you can follow the ladies to the store; you can see)
They just choose their own colors.
They never buy another kind of people's colors."

If a woman or her daughters have neither the time nor the proper materials to prepare ceremonial clothes, then traditional skirts, hats, sashes and purses can be bought from seamstresses in Thai camps, who spend weeks on each piece. These items even come sheathed in a protective plastic coating which is not removed when worn. Though many women must spend more time making paj ntaub for sale rather than for personal use, the ideal is still to provide for your family first, be it through labor or purchase.

Strength is the most important criteria used to measure the value of a piece made for sale. It is a matter of pride for Hmong women to stand by the quality of the work they sell, whether made by themselves or by relatives in Thailand. They check to see if all layers of the appliqué are thoroughly anchored to the backing piece, and will reinforce them if not satisfied. They can guarantee their American customers that the pillow cover, the wall hanging they buy is machine washable. Women will also incorporate items made for sale into ritual gift-giving exchanges, particularly in relationships established with Americans. As with family gifts, they try to insure that the pattern on the piece represents their sub-group, even if the recipient hasn't the least idea of the design's meaning. If she presents a story cloth for a wedding gift, the giver often makes sure that an even amount of figures are represented, avoiding the unlucky symbolism of odd numbers.

Hmong women technically judge the story cloths that pass through their hands according to the density of the satin stitches used to fill in a design. Pang Xiong draws her thumb across the thickly applied satin stitching, and nods approvingly when she cannot see the background cloth. But story cloths must pass a moral judgment as well. A good piece tells a true story, a history; it is a testament to experience (fig. 6 right). Story cloths retell myths that explain the origin of clans; they present the ethos of a people through their folktales. Story cloths testify to a rigorous recording of the phenomenal world, as seamstresses ply layer upon layer of varicolored threads to realistically portray a bird's plumage, or the mane of a lion. The technology common to village life in Laos appears in all its ingenious varieties—but so does the technology of war, with excruciating details of bombs, bullets and yellow rain.

Scholars studying traditional culture have come to understand that changes induced in a tradition by influences outside of its cultural context can themselves be reincorporated into that culture. Most Hmong craftswomen will agree that the creation of story cloths was suggested by relief workers concerned with the market appeal of paj ntaub. Yet they bridle at the idea of outsiders suggesting topics; for how can a stranger know what it means to be Hmong? Discussing the creative process of a story cloth artist, one woman states:

The artist, he thinks in his mind, all the time
until he knows how to draw it.
He knows how to draw it,
because everything is in his mind.
The same way I do my sewing.
Then, he draws the picture *by himself.*
Then, he closes his eyes,
he can see the ladies,

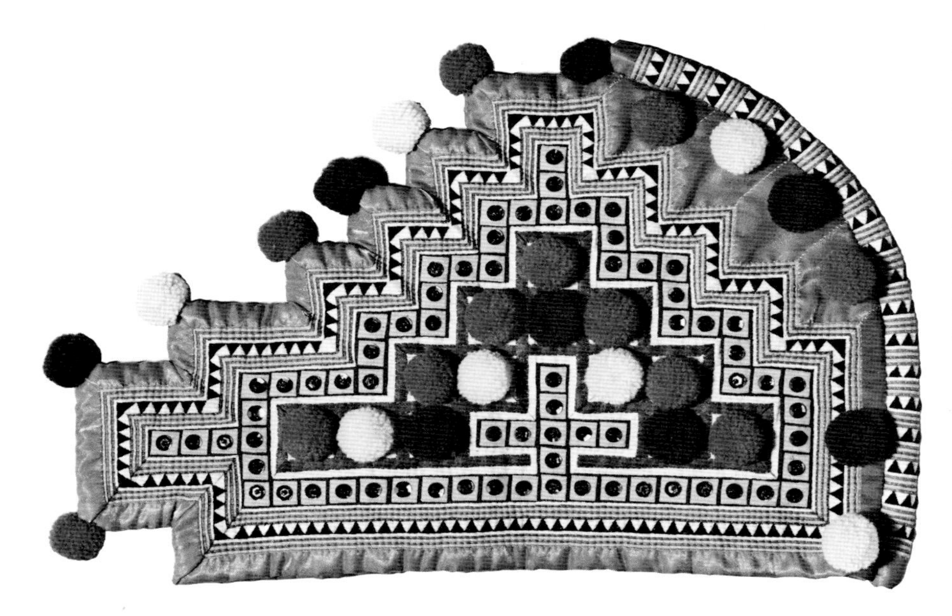

***Figure** 7. Young woman's festive hat, "Cockscomb Style", based on Green Hmong tradition. Artist unknown, made in California, c. 1986. Cotton blend, nylon, acrylic yarn pompoms, sequins. 13.5" × 8.5". Collection of Sally Peterson.*

Hmong women of all ages continue to sew paj ntaub for festive occasions. Styles, fads, and trends within Hmong communities rearrange traditional elements, and incorporate new ideas. This hat, currently in vogue, is based on a child's hat design of the Green Hmong. Women now add sequins and bangles, which have light-catching properties similar to the silver coins traditionally used to decorate paj ntaub.

he can see the men.
He draws the picture,
He thinks about his country.
He draws, what is it, where is it, who is it.

Duplicates of most story cloth themes circulate in quantities through the networks of Hmong paj ntaub marketing. Yet artists and needleworkers will individualize cloths according to their own aesthetic standards or creative inspiration. Each story cloth, each telling, has the capacity to transform the myth, the story, and the history, as Hmong artists express the present-day collective consciousness of their community (fig. 6 left).

More and more Hmong households have adopted the American practice of hanging textiles in their homes, and many display story cloths as well as traditional paj ntaub. Others would like to, but ironically, cannot afford to keep favored pieces, for relatives in the camps need the money from their eventual sale. Story cloths not only store memories, but serve as an archive for illustrating a cultural heritage to American-born children; children who can read the English captions, translate them back into Hmong, and have their elders explain the meaning. Though story cloths originally were developed for non-Hmong audiences, recently several beautifully designed cloths, potent with the national symbols of Laos, have been labeled in that country's language, and sold specifically to members of Hmong communities.

The phenomenon of consciously investing new forms of paj ntaub with deeply-felt, cultural meaning occur in other contexts as well. Several Pennsylvania women were invited to participate in the Kohler Art Center's 1985 "Hmong Artist's Conference and Exhibit" in Sheboygan, Wisconsin. The women prepared samplers exhibiting their best work, and labeled them with their names, birthdates, and home province. Such samplers are an emergent expressive form, encapsulating traditional design and workmanship, yet also adopting the "wall hanging" form required by marketing, and the very Western emphasis upon signing one's work. Formerly, the measure of a woman's skill was displayed by the clothing of her family; paj ntaub enhanced the beauty of an individual, and cemented one's identity; the contours and movement of the body in turn heightened the aesthetic appreciation of the needlework. Now an artist's talents are exhibited according to Western standards and practices; signed, hung and sold. This method has begun to be adopted by the Hmong, and for the Hmong. Pang Xiong, the architect of these samplers, plans to make one for each of her six children. They will express both her heritage and her legacy; her signature on her family's history. They will provide a way to reach out and touch the generations she will not live to see. She says,

"Someday, very, very, cool my heart,
I will make a piece for each of my children.
And they will think of me, my sewing.
And I will put my name,
I will put the letters in Hmong,
in English,
in Lao,
and in Thai.
And it will say
Don't forget your culture!
All your whole life,
and your children's,
and your grandchildren's life!
Ever, ever."

Suggested Reading:

Adams, Monni. "Dress and Design in Highland Southeast Asia: The Hmong (Miao) and the Yao" *Textile Museum Journal* (1974) 4:1

Cambell, Margaret, Nakorn Pongnoi and Chusak Voraphitak. *From the Hands of the Hills.* Hong Kong: Media Transasia, 1978.

Dewhurst, C. Kurt and Marsha MacDowell. *Michigan Hmong Arts.* Catalogue for the 1984 Exhibition, Kresge Gallery, Michigan State University. East Lansing, Michigan: The Museum, Folk Culture Series 3:2(December, 1983).

Graham, David Crockett. *Songs and Tales of the Chu'an Miao.* Washington, D.C.: Smithsonian Press, 1956.

John Michael Kohler Arts Center. *Hmong Art: Tradition and Change.* Sheboygan, Wisconsin: John Michael Kohler Arts Center, 1986.

Lewis, Paul and Elaine. *Peoples of the Golden Triangle: Six Tribes from Thailand.* London: Thames and Hudson, Ltd. 1984.

Yih-Fu, Ruey, "A Study of the Miao People," translated and summarized by V.T. Yang, in F.S. Drake, ed. *Symposium on Historical Archaeological and Linguistic Studies on Southern China, Southeast Asia and the Hong Kong Region.* Hong Kong: Hong Kong University Press, 1967. pp 49 58.

Sally Peterson, a former schoolteacher with a Masters of Science in Education, is presently a doctoral condidate at the University of Pennsylvania, currently at work on a dissertation entitled "From the Mind and Heart: Paj Ntaub Textiles of the Laotion Hmong." The dissertation discusses the historical background of this art and its contemporary production in refugee camps in Thailand and the United States. Ms. Peterson served as staff folklorist for the Hmong Community Folklife Documentation Project sponsored by the Folklife Center of Philadelphia's International House, which was funded through grants from the Folk Arts division of the NEA, the Pennsylvania State Council on the Arts, and the Sun Company. She has taught folklore courses at the University of Pennsylvania. She presented several Hmong paj ntaub artists at the Smithsonian's 1986 Festival of American Folklife and is presently conducting fieldwork in Pennsylvania's Hmong communities for Craft and Community: Traditional Craftsmanship in Pennsylvania, *a future traveling exhibition sponsored by the Balch Institute and the state's folklife office and scheduled for 1989.*

More For Warmth Than For Looks

Quilts of the Blue Ridge Mountains

Geraldine N. Johnson

Plate 5. Strip Quilt with fan quilting made by Donna Choate, Sparta, North Carolina. Geraldine Johnson, BR8-1-20544/36A. We are grateful to the American Folklife Center at the Library of Congress for providing prints from the collection created by the Blue Ridge Folklife Project. Photograph identifications are followed by the photographer's name and the project negative file number.

Toward the end of my stay in the Blue Ridge as a part of the American Folklife Center's research team, I interviewed Zenna Todd, a traditional quilter from Ennice, North Carolina. During the course of our conversation, she told me the following narrative and later alluded to parts of it several times, an indication of its importance in her repertoire of narratives:

> I'll never forget the first quilt that I cut out by pattern; it was a Monkey Wrench. My mother-in-law, she was going to show me how to quilt, you know, and how to do it. So she helped me to get started. The lining was kind of a deep rose color, and I said to her, I said, what kind of thread should we use to quilt this with. Oh, I was really tickled to get started, you know, on that quilt, and she says, well, I'd just use black. Said you've got an awful lot of dark colors in it. So we hanged the quilt from the ceiling with cord, and put it in a frame, and she helped me to get started. She didn't tell me to pull the knots through the lining and have them on the inside so they wouldn't show. She says, well now, you just go ahead and quilt all the way across there, and I'll be back tomorrow and see how you're doing. So I quilted all the way across one side. She didn't tell me about the knots, and where I'd tied those knots and I hadn't pulled them through, and there they showed, just them black knots on the underneath side. So when I rolled the quilt up, I rolled it up so we could walk under it and around it, and I looked up under it, and it looked like flies a-setting on the quilt. I said when she come back, I said, my goodness, I've just ruined this quilt. I said, I've got, it looks like flies a-setting on the lining. She says, my goodness, says, why didn't you pull them through. And I says, why, you didn't tell me.

Mrs. Todd's narrative is both amusing and instructive to a local audience; in addition, it makes several important points about Blue Ridge quilting. First, this woman, like so many others in the region, learned how to quilt from her mother-in-law after she was married. She did not set up housekeeping with the proverbial dozen quilts or an elaborately stitched bridal quilt.[1] Second, the quilting process itself was, and still is, a solitary affair performed in the home with quilting frames suspended from the ceiling. Quilting bees are relatively modern devices used primarily for fund-raising by local groups. Finally the quilts were pieced in traditional block patterns and quilted with thread of a contrasting color. Elaborate patterns radiating from the center are uncommon, and thread colors were seldom chosen to blend in with the color of the quilt top or lining.

These observations contradict some common notions about quilting, and at the same time reinforce the importance of continuing serious investigations into regional quilting styles. Although many scholars believe that this particular area of women's studies has been examined in microscopic detail, we have done very little to examine the entire range of quilts created in any given region. We have poked at quilt tops until they are ragged, documented quilting bees ad infinitum, and more recently, investigated ethnic sources of quilting styles.[2] One reason for this narrowed vision seems to be our scholarly preoccupation with the Pennsylvania-German quilting model; individual quilters or communities of quilters that do not fit the stereotype are routinely ignored. We need to begin to examine the entire scope of a woman's handwork and produce more descriptive essays dealing with regional quilt types and quilting techniques. Finally we also should document the quilter's words and narratives to better understand the history, vision, and spirit of women who create such intriguing items.[3]

Peering more closely at specific regions gives us an opportunity to examine the impact of specific socioeconomic forces. The quilting revival, for example, has now had a significant effect on traditional quilting techniques. Quilting books, magazines, and newsletters clutter our libraries and newsstands. No corner of our vast country is safe from tourism, and federal programs occasionally reach those for whom they are intended. All these influences should be considered particularly when we look at any potentially marketable craft.

But, at the same time, we must remember that some privacy remains in American life. Commercial ventures, the media, and the federal government often fail to impinge upon the everyday lives of the resilient folk. One researcher said that it would be "difficult for fieldworkers to find craftspeople not influenced by the 'revival' and its educational institutions."[4] Such is not the case. Many traditional craftspeople carry out their work unfettered and uninterrupted by scholars, book salesmen, craft shop owners, social workers, and probably even field researchers for the Library of Congress.

Occasionally we did intrude, however, and the observations made in this paper are based on tape-recorded interviews with sixteen Blue Ridge quilters and informal discussions with many other quilters, craft shop owners, and residents in parts of eight rural counties—Carroll, Floyd, Patrick, and Grayson in Virginia, and Alleghany, Ashe, Surry, and Wilkes in North Carolina. I located informants by visiting craft shops, talking to county extension agents, and simply driving around the countryside. Sixteen hundred photographs, primarily of quilts, provide the visual documentation for this essay, and 102 pages of field notes add some contextual background to these mechanical images.

In searching for Blue Ridge quilts and quilters, I looked for some pattern in the visual and verbal images that bombarded me each day. Was it geographical? Did North Carolina quilts and quiltmaking techniques differ from Virginia's? Did quilts "up the mountain" vary from their counterparts "down the mountain"? No such simple answer emerged. Instead of a pattern of geographical variation, I found a somewhat blurry pattern of socioeconomic differences. Women living within one or two miles of one another created items that reflected their unique lifestyles, purposes, values, and finally individual styles. I chose to call these two types of quilts the plain and the fancy.

In using these two terms, I am not simply referring to the surface appearance of the quilt as most folk art historians do.[5] Rather I am speaking of the cluster of conceptual and behavioral processes shared by the women who make each type of quilt. I am focusing on the fabrics used in the quilt top and the techniques used to piece or appliqué it, the filler or lining the quilters use, the quilting thread and the stitches they make, the way the quilt is bound, and finally the use to which the quilt is put. Plain quilters share a common set of values in these and other matters as do their fancy counterparts.

Plain quilting, with its roots firmly planted in tradition, was born of necessity and nurtured by both white and black cultural traditions in the area. As one woman explains, "Just so we had quilts for our own use. That's all we thought about in them days. That's how people kept warm then, you know. They didn't keep their houses warm all night like they do now. We depended on those quilts to keep warm." To a lesser degree, fancy quilting also existed in the Blue Ridge, but the tradition has been strongly influenced by the quilting revival and a host of outside forces, especially federal and state poverty programs, tourism, and national publications.

Several words of caution are necessary here. First, the words "fancy" and "plain" come from the quilters themselves. Fancy quilting is a label promoted by quilting books and newsletters, but the women of the region also call themselves and others "fancy quilters."[6] Zenna Todd, for example, tried to describe a fancy quilt to me that same afternoon:

> A fancy quilt I would call one that was pieced by a pattern and quilted around each piece on each side of a seam and then if it was put together with say one piece block and then a solid block. Then do some kind of real pretty design in the solid block. Then you do the border then to correspond with the quilting you did in the solid. Now that's what I would call a fancy.

Next she went on to discuss the plain quilt. "The other kind," she said, "would be just something that you would need to keep the bed warm.". The term "plain" then is used less often by the quilters to refer to women who make primarily utilitarian quilts.

Second, there is considerable cross-over between the two categories. Most fancy quilters began as plain quilters; some women now make both types—the plain to use at home and the fancy to sell. "If I make a fancy one, I sell it," Ruth Holbrook of Traphill, North Carolina, says. Then she describes how she makes the rag quilts as she calls them:

> The ones that I use at the house, there's not much work in them. I stick them on the sewing machine and sew them up, and then quilt them with stitches about a quarter or eighths long so they'll hold together, and throw them on the bed and go on.

Finally, little communication takes place between the two groups, and there seems to be little familiarity with the types of quilts made by a neighbor who participates in a different quilting network.

Plain Quilts

Twelve out of sixteen quilters I interviewed could be called plain quilters. Sociologists would probably place most at the lower end of the Blue Ridge socioeconomic scale, and because of this, the women share a similar world view and set of domestic values. The quilts they make display certain common characteristics that readily reflect the unique vision of their creators. They are born of necessity and meant to be used when people "got good and cold"; because of this they are made quickly from bits and pieces of dark fabrics generally found in today's clothing. In working with very limited resources, these quilters show as much ingenuity as their needle-wielding ancestors did. They stitch block patterns almost exclusively with the LeMoyne Star, a favorite motif. The blocks are then stitched into strips and later into standard sized quilts. In terms of quilting process, then, the greatest continuity of tradition is found in the plain quilt.

In function, the plain quilt was, and still is, made because it is needed as a bedcover. Blue Ridge winters are cold, and those interesting vernacular houses are drafty and cold. Rug weaver Mazie Beamer describes her large I-house for me:

> It was just a frame house. There was no insulation. They didn't storm-side houses then; they just put up their weather boarding, and then they sealed with beaded sealing inside, and there was no way . . . When the wind blowed and the snow come, it snowed in the house too. I know when you get up of a morning, you'd have to get upstairs to the attic and scoop up, sometimes the snow would be six inches deep up there, and you gotta get that out before you got the house warm enough for it to melt and run down through. So you always had to move around when it was that kind of weather.

Obviously, she continues, "When you lived in a cold, cold house, you had to have a lot of quilts to keep you warm." Roxie Ray's father slept with anywhere from five to seven quilts on his bed, and another woman claims, "We couldn't turn over" at night because the quilts were so heavy. Although most Blue Ridge homes are warmer today than they once were, these quilters still cling to their old habits of making quilts from heavy materials, filling them with thick batting or blankets, and creating an item that weighs heavily on the body at night.

The plain quilt represents a salvage craft at its very best. Tops are pieced with any kind of material found around the house and farm—feedsacks, old clothing, and scraps from homemade clothing. "Whatever you had you had to use it," said Roxie Ray, a quilter from Poplar Springs, North Carolina. "You had to figure out some way to use it because people didn't have the money, and my folks wasn't the only ones that didn't have it. It just wasn't there." Her ingenious family made strip quilts from old sandpaper belts retrieved by her father from the furniture factory in nearby Elkin:

> It was sandbelts that run the sander at the furniture factory where my Daddy worked. When the sand was wore off them, they'd take them off and put a new one on. They'd reach across this room and more. One of these long belts, you know, that run those wheels, and they'd just throw them away. Well, my father got to bringing them home, and he found you could put them in a tub of water and soak them, and all that sand would come off. Then mother would take them and boil them, and they'd be white, and then she'd dye them pink, or green, and make strip quilts out of it like that. And the lining, top, and back. And she would tack them though.

Figure 1. *Log Cabin quilt started by Mamie Lee Bryan. The five blocks were "too slow" to piece so she pieced the rest of the quilt in blocks and strips. Lyntha Eiler, BR8-2-20414/25.*

Figure 2. Quilts made by Carrie Severt of Ennice, North Carolina, airing out on the front porch of her home. Geraldine Johnson, BR8 GJ 13-8 (original in color).

Later some quilters could afford to buy special fabrics for their quilts, and as Zenna Todd points out, their quilting improved:

I didn't do the fancy thing about quilting, like cutting out by patterns. At that time we didn't have too much to do with, and we would just sew them up every how the pieces come, you know. Call it crazy quilt. But then as the years advanced, we got on up where we could buy a little better material and cut out by patterns and piece.

But most plain quilters still use scraps from sewing and old clothing given to them by family and friends. If they buy fabrics they still cling to those standards of the past. White, for example, is not a popular color in these quilts. "Most of the time, we tried to make the quilts dark regardless of the pattern," Roxie Ray recalls, "and we tried to get dark outing. Gray outing they called it, to make the linings out of." White is seldom found in quilts meant to be used; instead the brightly colored solids, large prints, and plaids of everyday clothing predominate. Finally, because so many fabrics used in sewing today are man-made, plain quilts are often created from both woven and double-knit polyester.

These quilts are frequently filled with homemade cotton batting, blankets from the local Chatham Blanket factory in Elkin, North Carolina, old clothing, and less often, store-bought Mountain Mist filler. Zenna Todd recalls that her mother-in-law used to make her own warm wool batting:

She would buy this wool when people would shear their sheeps. She would go and get this wool and wash it, and then she had cards, what she called cards. I had never seen any until after I was married. She would card this wool, and it would be about a three by six inch little batts. She'd lay them in a box; when she got ready to fix her quilts, she'd get them out and put them on there. Oh it just made one of the wonderfulest quilts you've ever seen. It would be so soft and so warm. That real sheep wool. But it was a lot of work in it, but you know, people had more time than they had money at that time.

Wool seldom appears as a filler in today's quilts except in the form of new blankets or worn-out clothing. When old clothes are used as filler, the seams are ripped apart, the worn parts cut out, and the pieces simply laid on the lining or basted together to form one piece.

The linings and joinings, on the other hand, are often made from feed sacks, either dyed or not, old sheets, or curtains. Again, Roxie Ray remembers the fabrics used to line the quilt and to set or join the blocks in the top:

We used to buy our linings out of feed sacks or get domestic and dye them. Plain old factory cloth. We'd dye it with different colors, and sew a seam and that would just be seventy-two inches wide. It was only thirty-six inches. And then two and half for the lining. But everybody back in my days, they couldn't buy stuff to set them together with, so we used whatever we had. Costed too much especially where there's a big bunch of kids to sew for. They had scraps, they called them, and they used that.

dren.

One silk quilt Mrs. Bryan thinks "more of . . . than I do of any of them" is actually a counterpane completed by Mr. Bryan's mother sometime before 1958. It is appliquéd in an elaborate Dutch Girl pattern and tufted around each square. Mrs. Bryan wanted to put the fragile counterpane to better use, so she bought silk pieces for one dollar and turned the counterpane into a string quilt:

> I kept the counterpane a long time, and I decided that I didn't want to use it on the bed just for a counterpane, and I was going to make a quilt out of it. So I just went and bought me some silk pieces . . . and made a silk top to it. It's beautiful.

After she had stitched the silk squares together, she used white thread to quilt the entire piece in the fan or squared fan pattern.

Obviously this heirloom was valuable to the Bryans; the fact that Mrs. Bryan actually paid money to buy fabric is a testimony to that fact. She also spent a considerable amount of time piecing the quilt; "that was the hardest one I've ever pieced in my life," she says. "I had a job with that quilt." Thus the strip piecing and white fan quilting were not simply utilitarian devices for Mrs. Bryan, but instead clear examples of her Afro-American aesthetic values at work.

Mamie Bryan also started what she labelled a Log Cabin quilt, but the item that emerged represents a battleground of personal values more clearly than most quilts. She made four or five Log Cabin blocks that closely resemble the patterns suggested by Vlach; later she said she just got tired of it because it went so slowly, and she created the rest of the quilt from her own improvisational blocks:[9]

> His mother had a log cabin quilt . . . and I wanted to learn how to make one. So I started mine, but I got tired of it. I got along too slow. So I quit. But now you can tell it. Here's the blocks. Them's the blocks I got pieced, and I got tired of that log cabin. Now she called it a log cabin quilt. Blocks. So I got tired of that, and I says I'm going to piece my own to get the quilt done. So I just pieced mine any way I wanted. All of them's in blocks and strips. . . . I said well I didn't have but four blocks. I said I'll put it right in the middle of my quilt. I couldn't finish it. It was too slow.

Did fatigue or impatience cause her to change her pattern, or did the improvisational blocks seem visually more appealing to her? We can only guess.

Donna Choate, on the other hand, is a black quilter whose mother "came up with white people." Only one out of six of her quilts is a strip quilt; one was simply a quilted floral sheet, and two others were rather precise pieced patterns. "Black people had it pretty rough," she says, and when she visited her friends, she noticed that "their quilts were not as good." Design or pattern is the characteristic that distinguished her family's quilts, and it is a value that remains with her until today:

> Well, I would think the design would be the main thing about a quilt. Because if you just piece up a strip just in any form, amount or any, it doesn't harmonize, it's not going to be very pretty. I'd rather piece my pieces, make squares, and put them together. Now a lot of people they have strip, a strip of this kind, a strip, they go to the store and buy remnants, you know, and make quilts. And they have all kind of colors. But mother taught us to use designs. If I was to make one now, it'd be some kind of design, I don't know what it would be.

A nine patch pattern completed by Mrs. Choate several years ago, however, showed that same random arrangement of blocks suggestive of black improvisation in quilt making.[10]

Not far from the Choate farm lives Carrie Severt, a quilter who uses approximately twenty to twenty-five quilts in her home. About one-fifth of them are strip quilts consisting of large squares and rectangles of dark brown, gray, blue, and black. The rest of her quilts include such familiar pieced patterns as Lone Star, the Tree, and the Wheel. Several others are similar to Mamie Bryan's quilts; the patterns tend to be less discernible because Pennsylvania-German quilting standards are not carefully heeded by Mrs. Severt.

The Severts' handsome rented farmhouse is made even grander on days when Carrie Severt airs out her quilts. "If you ain't used them too much," she says, "airing does them as much good as washing them." She washes the heavy quilts only once a year, but airs them as she feels it is necessary.

Carrie Severt gets her quilting patterns from neighbors, friends and family members, and makes her own cardboard and sandpaper templates to use in piecing. Like most plain quilters, she refuses to buy patterns or make appliqué quilts. Once she bought some appliqué patterns, but found the process entirely too wasteful:

> I ordered me a bunch of patterns one time out of a magazine some way, but I never have thought too much of them. They're pretty, but it takes a whole lot of stuff to fix one of the things. You've got to have material to sew these patterns down on it, and some of them it takes great big old long pieces to put them designs on there.

Thus pieced patterns better suit her thrifty nature.

Carrie Severt is an avid quilter, and during one winter pieced over forty quilt tops. For her it is not simply another household chore, but an activity that engages her emotionally and intellectually:

> But, law, I'd rather quilt than eat. I love that quilting. I ain't too good a hand at it, but I just dearly love it. My husband gets so mad at me he could kill me. He said I'd sit here and piece them old quilts and let him starve to death. I told him I'd rather quilt than eat. But I never let him get hungry. I always fix his meals.

During the winter, she quilts alone in her bedroom after helping her husband with the outdoor chores. He may grumble about her devotion to quilting, but he good-naturedly draws off the fan patterns for her with a piece of chalk and a string:

But I always make my husband lay mine off. Cause he can do a better job than I can. He can keep it more evener than I can. But he's always laid mine off for me. I'll make out like to him I can't lay them off. I could.

The Wheel quilt is one of Carrie Severt's favorite patterns. It allows her to use efficiently the many scraps of fabric given to her by friends and neighbors. She will use any type of fabric for her quilts; thus polyester double-knit, flannel, and even blanket material, often appear in the spokes of her wheels. White is the only color banished from her color schemes; "You can use a little white in the quilt," she says, "but I don't like too much white. It's too easy to show dirt." She makes no attempt to coordinate the colors or patterns of fabrics even in the four sections of background material. The result is a bold quilt that adds a riot of color and pattern to her simply decorated, almost austere, bedrooms.

The Lone Star and Tree quilts illustrate Carrie Severt's preference for solid, rich colors. The Tree quilt is also a fine example of her lack of concern for exact repetition and precision in creating the blocks in a quilt. Some trees face different directions, and others have fewer branches than their neighbors. The joinings are not of equal width, and corners frequently do not meet. A rigid adherence to a superimposed set of rules is not a part of Mrs. Severt's aesthetic sensibility. Improvisation, in other words, may play a greater role in white quilting traditions than we had previously thought.

Naturally most women do not fit neatly into one category or the other. Quilters like Ila Patton have always made both plain and fancy quilts. Other women, such as Ruth Holbrook, are plain quilters who were plucked out of their community, sent to college, and taught the rules of fancy quilting. Still other women, such as Josie Goad, have adapted their plain quilting techniques to the demands of the tourist market. The quilt patterns she uses are familiar, the colors bold, the linings often figured sheets, and the familiar fan quilting predominates, but the quilt has been refined slightly to make it a more appealing item.

Ila Patton's quilt collection clearly represents the work of a woman who could piece such contemporary and complicated patterns as the Cathedral Window, but preferred the simpler strip quilt stitched in elaborate fans with contrasting thread. Mrs. Patton also made a regional favorite, the Nine of Diamonds, a simple nine patch turned on its point. One is joined with navy blue joinings and quilted in diagonal lines drawn on with flour and water:

We would dip yarn string in, take a little flour and make a little paste and put that yarn string in it and fasten it from one corner to the other and just flip it, and it would draw these lines clear through, and I believe that's the way this is laid off.

Ila Patton also uses "secret tacking" to stitch her quilts; one long stitch, about an inch long, is hidden in the filler and only the small stitch shows. It is, she says, "a little easier and quicker done."

Basically plain quilters use their ingenuity to create an item that is both useful and visually intriguing. This quilting style most clearly preserves the traditional process of quilting—using scrap materials to make a product for immediate use. These everyday quilts have not received the attention they deserve, and the unique principles of design that underlie them deserve further examination.

Fancy Quilts

The fancy quilt, on the other hand, has been analyzed, discussed, and photographed in great detail. Four of the quilters I interviewed are considered fancy or "quality" quilters by their community, and they consider their own work to be fancy quilting. "I call it fancy quilting; I don't know what other people call it," one woman said.

Although these women often live within a mile or two of their plain quilting neighbors, they are only vaguely familiar with the quilt made for "service" because their networks are limited to other fancy quilters. Most are college educated, and a few are former school teachers. They get some of their quilting information and inspiration from printed sources—books, magazines, and quilting newsletters. Generally they enjoy a higher socioeconomic status than plain quilters. One woman, for example, quilts with her husband each winter; "it's good therapy," she says. They try to complete four or five quilts before they move to Florida for the rest of the winter months.

All fancy quilters grew up in families with strong quilting traditions. Most began as plain quilters, but soon improved their aesthetic and technical skills. "I've changed from plain quilting to fancy wreaths and fancy designs," says Lura Stanley. "Now I quilt for the beauty of a quilt. I make quilts just for the beauty and not really for the service." These women seldom speak in reverential tones about the quilting of their forebears. Crystal Cruise of Meadows of Dan, Virginia, recalls that her mother's quilts were "not what I would call pretty." She continues:

My mother never did a nice job of quilting. She did a lot of quilting, but it was never what I considered a nice job. I guess she didn't have the time. She was a very busy person raising that many children, and my father was sick for fifteen years. I expect it was more or less for warmth that she quilted.

The women recognize that their mothers and grandmothers quilted in the fashion of the day, "more for warmth than beauty," but they also believe that their ancestors just did not know as much about quilting.

These four women have been directly and indirectly influenced by the complex forces that struck the region after 1930. Craft shops grew up along the Blue Ridge Parkway bringing new ideas to the region and offering a sales outlet for the local women who sought both the income and prestige associated with handcraft sales. The most recent quilting revival, which apparently reached the area in the early 1970's made the craft a socially acceptable and even a desirable skill. Nora Glasco, a fancy quilter from Ennice, North Carolina, most clearly dates the beginnings of that revival in a rather poignant narrative:

My father died about seven or eight years ago, and we were going through the house; they lived in an older type house, and we were going through and kept seeing these raggy quilts. Some of them were just threadbare, but they were beautiful. They were the older type materials. We burned a lot. A few months later, some people came down and told us that these quilts were worth a lot of money.

Craft shop owners from major urban areas now scour the region looking for quilters; local professionals of some prestige—the minister or physician, for example—admire the woman's handwork. But most important are the family members who have a new appreciation of the woman's technical skill and aesthetic judgment and in this subtle way encourage her to spend long hours at the quilting frame producing an item they know will eventually be theirs.

Federal and state programs have also intervened on several levels to influence regional crafts. Government sponsored craft outlets tried to help the quilters improve their skills and thereby increase the marketability of their quilts. One craft shop manager told a quilter that creativity was the essence of craft and urged her to be more creative in her work. Zenna Todd's response is almost a classic statement of the power of tradition even in the mind of the fancy quilter:

They wanted me to come up with some kind of pattern just, you know, that I could do, something that I would think about creating myself. Very creative. But I've never got in on that. I teld them I didn't want to concentrate that much on it. I don't mind changing something just a little bit, or maybe doing it a different way to what somebody else has done, but they said that that was really craft when you done that. And I guess it is.

Finally an OEO craft program administered by Appalachian State College in Boone, North Carolina, affected the lives of both low and middle income quilters in the North Carolina portion of our region. Quilter Ruth Holbrook learned through that program that, although she knew how to quilt, she was doing everything wrong:

I just used the same material that my dresses were made out of. I didn't press my seams open. I did use big thread. I quilted them all in fans. Didn't know no different. Or diamonds. After I read those books, and

Figure 3. *Carrie Severt's Wheel quilt. Lyntha Eiler, BR8-7-20346/21.*

that lady told me I was doing everything, I knowed how to do it, but I was doing it wrong. I got to matching my colors and material, and things like that. I can sell them faster than I can make them. In fact, they're most of the time sold before they're put in the frame.

Now she makes enough plain quilts to "keep my bed warm," and sells the fancy ones she learned how to make at the college.

In the hands of the fancy quilters, the craft is no longer a salvage craft. These women spend both time and money shopping for fabrics to use as quilt pieces, filler, and linings. As Ruth Holbrook quickly learned, used fabrics have no place in the products of a college trained quilter.

Relatively rigid rules dictate the colors, patterns, and fabric content of a fancy quilt. Fabrics for the quilt top should be a small print in colors that sell well; local women chuckle about the popularity of so-called "earth tones," especially brown. Those were colors seldom found in a quilt until the quilting revival. The print should be nicely coordinated with solid colors, and both should be a cotton or a cotton-polyester fabric. The filler is most often Mountain Mist polyester or a cotton-polyester blend, which gives the quilt a nice, puffy look. The lining should be a solid color, preferably a white or off-white sheet or unbleached muslin. Finally the edges of fancy quilts are usually bound with bias tape, either homemade or store bought, in a color that matches the quilt's top or lining.

Technically these quilts are also very similar. They are quilted in white thread which usually matches the lining, and the quilting is done "by the piece" with elaborate quilting patterns in the solid blocks and around the border. An astonishing amount of creative research goes into developing a unique quilting pattern. Some women borrow patterns from neighbors; others adapt them from pattern books. Nora Glasco traced the outline of an overturned bottle; "it was shaped so pretty," she says, "that I copied it off and made a quilt pattern." These quilters also follow the well-known rules set down for fancy quilting stitches. "They all want them little fine stitches," Ruth Holbrook says. In piecing, the quilter must use sixteen stitches to the inch and in quilting, ten to twelve stitches to the inch.

Although many women may violate one or more of these rules on occasion, their overall purpose in adhering to the general principles of fancy quilting seems clear. They are creating an item with a selfconscious eye to both the past and the future. They are recreating the quilt as they believe it existed in the past. The model they follow, however, is not that of their own region, but rather the Pennsylvania-German model which has set the standard for this most recent quilting revival. Lura Stanley, for example, searches for hard-to-find small calico prints because "those calicos of a long time ago were small flowers." One craft shop owner bans polyester from her shop and urges her quilters to use cotton filling."She says it's the old time way of doing it," I was told. Many quilters refuse her request because "it's very hard to quilt, and it just doesn't hold up as well." This careful probing of the past brings with it a corresponding look into the future. Quilts are now made for succeeding generations. "I hope my quilts are here for the . . . 21st century and maybe longer if they're taken care of," says Lura Stanley.

Finally many of these quilts are made to be sold, and their mobility is astounding. Anyone who believes that quilts are still being pieced by little, white-haired women who quilt them alone in their living rooms or with the church quilting bee is hopelessly romantic. Quilts are moving from one end of the continent to the other. Quilt tops pieced in Georgia and Washington are quilted in the Blue Ridge and later shipped back to Washington or on to New England. Quilts are pieced by one woman and quilted by others who send them to a third for resale. Regional patterns at this level are breaking down as quilts move rapidly into and out of a specific community.

One tie that binds these communities together is use; most women who make and women who buy fancy quilts use them in bedrooms as bedspreads. They are an investment meant to be seen and appreciated in an appropriate environment. Only in craft shops did I see quilts and quilt patterns used in unconventional ways. Craft shops frequently display quilts hanging from a wall or covering tables. A quilt pattern on a pillow, obviously, is the most common revival form of quilting, and several fancy quilters make pillows as gifts or for sale in local shops. Very few use them in their own homes.

While many fancy quilts are sold, others are given as special gifts to members of the community. The highest use to which a quilt can be put, however, is to serve as an heirloom for children and grandchildren. The quilters expect their children to use these quilts—as bedspreads more than blankets perhaps—but basically they are to be cherished as a legacy from a skilled parent or grandparent. Scorned is the child who does not appreciate such a gift. "I made my son two real fancy quilts," Ruth Holbrook told me. "He didn't appreciate them. He throwed them on the bed, and he smoked and burnt holes in them. Won't get no more."

Lura Stanley, for example, is a fancy quilter who never sells her quilts, but gives them to her children and grandchildren as gifts. "My grandchildren know how to work me," she says with a laugh. She knows that people could not afford to pay her what these quilts are worth to both her and her family:

The money doesn't excite me at all. I would not sell a quilt. I give my quilts. There's too much time and effort put in a quilt for me to sell. I'd have to have more than people would give for my quilts. They're large; they're large enough for spreads, and there's so much time in them that I don't think people would pay me what I'd have to have for my quilts, so I just give them.

Lura is an unconventional Blue Ridge quilter in many ways. She quilts with a hoop instead of a large quilting frame. This makes her quilts looser than some, but also makes it easier for her to quilt the elaborate circular patterns she finds so appealing. She draws all of her own quilting patterns onto the top of the quilt using a homemade stencil and a soft lead pencil. In making the circular feather wreath, for example, she uses a handy saucer to draw the basic circle and then draws each feather by hand.

Lura does not consider herself the best at making quilts; her work is "passable" she says. When she started quilting some fifteen years ago, she began with the Drunkard's Path, which she quilted "in the seam" instead of one quarter inch from the seam. She did not want her big stitches to show; now her stitches are smaller, but she still uses linings with small prints to hide the stitches on the quilt's reverse side. Because she matches her quilting thread to each color in the quilt top, this patterned lining also masks the variety of thread colors on the back. "I ignore my lining when I'm quilting, and I quilt for the top of the quilt," she says, "the color that the material is."

Mrs. Stanley considers a quilt a "beautiful art work" and thus places her emphasis on the pieced or appliquéd quilt top pattern, which she purchases or creates herself. Her prize quilt seems to be a Sunburst pattern copied from a magazine and pieced in the familiar earth tones:

I got it from a little tiny picture in a magazine of some famous quilt in a museum somewhere. Just a little tiny picture, and I thought that was so pretty. It was in color. But it didn't show the outside of the quilt; it just showed the center.

She had no idea how to fill in the border of the quilt and finally made up her own pattern of LeMoyne Stars pieced from various shades of orange, beige, and brown.

Again, toward the end of our Blue Ridge stay, the whole process of field teamwork blossomed during one fascinating morning of work. As I interviewed Mrs. Stanley, Lyntha and Terry Eiler photographed her quilts by hanging them over a line strung between two trees. It was the first time Mrs. Stanley had ever seen them displayed this way, and instead of a mundane discussion of each quilt, I recorded a wonderfully spontaneous outburst of praise for each quilt. "I didn't know they were so pretty," she said softly at first and then much louder. "I had really never seen them outdoors," she continued. "Isn't that gorgeous? It is really." Finally she concluded, "I don't usually brag on my handiwork, but when I see them a-hanging out on the line, they do look so pretty." Clearly the folk aesthetic—the joyous outburst when confronted by the attractive item—was evident in her remarks and reserved for the patterns, color combinations, and quilting on the quilt top.[11]

Nora Glasco is another fancy quilter who quilts primarily for other people. She, her mother, and her sister used to quilt from ninety to one hundred quilts a year during their peak quilting period. Working from an unfinished store front, they quilted tops for customers both within and outside the region and stitched their own quilts for resale at a nearby craft shop.

The Log Cabin quilt Nora was working on alone when I saw her tells us much about Blue Ridge fancy quilting. The top, a pattern fairly common in the area, had been pieced in Georgia and was sold already to a New England woman. Mrs. Glasco would do all the fancy quilting for forty dollars. The quilt colors are the modern earth tones; the pattern is small and the solid colors blend well with the pattern. Mrs. Glasco was quilting it "by the piece" and trying to plan a fancy quilting pattern for the border around the edge of the quilt. The final product would surely be an elaborate but mellow quilt that would fit into any modern bedroom decor.

Mrs. Glasco has an older Lone Star quilt pieced from old neckties by her grandmother some thirty years ago. The juxtaposition of patterns now seems jarring to her, and she talked to me about tearing the quilt top apart and adding rows of solid colors to it to give it a more contemporary appearance. Surely the values of the quilting revival have influenced both the technical skills and aesthetic sensibilities of the fancy quilters.

The Process

In terms of performance, Blue Ridge quilting is, and always has been, a solitary, or at most, a family affair. Again, climate and vernacular architecture may have caused this. Rooms in private homes are relatively small and not conducive to eight or ten women moving about a rather large quilting frame. Churches in the area lack large social rooms, and thus there seems to be no suitable place for women to gather. In any event most women prefer spending two or three solitary days stitching on a quilt suspended from the ceiling of a small bedroom or living room.

I heard of only three quilting groups, all of which were relatively modern innovations. We observed two of these groups at work. One, organized by the local Homemaker's Club in North Carolina, is held in an old abandoned house. A second group of women filled the basement of the Baptist Church in Meadows of Dan, Virginia. Even this so-called quilting bee reflects the area's major thrust toward solitary quilting. The entire group gathers on the first day to put in and begin work on the quilt. Then the women come in by ones, twos, and threes each day until the quilt is finished. Crystal Cruise, the group's organizer, describes the process:

Sometimes you'll be in quilting all by yourself, and sometimes you'll have somebody with you, you know. You don't hardly ever meet all in a group.

Maybe the first day, but where you're having this group quilting, you don't always have them all there.

Mrs. Cruise remains the primary force behind the church group's quilting. She pieces many of their quilt tops, and each year she and her husband quilt four or five quilts, including elaborate appliqué patterns which she purchases in kit form. When I visited her, she was piecing a Grandmother's Flower Garden sent to her from the state of Washington. She tried to stitch the fifteen hundred hexagons together by hand. Finally, overwhelmed by the task, she threw the bundle down in disgust, and her husband solved the mathematical puzzle after she fled the house. She asked the church ladies to quilt the top for sentimental reasons even though she knew that some would not do a good job. Occasionally she brings the quilts home and tears out the most offensive stitches. "On my own quilts," she warns, "I would not recommend group quilting."

Ten women gathered at the Meadows of Dan Baptist Church one Thursday morning. Four team members recorded the event on film and tape. The highly self-conscious women still managed to discuss the two major events of the week—a local woman had won the title of Miss America and the National Park Service had once again provoked the community. Family and community gossip intertwined with comments about the quilt and quilting itself. After the obligatory covered dish dinner and a visit by the minister, the group continued to quilt until four o'clock. Once a woman took me off to the side to tell an off-color joke, and the minister discussed local politics with me in some detail. The event was surely contrived, but then most Blue Ridge quilting bees are more or less.

The strong emphasis on the social dimension of quilting keeps us from looking deeper into a woman's psyche to discover other forces that drive her to the quilting frame and threaded needle. The solitude, sense of comfort, and a need for beauty are all aspects of the craft that deserve further exploration. As we delve into quilting from an art historian's or sociologist's point-of-view and search, as we must, for the item's regional boundaries, the subtle nuances in the woman's personality must not be overlooked.

Conclusions

Blue Ridge quilts, like quilts everywhere, are intimately tied to the region in which they are created. Basically they were used to keep warm in an area with low income, cold winters, and drafty houses. In our search for deeper social and aesthetic meanings, we cannot ignore this basic and fundamental fact. If we do we may well overlook that very interesting body of quilts tucked away in closets throughout the country—the plain quilt.

Farm wives showed tremendous ingenuity and skill in creating quilts from the remnants of their environment—the scraps, feedbags, and worn out socks that eventually reappeared in quilts. Their pieces did not match and their stitches were sometimes too large, but these quilts too reflect an aesthetic that has only begun to be explored among some black quilters. White non-Pennsylvania-German quilts also deserve attention.

Now that Appalachia has been discovered as a fashionable area of poverty and old-timey ways, fancy quilts in particular illustrate the results of government intervention, folk craft enthusiasm, and the quilting revival in general. The Blue Ridge Parkway, slashing through the region, provided a market for women who wished to sell quilts that met certain standards. Federal poverty programs, on the other hand, attempted to squash local quilting traditions and replace them with those deemed aesthetically and technically superior. Thus if the Blue Ridge experience is any example, future studies of quilts should also examine the positive and negative aspects of the quilting revival as it is manifested in regional tourism and federalism.

Basically, however, these quilts—both plain and fancy—illustrate for me the values I heard so often articulated in the personal narratives, jokes, and gossip these women shared with me—the value of home, family, and community. Nora Glasco expressed it verbally when she compared her seventeen years in the Hanes textile mill with work in her home and church:

When you go into a factory, so much of the time, I speak for a lot of people, I think, when I say this, you feel like that you just go in and your life is just revolved around a machine. When you're home doing your housework, doing things for the neighbors, working with your church, working with craft groups and things, you feel like you have a broader view of life and you feel like your life is more wholesome and worthwhile. You don't make any money, but you sure do enjoy yourself a lot more. Factory work is fine for those that enjoy it; I did not enjoy it, only for the people.

Zenna Todd's Crazy quilt illustrates those same values in material form. Pieced from her children's old clothing, the quilt contains, in embroidery, the family's secrets and jokes. Sewing materials, an old phonograph, a pet duck, and even Mrs. Todd's own hand, complete with the nail polish her children tease her about, are all recorded in this document. Fancy or plain—directly or indirectly—the Blue Ridge quilt is both a protector and documentor of family life.

We folklorists, then, who are particularly interested in the values and creative activity of women need to discover what women are really saying and doing. We need to investigate regional styles in quilting as well as other types of handwork. We need to investigate socioeconomic factors as they relate both to the item and to the process. Finally we need to document the entire range of materials created by women in their domestic careers. "Now do you reckon that they will enjoy seeing quilts like this?" Mamie Bryan asked. The answer should be yes.

[1] For discussions of the Bride's Quilt and other related popular belief, see among others: Mary Washington Clarke, *Kentucky Quilts and Their Makers* (Lexington, Kentucky: The University Press of Kentucky, 1976), p. 6; Florence Peto, *American Quilts and Coverlets* (New York: Chanticleer Press, 1949), p. 19.

[2] Several quilting bibliographies have now been published. See Simon J. Bronner, *Bibliography of American Folk and Vernacular Art* (Bloomington, Indiana: Folklore Publications Group, 1980); Susan Roach and Lorre M. Weidlich, "Quilt Making in America: A Selected Bibliography," *Folklore Feminists Communication,* 3 (1974), 17-28. Many contemporary studies listed in the above bibliographies focus primarily on the quilt top as a work of art. See, for example, Jonathan Holstein, *American Pieced Quilts* (Washington, D.C.: Smithsonian Institution, 1972) and *The Pieced Quilt: An American Design Tradition* (Greenwich, Connecticut: New York Graphic Society, Ltd., 1973); Lenice Ingram Bacon, *American Patchwork Quilts* (New York: William Morrow and Co., 1973); Effie Chalmers Pforr, *Progressive Farmer Award Winning Quilts* (Birmingham, Alabama, 1974). Susan Stewart explores the social and religious dimensions of quilting in "Sociological Aspects of Quilting in Three Brethren Churches in Southeastern Pennsylvania," *Pennsylvania Folklife,* 23 (1974), 15-29. Finally, for comments on black quilting traditions, see John Michael Vlach, "Quilting" in *The Afro-American Tradition in Decorative Arts* (Cleveland, Ohio: The Cleveland Museum of Art, 1978), pp. 44-75.

[3] Two contemporary works attempt to place the quilts within the context of the quiltmakers' lives; see Clarke, and Patricia Cooper and Norma Bradley Buferd, *The Quilters: Women and Domestic Art* (Garden City, New York 1978). Some older works captured the spirit of the quilter as well; see, for example, Ruth E. Finley, *Old Patchwork Quilts and the Women Who Made Them* (Philadelphia: J.B. Lippincott Co., 1929). For the best discussion of the history of the quilt, see Patsy and Myron Orlofsky, *Quilts in America* (New York: McGraw-Hill, 1974).

[4] Peter T. Bartis, *Preliminary Research Survey for the Blue Ridge Folklife Project* (Washington, D.C.: American Folklife Center, 1978), p. 20.

[5] No one considers the quilt to be a "painting" more than Jonathan Holstein. See *American Pieced Quilts,* p. 7; *The Pieced Quilt,* p. 8. Holstein's assumptions about the quilter's vision of her own work seem naive, and more discussion with women who quilt might help him modify some of his remarks. Unfortunately Vlach suggests that Holstein's quilt collection is the Euro-American norm to which he compares Afro-American quilts, p.44. Several other books serve as excellent guides to quilt top patterns and names; see Carrie A. Hall and Rose G. Kretsinger, *The Romance of the Patchwork Quilt in America* (New York: Bonanza Books, 1938); Margaret Ickis, *The Standard Book of Quilt Making and Collecting* (New York: Greystone Press, 1949; rpt. New York: Dover Publications, 1959); Carleton L. Safford and Robert Bishop, *America's Quilts and Coverlets* (New York: E.P. Dutton and Co., 1972).

[6] For a short list of quilting newsletters, see Roach and Weidlich. Observations made in this paper are based on my examination of issues of *Quilter's Newsletter Magazine,* 6700 West 44th Avenue, Wheatridge, Colorado, 80033.

[7] The "sea wave" is also referred to as the "fan" and is "by no means exclusive to Wales" according to Averil Colby in *Quilting* (New York: Charles Scribner's Sons, 1971), p.50. Colby states that the pattern was generally used in borders, but Mavis Fitzrandolph in *Traditional Quilting: Its Story and Its Practice* (London: B.T. Batsford Ltd., 1954) includes a photo of a quilt with an over-all "sea wave" pattern which looks very much like a fan. Joyce Joines Newman in *North Carolina Country Quilts* (Chapel Hill, North Carolina: The Ackland Art Museum, 1978) finds that fan quilting predominates in the more "unsophisticated" quilts of the Scots-Irish in one of three North Carolina regions. For further discussions of fan quilting, see Josephine Lombardo, "Folk Crafts," in *Introduction to Folklore,* ed. Robert J. Adams (Bloomington, Indiana: Indiana University, 1973), pp. 90-9.

[8] Vlach, p. 44.

[9] Vlach, p. 73.

[10] Vlach, p. 67.

[11] Michael Owen Jones discusses the problems of investigating the "folk aesthetic" in "The Concept of 'Aesthetic' in the Traditional Arts," *Western Folklore,* 30 (April 1971), 77-104, and *The Hand Made Object and Its Maker* (Berkeley: University of California Press, 1975), pp. 229-35.

Geraldine Johnson earned her doctorate from the University of Maryland and her thesis was "Rag Rugs and Rug Makers of Western Maryland: A Study of Craft in Community." She previously got degrees from the University of California in Los Angeles and the University of Minnesota in Duluth. She currently does site evaluations of grant funded activities funded by the National Endowment for the Arts/Folk Art Programs, does work for the Smithsonian's Festival of American Folklife, for the United Planning Organization, and research for "Craft and Community: Traditional Craftsmanship in Pennsylvania," an exhibition co-sponsored by the Pennsylvania Heritage Affairs Commission and the Balch Institute for Ethnic Studies. She has presented papers on rugmaking at the American Folklore Society, the Virginia Folklore Society, and for a symposium on the subject organized for the Library of Congress. Her publications include Weaving Rag Rugs: Women's Craft in West Maryland *(1985), and a more recent series "Plain and Fancy: The Socioeconomics of Blue Ridge Quilts" in the Autumn 1982 issue of* Appalachian Journal *and "More For Warmth Than for Looks: Quilts of the Blue Ridge Mountains" in the Fall/Winter 1982 issue of the* North Carolina Folklore Journal.

Figure 4. *Crystal Cruise piecing a Grandmother's Flower Garden while her husband, Levy, watches. Geraldine Johnson, BR8-1-20343/35A.*

The Folklore Of The Australian Wagga

A Distant Cousin of the Pennsylvania Hap

Annette Gero

Waggas are Australian quilts of the late 19th and 20th century—utilitarian, constructed out of necessity, and often extremely crude. They were used mainly in the country as bed or verandah quilts, by drovers on sulkies, and by swagmen. No country property was without its quota of waggas.

The origin of the wagga is not known but comforters or quilts such as the Pennsylvania hap or many North Country English quilts are known to have similar methods of construction. However, documentation of the latter two is much earlier than the first records of the waggas. Jeannette Lasansky, in her article in *Uncoverings*,[1] reports that Pennsylvania haps are listed in estate inventories and auctions as early as 1835. Sybil Lewis and Dorothy Osler from the Heritage Committee of the English Quilters Guide[2] have made reference to late 19th and early 20th North Country English quilts "of real 'rag-bag' quality of which most have been of very pedestrian designs . . ." made by the poorer classes out of necessity, probably from cut down old blankets and worn out clothing. During my travels I have heard of similar quilts in both New Zealand and Canada. Ruth McKendry discusses such quilts in her book on Canadian bedcoverings[3] and several others are featured in the exhibition catalogues *Pieced Quilts of Ontario*[4] and *Alberta Quilts*.[5] As all these places were at one time a British colony, it can be surmised that perhaps the haps and the waggas, and these other related quilts are all descendants of an early British quilt type. Indeed, the word hap is a Northern English dialect word meaning a warm covering of any kind but generally one of coarse material.[6]

The word quilt is derived from the Latin *culcita* meaning a sack filled with stuffing and used as a covering for warmth and this is exactly the definition of a wagga. The wagga consisted of a stuffing, often food sacks such as chaff bags or cut down woollen clothing, covered on both sides with pretty cotton fabric such as cretonne, often in patchwork, and quilted or tied through the layers to hold it together. They appear to have been made in every state in Australia and by both men and women.

The origin of the word wagga remains a mystery but it is thought to be derived from the Wagga Lily flour sacks made by the Murrumbidgee Co-op Milling Co. Ltd, in Wagga Wagga, New South Wales (NSW) (which were used as stuffing). These food sacks were of extremely fine quality, woven closely and warm, thus ideally suited for incorporation into a wagga.[7] *The Macquarie Dictionary* (Dictionary of Australian English) defines a wagga as: "n. a blanket made from hessian bags or similar material; also Wagga blanket, Wagga rug—from Wagga Wagga town in NSW."[8] Furthermore, an article called "Useful Australian Inventions for the Household—Wagga Rugs and Billy Cans," which appeared in the women's magazine *New Idea*, August 15, 1951), reports:

> With the price of wool soaring to such heights it seems that many Australian families will not be able to buy woollen blankets, therefore they will be forced to seek substitutes, possibly in Wagga rugs and Murrumbidgee blankets. Both the Wagga rugs and the Murrumbidgee blanket are purely Australian commodities, and while they were, in the first place, the inventions of bushmen, it was the women of the outback who converted them from crude bush blankets to blankets fit to be seen in use in any home.
>
> There is not a great deal of difference between a Wagga rug and a Murrumbidgee blanket. The Wagga rug (also called the Sydney blanket) merely consisted of two chaff bags or corn bags carefully opened and stitched together. The Murrumbidgee blanket consisted of three or more wheat sacks stitched together without first being opened out, thus giving a double thickness of material.

***Plate 6.** Detail of wagga, maker unknown, made from furnishing fabrics ca.1935, New South Wales, Australia. 53" × 63". Collection of Annette Gero.*

Figure 1. Double sided wagga quilt made by Fanny Jenkins (a dressmaker), Daylesford, Victoria, ca.1910. Cretonne-covered wagga quilted in squares from the centre outwards. The stuffing consists of many layers of blanket pieces and patches of woolen clothes tacked flat. The cretonne is a green floral pattern on one side and red on the reverse. 42" × 50". Collection of Annette Gero.

This is the most typical of the waggas as it is covered with a pretty cretonne which would have cost around 3d per yard. Other examples are stuffed with food sacks rather than cut down clothing or blankets.

Figure 2. Fanny Jenkins, ca.1896, b. Castlemaine. Courtesy: Amy Oglethorpe.

In pioneer homes, where such blankets were used . . . some were neatly bound with coloured binding, some were given an attractive fringe, while some were even covered with cretonne or other cheap material. In one home I saw Wagga rugs on every bed.

Whilst researching old Australian patchwork and waggas I was fortunate to be interviewed on the ABC program *Australian All Over.* I received hundreds of letters from people with waggas or the remembrances of them. The folklore of the wagga is perhaps best expressed by quotations from some of these letters. A farmer from Gerogery (NSW) describes his method of construction.[9]

In our district the bush blanket was called a *wagra*. It always consisted of the same material. Superphosphate manure was supplied in jute bags. If it was used immediately the empty bags were soaked in the dam for several days and then thoroughly washed. They were opened carefully at the seams, sewn together, and then covered with "cretonne," a cheap cotton material with rather pretty patterns (at 3d per yard). Though heavy they were very warm and lasted for years and us children always had one or two on our beds.

A lady from Toowoomba, Queensland said:

I listened with great interest to the discussion on the old "wagga" or "wogga" type of blanket and was transported back in time to my childhood in north Queensland where I was born and bread [sic]. During the years of hardship brought about by the great depression, I can very clearly remember my mother cutting up old coats, woollen trousers, in fact anything woollen and painstakingly piecing them all together in a large rectangle and then covering them with perhaps an old curtain [which still had some wear in it], quilt or cheap calico bordered with some bright material.

I can remember having my tonsils removed in 1940 or 1941 and the nursing staff being very puzzled at my bellows after the operation to "take the 'waggas' off me"!

Occasionally, on a very cold night when I am abed with electric blanket "stoked up" and a feather doona tucked up to my chin, I think of the days in north Queensland and the comfort we children derived in the cooler weather from our own personal "waggas."

Two other recollections state:

When I was about 11 years of age my Mother had a second-hand "Astrachan" short coat given to her by a friend who was much better off financially than she was. However what she lacked in money she made up for in pride and refused to wear it.

I tried it on and decided that without any alteration it would make a splendid overcoat for me. I was a big girl for my age and I felt very grand in the despised Astrachan Coat. Alas I didn't bargain for the durability of Astrachan, and my own growth rate, so the old coat was discarded until one day Mum decided to cut it into squares and make a "Wagga quilt." The whole thing was covered with cretonne and I was unaware that the quilt that kept me warm at night, mostly consisted of the old Astrachan Coat. When I was married Mum decided that I should have it in my new home so, dutifully I took it, and although I had no use for it, until after my children arrived, it was comforting to know that it was there if needed. I had six children, and the "Wagga" as it was affectionately known, was

Figure 3. *The stuffing of a wagga quilt made by Catherine Sarah Fenner, Armidale, NSW, c.1940. Wool and cotton incorporating hand knitted garments. Machine and hand stitched. 31" × 66". Courtesy of the Museum of Applied Arts and Sciences, Sydney, NSW. Photo by R. Deckker.*

Figure 4. *Quilt of woolen suitings made by Caroline May West, Trundle, NSW, ca. 1930. Samples of suiting fabrics are arranged in a diagonal pattern of light and dark fabrics. Wool and cotton, hand and machine pieced. Hand quilted, 64" x 92". Courtesy of the Museum of Applied Arts and Sciences, Sydney, NSW. Photo by R. Deckker.*

becoming a bit "tatty". The cretonne covering needed renewing so I took it off with the intention of doing just that. Imagine my surprise after all those years to see the remains of the old Astrachan Coat.

K.W. from Millicent, South Australia
(Memories of an Old Astrachan Coat—also a Wagga Quilt)

How well I remember them. They were so much part of my childhood. Although we as children in the depression years knew the comfort of good woollen blankets and the luxury of downfilled satin quilts, we had many relatives and friends less fortunate in those desperate days. The extraordinary woman who was my grandmother made sure that these families shared our farm produce—milk, eggs, cream, butter, etc.—and to keep them warm from the bitter chills of frosty winter nights, out would come her hand-operated sewing machine and in no time 2 "thinnish" blankets would be quilted together with some "packing" and then covered in attractive cretonne—a good quality cotton material—in bright floral designs.

M.R. from Warracknabeal, Victoria. (*Wagga-Waggas*)

Chaff bags, tops of wool bales and flour sacks, blankets, socks and old clothing were all incorporated into the wagga. A farmer from Victoria remembers that they were used as knee rugs in horse drawn jinkers when he was a boy, should one of the children be taken to town to the doctors or visiting church on cold days:

About 1922 I can remember my mother still making them. She would take an old blanket that was too worn to use on the beds, she would then gather together old jumpers, cardigans and other items of knitted wool, and cut them up to produce flat, even pieces of material, even the sleeves would be opened out flat. She would then hand "tack" the pieces to the blanket on both sides until it was completely covered.

Many of the waggas that survive today have been covered and recovered as they wore out leaving a myriad of different cotton layers and pretty patchwork patterns.

Similar stories are also told of quilts made in North America. A letter in the "Home Loving Hearts" column (which served as a forum for exchanging ideas about domestic life) in the *Manitoba Prairie Farmers Weekly Free Press,* February 6, 1935, says:[10]

Quilt from Rags

Dear Hearts,

I will tell you how to make use of old clothes or socks that are beyond patching. Wash them clean and rip them apart. Take four twine socks, rip and wash also. When dry sew together in square. Now sew on the old pieces and sock tops to cover socks. When finished cover all with cheap print, and you will have a real warm quilt.

Just as the hap is called by other names in different parts of the United States—"suggan," or a "camp," "cabin," "hunting," "fishing" or "britches" quilt[11]—so too the wagga has been called a "wogga," a "bush rug" or a "bluey." It appears in Australian literature as early as the 1890s. Henry Lawson, in two short stories, tells the tale of poor people whose children slept beneath their patchwork wagga quilts.[12] Both Henry Lawson[13] and Banjo Patterson mention drovers with their wagga rugs. A drover's daughter tells the tale of her father "who did a bit of droving in all kinds of weather and would never camp out unless he has his wagga" and swagmen and the bagmen (nomadic work seekers such as shearers and fruit pickers) are thought to have gained their names by their "swag" or "wagga" that they carried. Albert Dorrington[14] in his story *A Bush Tanqueray* (c. 1901) mentions "sleeping in the wet without a bluey" and Mrs. Aeneas Gunn[15] in *We of the Never Never* (c. 1908) describes the bluey or bush rug. Even folk songs were written about the "blueys":

Back to Crajingalong
For that's the place where I belong;
Where a sun-kissed maid
Neath a gum tree's shade
Waits for me to go along to Croa-jinga-long;
No longer will I roam
From my old Australian home;
I'll hump my bluey
And I'll shout a coo-ee
Back to Croa-jinga-linga-linga-long.

Pat Dunlop

Waggas were also community-made quilts and during the Great Depression and the world wars—such groups as the Red Cross, the Country Women's Association (CWA) and St. Vincent de Paul made waggas to aid the needy. A doctor's wife in Maroubra (NWS) recalls in 1924: "The St. Vincent de Paul came and asked me could I help . . . so I got up a little group . . . These people at Happy Valley, some had no bedclothes, the wind used to blow through their tents. We collected all old woollen socks and sewed the good parts on to a piece of unbleached calico, the cheapest we could buy, and we made thirty-seven quilts padded with wool for those little kiddies . . ."[16]

A second form of the wagga is more commonly called the Depression rug or quilt. These bed coverings were constructed from samples of men's suiting fabrics obtained from tailors or factories or cut down trousers. Such quilts were predominantly made during the 1930s depression. Women carried a tremendous burden then. Domestic work was full-time repetitive never-ending labour and, as well, family survival depended on the initiative of the woman and her traditional women's skills. Sheets were made of patchwork, letter paper became steamed off labels from jam jars, children's clothes were made by hand from flour bags, as well as underclothes which were a luxury. Blankets, if one was lucky enough, were Depression quilts made from old coats or suiting samples or waggas: "We had a partly filled chaff bag for a mattress, and three bushel bags sewn together made a blanket or wagga."[17] One person remembered that: blankets and sheets were out of the question. "We didn't have sheets for years. Well, to be honest, we had three bags sown [sic] together and covered them with cretonne. My wife used to get some cretonne for 2s lld for a dozen yards."[18] Wendy Lowenstein, in her book on the 1930s depression in Australia, relates a story of a wagga Depression quilt which was stolen for its warmth.[19]

We're walking along in the dark and all of a sudden we hear someone snoring. 'A bloke's asleep on the front verandah,' I said. 'Listen, we're going to die if we don't get some warmth. This feller might have a lot of blankets.' So I snuck up on the verandah and there's a bloke curled up on a bed with a great big wagga rug made of hessian with coloured patches . . . That night we found an old A model Ford and curled up in the back seat under his wagga rug . . .

It was not only the unfortunate who made Depression rugs. They seem to have been very popular throughout Australia with all classes of people. Despite the humble origins of their fabrics, many of the patterns of their woollen patchwork quilts were artistically designed, stating that they were decorative as well as utilitarian objects. One was made by Elizabeth Blyth (b. in Tasmania 1844, d. 1923), the granddaughter of William Crowther, surgeon of Hobart Town during the colony's early days. In 1867 she was married to Joshua Hayes whose father John Hayes was the first white man to be born in Van Dieman's Land (as Tasmania was known then). Elizabeth was a school teacher and taught at the Pontville school. She used to drive a horse and buggy to and from school every day. One of her sons John Blyth Hayes was the Premier of Tasmania from 1922 to 1923.

Elizabeth made her wagga quilt during the war years sometime before her death in 1923. Although she came from such an eminent family, the quilt consists of 298 squares of woollen suiting materials from pieces of her son's suiting trousers which could no longer be repaired. The quilt is machine pieced, but hand worked around the edges and backed with a soft fawn linen or cotton joined in strips of about 24 inches wide. The quilt has served many generations and recently Elizabeth's great-great-grandchild has had it on her bed for extra warmth.

Lillian Head, who is now in her 70s, still has a cupboard full of waggas made from tailors, samples and offcuts, which she made together with her mother, grandmother and her aunts: "The back room of our house was turned into a sewing room with two sewing machines. We used to go to Blackmore's Tailors near St. Peters (Sydney) and pick up precut men's vests, which we took home to sew. The tailor often gave us swatches and offcuts from which we produced waggas; we gave many away. They were often lined with sugar bags which we got from grocers. We were still making them in 1927 when the Duke and Dutchess of York (later King George VI and the present Queen Mother), came to Australia to open Parliment House and I remember taking along a box of swatches to sew whilst waiting to see their carriage pass when they openned the Royal Agricultural Show that year." Lillian Head continued to make waggas until 1947. Many of these waggas also contained the woollen fabric from her father-in-law's trousers, old dresses and old coats.

Annie Thomas of Victoria also made a Depression quilt but from factory blanket samples. A wide range of colours has been pieced between black squares to obtain a cheerful piece of decorative art and the quilt has been in use ever since the Depression.

The third type of wagga is what I have called the "salesman's samples" quilt. These quilts were usually made from cottons from the 1920s to the 1950s and were made from the pinked edged material samples that were carried by travelling salesmen. The woman who could not afford purchased quilt fabric would wait anxiously for the travelling salesman to arrive, ply him with her freshly baked cake, and hope that he would leave his sample book behind. The samples were all one size, and just a good shape to incorporate into a patchwork quilt. Many medallion quilts made in the late 19th and early 20th century have borders of these salesmen's samples. In fact Sidney Myer, the founder of Myer Emporium in Victoria, started in business as a travelling draper with his cart and horse serving the little towns north of Bendigo.[20] One lady remembers the travelling haberdashery salesmen from her childhood days in Victoria: "We had travelling salesmen but being in a Depression we found them too expensive . . . we had two traders call twice a year. They sold everything from material, buttons, pins, ribbons, you name it, they had it. Both traders travelled in wagonettes drawn by two horses and when we would see their wagons coming down the lane my brother and I would rush to open the farm gate. They always rewarded us with lollies, so, of course, they were popular with us children."

The stories such as these of the waggas, the blueys and the Depression quilts are a real part of Australia's folklore. Although Australian women also produced extremely elegant and well made quilts during the 19th and early 20th century (see *The Quilt Digest 5,* 1987[21]) the waggas seem to evoke a particular emotion and fondness in all those who remember them. Now is the time to collect and document them before they slip away from us forever. Australia is rich in folk history and yet domestic crafts such as the wagga have only recently begun to be acknowledged and given due status.

This article is dedicated to Robin Lovejoy, (1923-1985) director and designer of drama and opera, who, with his familiarity with stage sets and his love of fabrics, has helped me identify many of these waggas.

[1]Jeannette Lasansky. "The Role of Haps in Central Pennsylvania's 19th and 20th Century Quiltmaking Traditions," *Uncoverings 1985* (Mill Valley, CA: American Quilt Study Group, 1986, pp. 85-93).

[2]Personal correspondence from Sybil Lewis and Dorothy Osler of the Heritage Committee of the English Quilters Guild, 1985.

[3]Ruth McKendry. *Traditional Quilts and Bed-coverings* (Toronto: Van Nostrand Reinhold Company, 1979).

Figure 5. *Sample book of men's suiting fabrics, ca.1940. The Australian Woollen Mills Pty Ltd, Marrickville, NSW. 10½" × 6½" × 2" on top of Depression wagga maker unknown made of tied suiting samples. The patches are in fact same size as those in suiting sample book. Collection of Annette Gero.*

[4]Dorothy K. Burnham. *Pieced Quilts of Ontario* (Toronto: Royal Ontario Museum, 1985, p. 10).

[5]Sandra Morton Weizman, and Elyse Eliot-Los. *Alberta Quilts* (Paperworks Press: Edmonton, Canada, 1984, pp. 15-20).

[6]*The Oxford English Dictionary* unabridged edition 1986.

[7]Jan Ross-Manley. In the catalogue *Wool Quilts Old and New/Exhibition Catalogue, June 16-30, 1985.* (Parkville, Victoria: Australian Wool Corporation and Running Stitch).

[8]*The Macquarie Dictionary,* Macquarie Library Pty Ltd (St. Leonards, NSW, Australia: Macquarie Library Pty Ltd., 1981).

[9]Quotations are from private correspondence to the author.

[10]Weizman. op. cit. p. 15.

[11]Lasansky. op. cit. p. 92.

[12]Henry Lawson. "A Child in the Dark, and a Foreign Father" in Leonard Cronin's (ed.) *A Fantasy of Man* (Sydney: Lansdowne Press, 1984, p. 141) and "Water them Geraniums" in Leonard Cronin's (ed.) *A Camp Fire* (Sydney: Lansdowne Press, 1984, p. 719).

[13]Margaret Rolfe. In the catalogue *Wool Quilts Old and New/Exhibition Catalogue, June 16-30, 1985.* (Parkville, Victoria: Australian Wool Corporation and Running Stitch).

[14]Albert Dorrington. "A Bush Tanquerary," in *The Bulletin Story Book,* 1901.

[15]Mrs. Aeneas Gunn. *We of the Never Never* (London: Hutchinson & Co. 1907, p. 27).

[16]Wendy Lowenstein. *Weevils in the Flour: An Oral Record of the 1930s Depression in Australia,* (Melborne: Hyland House, 1978, pp. 299-300).

[17]Ibid., p. 113.

[18]Ray Broomhill. *Unemployed Workers. A Social History of the Great Depression in Adelaide.* (University of Queensland Press, 1978, p. 93).

[19]Lowenstein, op. cit. p. 122.

[20]Alan Marshall. *The Gay Provider: The Myer Story* (Melbourne: F. W. Cheshire, 1961, p. 37).

[21]Annette Gero. "Quilts and Their Makers in Nineteenth Century Australia," *The Quilt Digest, Vol. 5.* (San Francisco: The Quilt Digest Press, 1987, pp. 58-71).

Suggested Reading:

Colby, Averil. *Patchwork.* London: B. T. Batsford, 1958.

Gero, Annette. "Quilts and their Makers in Nineteenth Century Australia," *The Quilt Digest, Vol. 5.* (San Francisco: The Quilt Digest Press, 1987).

Lasansky, Jeannette. "The Role of Haps in Central Pennsylvania's 19th and 20th Century Quiltmaking Traditions," *Uncoverings 1985.* Mill Valley, Ca: The American Quilt Study Group, 1986.

______. "Typical Versus the Unusual: Distortions of time," *In the Heart of Pennsylvania/Symposium Papers.* (Lewisburg, PA: The Oral Traditions Project, 1986).

Lowenstein, Wendy. *Weevils in the Flour: An Oral Record of the 1930s Depression in Australia.* (Melborne: Hyland House, 1978).

McKendry, Ruth. *Quilts and Other Bed Coverings in the Canadian Traditions.* (Toronto: Van Nostrand Reinhold Ltd., 1979).

Walker, Murray, *Colonial Crafts of Victoria, Early Settlement to 1921/Catalogue of an Exhibition at the National Gallery of Victoria (Australia), November 1978—January 1979.*

Annette Gero is one of Australia's first quilt historians and has a doctorate in biochemistry from the University of New South Wales, Sydney. She has lectured and written extensively on the history of old quilts including: "Collecting American Antique Quilts" in the Australian Business Collectors Annual *(1984), the introduction to the exhibition catalog* Wool Quilts Old and New *published by the Australian Wool Corporation (1985), "Australian Quilt Makers From Our Past: Alicia Florinda Tye (1864-1959) and Mary Ann Bruton (1851-1939)" in* Australiana Vol. 8, No.2 *(1986), "The Quiltmaker's Art" in* Craft Arts (1986), and *"Quilts and Their Makers in Nineteenth Century Australia"* in The Quilt Digest, (1987). *Her paper entitled "Patriotic Australian Quilts" was presented at the American Quilt Study Group's 1987 meeting and will be published in* Uncoverings 1987. *Annette has one of the major collections of antique quilts in Australia which has been exhibited widely including the Regional Galleries and the National Trust. In 1986 she was elected a Fellow of the Royal Society of Arts (London) in recognition of her contribution toward quilt research.*

Figure 6. *Wagga Lily Flour advertisement from 1925. From the* Goulburn Cookery Book *compiled by Mrs. Forster Rutledge, 31st edn. Collection of Jan Ross-Manley.*

Template Quilt Construction And Its Offshoots

From Godey's Lady's Book of Mountain Mist

Virginia Gunn

Carrie Hall, co-author of *Romance of the Patchwork Quilt in America*, called the mosaic quilt of 1885 the "grandmother" of the 1930s "grandmother's flower garden" quilts. Honeycomb, hexagon, or mosaic quilts have been perennial favorites of American quiltmakers for almost two centuries. This six-sided pattern, the only patchwork design offered in an American magazine in the first half of the 19th century, appeared in the January 1835 issue of *Godey's Lady's Magazine* (fig. 1). A century later, the Stearns & Foster Company of Cincinnati prominently featured the same design on their Mountain Mist quilt batting wrapper (fig. 2).

Godey's titled the pattern "hexagon patchwork" and also referred to it as a "honeycomb" design. Their instructions called for basting fabric patches over carefully cut paper hexagons, before sewing them together "neatly over the edge" (fig. 3). A century later, American women had discarded this paper template method of construction. They sewed their "grandmother's flower gardens" together with a running stitch method, adding 1/4" seams to the design traced on fabric and joining pieces with a small running stitch. Thus, the hexagon quilts of the 1800s-1830s, the mosaic quilts of the 1870s-1890s, and the flower garden quilts of the 1930s, have identical designs, but two different methods of construction. Clothing construction techniques, domestic education of young females, recommendations of tastemakers and fashion periodicals, and rural traditions and preferences all influenced the methods quiltmakers used.

Late 18th/ Early 19th Century Quiltmaking

English quilt historian Averil Colby, author of *Patchwork* (1958) and *Patchwork Quilts* (1965), believes English patchwork originated in well-to-do households and filtered down to the cottages of the poor. Originally English women used the quick running stitch method for piecing patterns based on rectangles and squares, but by 1770 upper-class women began basting expensive chintz and silk fabrics around paper shapes to fashion precise geometrical pieced designs.

Colby notes that English and American patchwork have many similarities in patterns, materials, and methods of working. Surviving quilts from the late 18th/ early 19th century suggest that American women mastered all the fashionable English techniques of quilt construction: whole cloth quilts, appliquéd quilts, pieced quilts utilizing running stitch methods, and pieced quilts utilizing paper template methods. It is not surprising that Americans were familiar with sewing techniques of the more affluent classes, for the majority of colonials came from England and migrated to new shores for reasons other than poverty. This premise is reinforced in stories which recall early 19th century quiltmaking in America.

In her tale, "The Patch-Work Quilt," appearing in the January 1844 *Graham's Magazine*, Ann S. Stephens speaks of a "rising sun" pattern composed of diamond-shaped pieces of calico with a center star radiating out over the quilt. The maker obtained the pattern from "an old English woman in the neighborhood, who has seen such things in her country." The diamond pattern could be precisely pieced over paper, as well as joined by running.

In another story entitled "The Patch-Work Quilt," appearing in the March 1846 issue of *The Columbian Lady's and Gentleman's Magazine*, Miss C. M. Sedgwick discusses a "beggar's patchwork formed of hexagonal bits of calico and silk." This quilt contained fragments of treasured gowns. Quilts of this type functioned as "story-books—family legends—illustrated traditions," rather than warm bed-

***Plate** 7. This unfinished silk quilt top still contains the paper templates used to shape the pieces of silk. The haphazard "mosaic" arrangement of brightly colored hexagons reflects late 19th century taste. However, cues from the paper templates and fabrics indicate that this top was made in the early 20th century, demonstrating that not everyone preferred "colonial revival" to Victorian template quilts. Author's collection.*

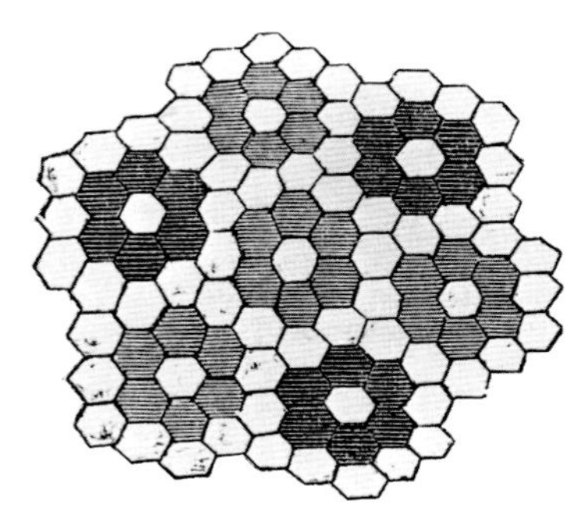

Figure 1. This engraving of hexagon patchwork appeared in the "Fancy Needle-work" section of the January 1835 issue of Godey's Lady's Book.

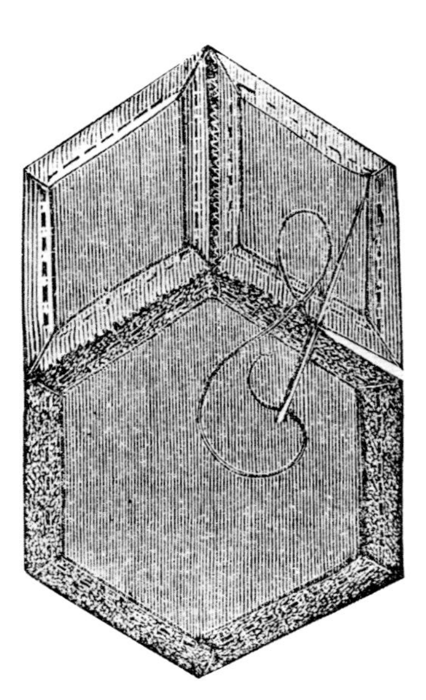

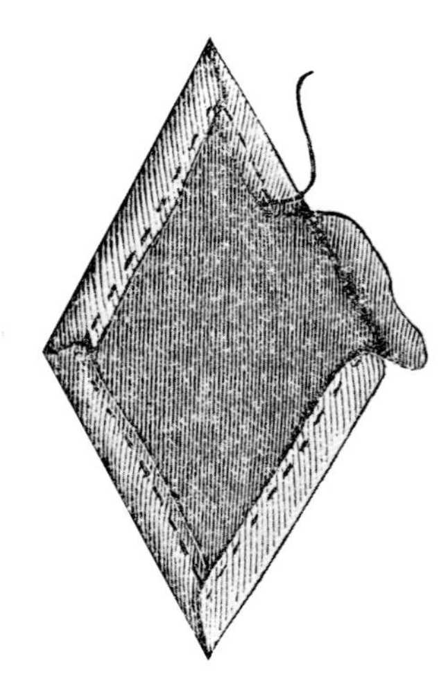

Figure 2. This engraving from the August 1880 issue of Peterson's Magazine *clearly illustrates the template method of construction in patchwork. The overhand stitch joins the fabric covered templates together in the same manner that it attached the bodice to the skirt in 19th century dress construction.*

dcoverings and were often made by the paper template method.

In colonial households, only the wealthy could afford to import quilts or had the leisure time in which to make them; hence, they became status symbols. With the Industrial Revolution, white cotton fabric became more abundant and less expensive. The aspiring middle classes became involved in quiltmaking. Although blankets provided more economical bed coverings, parents encouraged daughters to make quilts. Handsome quilts added to the value of a girl's dowry, and symbolized the fact that their maker possessed sewing skills essential to a family's well-being and survival. Stephens noted that young girls hung out their handmade linens and patchwork quilts each spring and fall as a sign that they had been properly trained for matrimony. Women had to know how to sew, for clothing of this period was made by hand, usually in the family home. A woman with a wealthy husband might be able to obtain help with sewing, using the services of tailors and seamstresses, but she rarely escaped sewing altogether.

To encourage daughters to learn necessary sewing skills, mothers allowed them to make small quilts for their dolls. In 1842, American pioneer educator Catherine Beecher, author of the widely used book *A Treatise on Domestic Economy*, suggested:

> When a little girl first begins to sew, her mother can promise her a small bed and pillows, as soon as she has sewed a patch quilt for them; and then a bedstead, as soon as she has sewed the sheets and cases for pillows; and then a large doll to dress, as soon as she has made the undergarments; and thus go on, till the whole contents of the baby-house are earned by the needle and skill of its little owner. Thus, the task of learning to sew, will become a pleasure; and every new toy will be earned by useful exertion.

It is likely that this method of teaching enjoyed wide use in America, for Beecher, who was born in 1800, remembered being taught in that manner by her own mother. Throughout the century, records indicate that patchwork was considered an excellent way to introduce plain sewing.

Sewing little squares together taught girls to handle a needle and thread and to perfect basic stitches—the running stitch and the backstitch. A child could also learn the hemming stitch while finishing the edge of her quilt project (figs. 4-6). Ellen Lindsay, in the February 1857 *Godey's*, asked:

> What little girl does not recollect her first piece of patchwork, the anxiety for fear the pieces would not fit, the eager care with which each stitch was taken, and the delight of finding the bright squares successfully blended into the pretty pattern. Another square and another, and the work begins to look as if in time it might become a quilt.

Some little girls completed bed-size quilts, although not everyone agreed that young children should do this. Six-year-old Mary Sutliff of Warren, Ohio completed 49 nine-patch squares to form the quilt inscribed by her mother "March 4 1861/the day the first Republican/ President A. Lincoln inaugurated/Amen." In 1850 Miss Electa Chase of Milan, Ohio, aged seven years, entered two pieced quilts in the Huron and Erie County Fair. The judges seemed impressed with her industry but the two women committee members doubted "the propriety of encouraging such young children to sit closely to sewing."

Skills gained sewing patchwork squares translated to garment construction, for skirt seams were usually 1/4" wide, just like patchwork seams (fig. 7). Prior to 1865, women formed skirts from total widths of fabrics. They seamed lengths of fabric together near the selvage, which was retained to prevent raveling. In clothing construction, as in pieced work, this narrow seam was pressed to one side rather than open.

It is likely that little girls of the early 19th century also made "rosettes," units of hexagons joined together using a foundation of paper templates. Joining hexagons taught the overhand or "over and over" stitch, another essential stitch in clothing construction or plain sewing (fig. 8). Women used overhanding to join skirts to completely lined and hemmed bodices, to join selvages and make flat seams on linens and bedding (fig. 9). Little girls would have needed to master this stitch in order to sew successfully. Thus, American women would not have found it strange for the 1835 *Godey's* to suggest using the template method and overhand stitch to make patchwork doll and cradle quilts or kettle-holders. Seaming hexagons and later "stars, triangles, diamonds, waves, stripes, squares, &c." provided educational amusement for little girls.

A number of women chose the paper template method for constructing elegant quilts of expensive silks or imported printed cottons. In *Uncoverings 1986*, (Mill Valley, CA: American Quilt Study Group, 1987) Tandy Hersh analyzes the outstanding template pieced quilt made by a Quaker girl at Primitive Hall near Philadelphia in 1842. However, the majority of American women seemed to prefer piecing large quilts with a running stitch rather than the over-and-over stitch. With many demands on their time, they probably found the running stitch and designs based on squares and rectangles easier and quicker. Although manufactured fabric became readily available after 1830, paper remained a scarce commodity in many rural frontier homes. At any rate, the running stitch method became more highly developed in America.

By contrast, Colby points out that the majority of English needleworkers became preoccupied with the hexagon shape, alone or in combination with other shapes. Instead of block style pieced or appliquéd quilts, English women began to concentrate on bedspreads composed of up to 3,000 to 4,000 small hexagon patches. Less ambitious needlewomen used this ornamental patchwork for smaller

Figure 3. *The Stearns & Foster Company featured their hexagon pattern, Number 25*—Grandmother's Flower Garden, *in a prominent position on their Mountain Mist batting wrapper with a 1939 copyright. Collection of Margaret Seebold.*

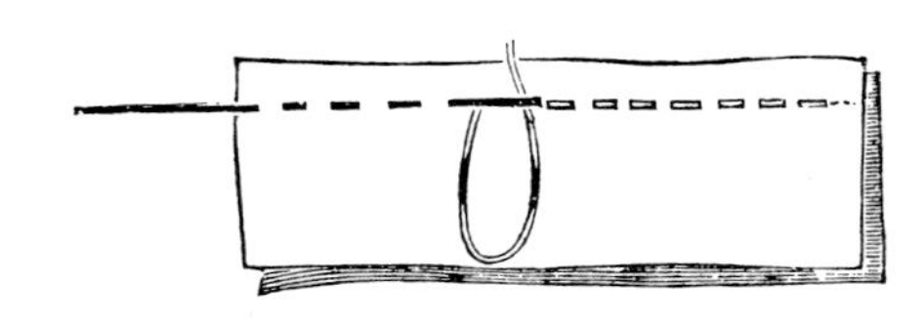

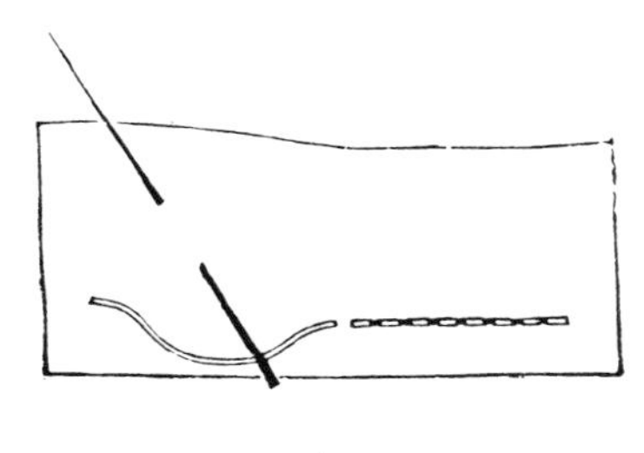

Figure 4. 19th Century children learned to do the basic running stitch as illustrated in this engraving from Louise J. Kirkwood's Illustrated Sewing Primer with Songs and Music for Schools and Families *(New York: Ivison, Blakeman, Taylor & Co., 1886).*

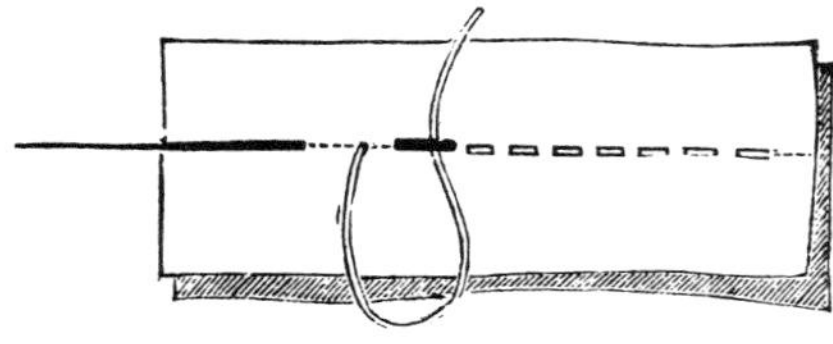

Figure 5. Little girls learned the backstitch variations for making strong seams as shown in Louise J. Kirkwood's Sewing Primer.

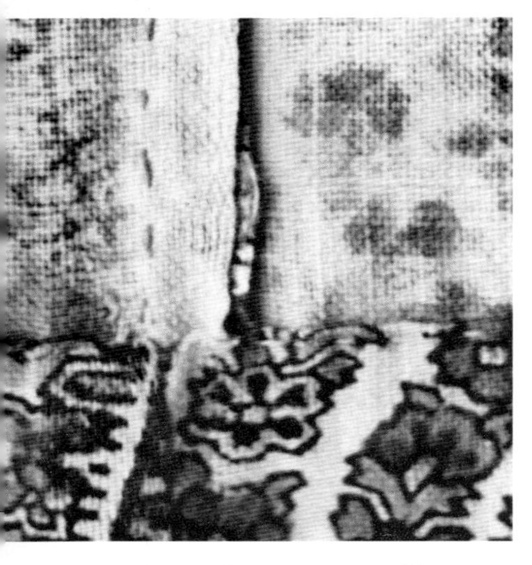

Figure 6. This photographic close-up shows the hem edge and skirt seam in a woman's printed cotton dress made in the mid-1860s. The seam is formed by using a running stitch placed 1/4 inch from the selvage. The seam is pressed to one side, also a common practice in running stitch patchwork. Collection of the School of Home Economics and Family Ecology, University of Akron. Photo by C. Douglas Gunn.

anti-macassars, ottomans, cushions, mats, and rugs. By 1850, hexagon patchwork utilizing paper templates had become the characteristic English work.

Mid-19th Century Template Work

Mid-19th century American publishers took pride in providing readers with the latest imported European patterns. In 1850 and 1851 *Godey's Lady's Magazine* began to seriously publish patchwork designs. They offered a series of thirty-five patterns copied from an English magazine, *The Family Friend*. Throughout the rest of the century, most patchwork designs published in America originated in England and reflected the English taste for paper template methods. *Peterson's Magazine* (1859) stressed that "mathematical precision is indispensible in cutting out the paper patterns, or the beauty of the work will be entirely destroyed." American women, who regularly used the overhand stitch in constructing clothing, would have found it easy to follow paper template directions. Quilts and smaller accessories made with paper templates began to enjoy high fashion status.

Godey's distributed 150,000 magazines each month. Women often shared and saved each issue and had them bound into books at the end of a year. Patterns appearing in *Godey's* and competing magazines like *Peterson's* and *Graham's* enjoyed wide circulation over a long period of time. They set the fashion standards for fancy and ornamental needlework (plate 7). Women received compliments by completing featured projects and adding these handmade touches to Victorian bedrooms and parlors decorated with purchased sets of furniture.

In 1858 English needle authority Mrs. Pullan came to America to direct the work table section of *Frank Leslie's Magazine*. In her popular *Lady's Manual of Fancy Work*, Pullan pronounced cotton quilts and counterpanes ugly and not worth making, but thought silk, velvet or satin fabrics basted over paper patterns could be converted into handsome cushions, chair-covers, and ottomans. American Florence Hartley, author of the *Ladies' Handbook of Fancy Ornamental Work* (1859), disagreed. She admitted liking the "genuine old fashioned patchwork" of calico quilts. However, Hartley's directions for doing patchwork called for the tin template, paper shapes, and silk fabrics preferred by the English. In fashion publications, cotton patchwork done with the running stitch method became associated with humble, useful, rural, and less fashionable origins.

As today's state quilt projects have demonstrated, mid-19th century women made significant numbers of cotton quilts utilizing the running stitch method and they also made the fashionable "template" style quilts in silk, imported cottons, and even wool. For example, Laurel Horton and Lynn Myer's study of South Carolina quilts, reported in *Social Fabric*, (Charleston: McKissick Museum, 1985) uncovered a number of paper template pieced quilts dating to the mid-19th century. Most originated in Charleston, a cosmopolitan center where women preferred to interpret the English template designs in expensive cottons rather than silks.

Antebellum women challenged themselves with template designs including hexagon, box, and star variations. In the mid-1850s a "young lady of Rhode Island," now identified as Adeline Harris Sears of Providence, began an ambitious autograph bedquilt in a box pattern variation. She mailed white silk diamond patches basted over card to notable people of that era, asking for them to return the patch with their signature added. Abraham Lincoln, Franklin Pierce, James Buchanan, and Charles Sumner are among those who signed patches. When *Godey's* reported on the project in their April 1864 issue, Adeline had collected 350 of the 556 autographs she incorporated in her 2780 piece quilt. She had been working on it for eight years. *Godey's* stated that it was a symbol of her mechanical, intellectual, and moral endeavor and believed she would finish it "if her life is spared." They gave further information on the overall design in the July issue, but noted that some might prefer to undertake only a sofa-cushion or table cover. (This quilt appears as Plate 60 in Patsy and Myron Orlofsky's *Quilts in America*.)

Late 19th Century Mosaic Template Work

In the late 1860s, styles of women's dresses and the methods used to construct them changed radically. Garments now featured shaped and gored skirts which no longer utilized the narrow 1/4" seam placed along a straight selvage. Seams became wider to prevent raveling along cut edges. As women began to use sewing machines, overhanding appeared less and less in clothing construction. Skills learned while sewing "nine-patches" or "rosettes" no longer translated directly to clothing construction.

Women's periodicals continued to offer occasional patchwork designs in the English style. They increasingly referred to these patterns as "mosaic" designs, suggesting that they would be appropriate in rooms decorated in the exotic middle Eastern or Turkish styles then fashionable (fig. 10 and 11). Needlework editors also recognized that patchwork now had more appeal in rural than in urban areas. The August 1867 *Demorest's Magazine* offered the familiar hexagon and box patterns in response to requests from "country readers" and stated that if any of their readers "possess any thing new, curious, or beautiful in the way of patch-work designs, they would be "happy to receive sketches or descriptions of them." S. Annie Frost, author of *The Ladies Guide to Needlework and Embroidery* (1877), noted that "some run the pieces together, some sew them on the sewing-machine, but the old-fashioned overstitch will ever be the best for patchwork." Her book inaccurately mentions basting pieces "over stiff card, or still better, pieces of tin." While recognizing both calico and silk patchwork, she felt the taste for both had nearly died out.

Women who continued to do template work in the post-Civil War era fabricated bold interpretations of the old patterns, often choosing strong color combinations. They applied template units to plain backgrounds giving their work interesting optical effects in which the geometric shapes seem to float on the quilt surface. In June 1877, *Peterson's* recognized such efforts and noted that the "box" pattern was again becoming very fashionable. However, after the Philadelphia Centennial Exhibition, a new craze for silk Crazy quilts began to sweep across the land, overshadowing paper template techniques. Crazy quilt construction featured the Log Cabin pressed technique done in a haphazard asymmetrical style which presented a strong contrast to precise, orderly template work. Some women combined both methods and added crazy work borders to a template style quilt.

The crazy work fad peaked in the mid-1880s. Strawbridge and Clothier's booklet *Crazy Patchwork* (1884) mentions that not all fashionable silk quilts are of crazy work. It includes directions for "patty-pan," a revival of the hexagon pattern, and for "tea-box," a new "oriental" name for the box design. The February 1888 *Godey's* reported that Miss Sara W. Kellogg of Brooklyn won the $50 prize in the "old fashioned silk patch work" category at the Second Canfield Art Needlework Competition held in New York City. It noted that her quilt was "very neatly and accurately made in a small octagon [sic?] design. The pattern was not intricate, but the points came together by a thread, and where hair-striped silk was used, the lines met and melted into each other."

Late 19th/ Early 20th Century Colonial Revival Quilts

In the 1890s, a reaction against Victorian clutter and excess slowly filtered down to the general public. Those tired of Victorian decor could select furnishings in the flowing art nouveau style or the more spare geometric "arts and crafts" styles. In America, they could also furnish rooms in a romanticized colonial style. Civil War Sanitary Fairs had featured colonial kitchens, as did the 1876 Philadelphia Exhibition. Visitors viewed rooms decorated with antique furnishing and witnessed reenacted quilting bees and apple parings. Interest in colonial revival gradually gained momentum. Women began to put on "colonial teas" to raise money for worthy causes. They dressed in old costumes and prepared tableaus of colonial interiors featuring appropriate accessories like spinning wheels and old-fashioned quilts. By the turn of the century, bedrooms decorated in colonial or early American style were popular and fashionable. Those not fortunate enough to own an antique quilt for their four poster bed began to think of buying one or creating a reproduction. Interestingly, the colonial bedrooms shown in interior decoration manuals often feature a quilt in a variation of the old hexagon motif (fig. 12).

Tastemakers identified hexagon variations as heirloom patterns, predating the Victorian silk models. Twentieth-century women chose "traditional" cotton fabrics for "colonial style" hexagon quilts. They usually constructed them with a running stitch instead of paper templates. Rural quiltmakers of the late 19th/early 20th centuries preferred the running stitch method and patterns based on squares and rectangles to the template hexagons associated with city fashion. It is likely they began making "colonial" hexagon patterns by the running stitch method and that this was picked up by urban editors and quiltmakers.

Although the *Delineator* (December) and the *Ladies' Home Journal* (October) both announced a revival of patchwork quilts in 1894, it took several decades before significant numbers of urban women began to make cotton quilts again. However, by 1915, Marie Webster, author of the pioneering book *Quilts, Their Story and How to Make Them*, believed that "more quilts are being made at the present time and over a wider area than ever before." While women turned to knitting during World War I, a continued interest in quilting and quilts can be traced throughout the 1910s and 1920s. Mary Alden Ferguson, writing for *Needlecraft Magazine* in February 1931, felt that:

> The great revival of interest in colonial furniture, and the consequent demand for "antiques" and their reproductions in modern homes, is doubtless responsible in large measure for the renaissance of quilting.

My mother, Helen Ruth Henry Railsback, remembers learning to piece and quilt in a small town in Kansas when she was six or seven years old in 1917-18. Her aunt started her on a nine-patch doll quilt made with the running stitch. She never learned to use paper shapes, for this method of construction was going out of favor for both patchwork and clothing. *Needlecraft Magazine* for May 1928 remembered the "'good old Colony times' when patchwork stints were the order of the day, and the 'over-and-over' seam afforded the very first lesson in the use of the needle which the small daughter of the house was encouraged to undertake." The cover of this issue, however, features a little girl piecing a block of squares with a running stitch.

The Depression Era Grandmother's Flower Garden

During the Depression of the late 1920s and 1930s, women found pieced work made an inexpensive and enjoyable hobby that helped to take one's mind off troubles. *McCall's Decorative Art and Needlework* (Winter 1932-33) pointed out that smart women insisted on "lovely new quilts made just like the old de-

Figure 7. *The closely spaced basic hemming stitch, illustrated in this diagram from the* D.M.C. Encyclopedia of Needlework *edited by Therèse de Dillmont (France, no date, c. 1870's), was used when attaching binding to quilts and clothing.*

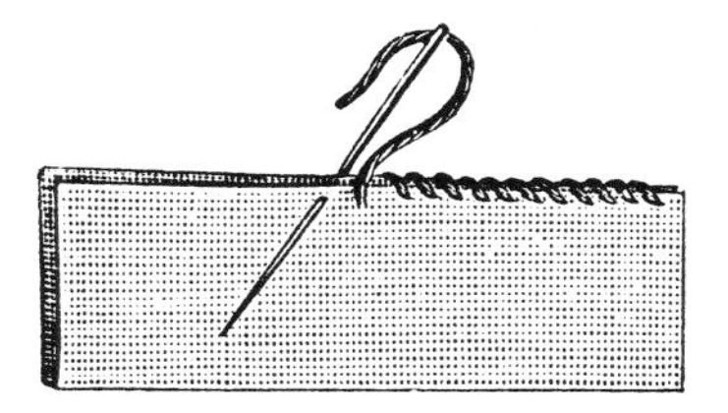

Figure 8. *This engraving from the* D.M.C. Encyclopedia of Needlework *illustrates the overhand stitch, the basic stitch used in template patchwork.*

Figure 9. *This photographic close-up shows the inside of a woman's silk wedding dress made in the mid-1860s. The top edge of the unlined striped silk skirt has been overcast and folded over. The folded edge is then gathered and attached to the lined and narrowly hemmed bodice with an overhand stitch. Collection of the School of Home Economics and Family Ecology, University of Akron. Photo by C. Douglas Gunn.*

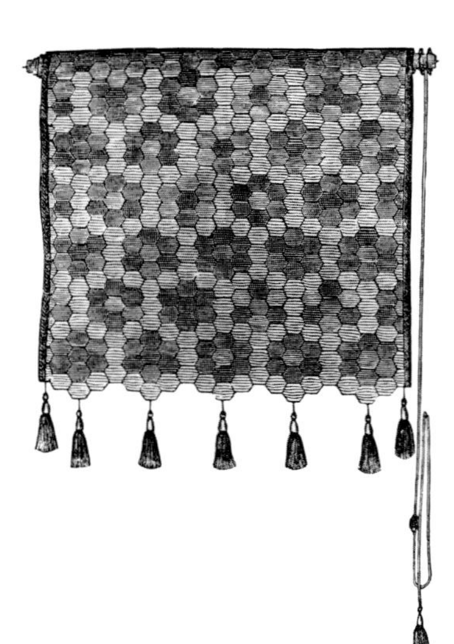

Figure 10. This engraving of a "Window Blind in Mosaic" appeared in the April 1871 issue of Godey's Lady's Book. *The rosettes of seven hexagons enclosed in a white ground were to be of a great variety of colors, irregularly placed.*

Figure 11. This engraving of a patch-work footstool or ottoman to be made with template construction appeared in the August 1880 issue of Peterson's Magazine. *The pattern featured colorful six-pointed silk stars on a ground of black velvet hexagons.*

signs" for their colonial bedrooms. The hexagon or mosaic, now most frequently called a "flower garden," reigned as a favorite design of this era. Catalogs, like the *Mountain Mist Blue Book* (fig. 13) and *Grandmother Clark's Old Fashioned Quilt Designs*, assured customers that grandmother and great-grandmother had prized this pattern. Only the *Double Wedding Ring* and *Dresden Plate* rivaled it in popularity.

Entrepreneurs offered new and easy ways to complete this popular design. The *Ladies' Art Company* of St. Louis presented "Grandmother's Flower Garden Quilt" as a ready-to-sew quilt. Precut patches cost $5.00 in colored prints or $6.50 in ginghams. Ruby McKim, in her 1932 catalogue *Designs Worth Doing*, gave the hexagon pattern four different names. She offered ready-cut materials for a "grandmother's flower garden" or "French bouquet" quilt for $4.00 and commented that "if quilts have taken the country by storm, then the hexagon Flower Garden, or the French Rose Garden—whatever your locality is calling it—well, it's a whirlwind!" The Grit Publishing Co. of Williamsport, Pennsylvania referred to the pattern as "Martha Washington's Rose Garden" in their *Colonial Quilts* catalog issued in 1932, the 200th anniversary of George Washington's birthday. They introduced it as the pattern "my mother taught me to sew with," and offered a full size drawing, color chart, and cutting guide with one-fourth inch seams allowed.

From 1931-33, the Stearns & Foster Company of Cincinnati ran a nostalgic and effective campaign to promote their quilt batting in *Needlecraft Magazine.* Each month they featured one of their "beautiful and authentic" patterns and reminded readers that these patterns had antique, pre-Civil War, colonial, covered-wagon, or log cabin origins. The interest in reproducing heirloom patterns led the company to create new patterns. These enjoyed success without displacing the older designs. In 1939, *Grandmother's Flower Garden* appeared on the Mountain Mist batting wrapper right near newer patterns. The pattern remained a favorite for quiltmakers during the following decades.

Women who continued to piece quilts in the 1940s and 1950s rarely, if ever, used the paper template method of construction. Young girls did most of their sewing by machine and seldom used even a small running stitch. In the quilting revival of the 1970s many women had to learn basic hand sewing skills from scratch. Interested in new techniques, they rediscovered the "English paper template" method of constructing "grandmother's flower garden" and "baby block" designs. Few realized that their great, great and ever-so-great grandmothers had been familiar with paper templates and the overhand stitch. American quiltmakers have loved and cherished honeycomb, hexagon, or mosaic variations for almost two centuries, by whatever names they have been called and by whichever method they have been constructed.

Suggested Reading:

Bullard, Lacy Folmar and Betty Jo Shiell. *Chintz Quilts: Unfading Glory*. Tallahassee, Florida: Serendipity Publishers, 1983.

Bullard, Lucy Folmer. "The Collector: Once Out of Time." *Quilt Digest 3*. San Francisco: Quilt Digest Press, 1985, pp. 8-21.

Colby, Averil. *Patchwork*. New York: Charles Scribner's Sons, (1958, 1982).

______. *Patchwork Quilts*. New York: Charles Scribner's Sons, 1965.

Gunn, Virginia. "Victorian Silk Template Patchwork in American Periodicals, 1850-1875." *Uncoverings 1983*. Mill Valley, CA: American Quilt Study Group, 1984, pp. 9-25.

Hersh, Tandy. "1842 Primitive Hall Pieced Quilt Top: The Art of Transforming Printed Fabric Designs through Geometry." *Uncoverings 1986*. Mill Valley, CA: American Quilt Study Group, 1987, pp. 47-59.

Virginia Gunn has a Masters in applied art from Syracuse University and is currently working on her doctorate in history. An Associate Professor at the University of Akron she has been involved with textiles all her life and has concentrated on quilts over the past fifteen years. She has lectured widely on the subject of textile conservation, including papers delivered at the Canton Art Institute in conjunction with a show, Ohio Quilts: Another View *as well as at Wooster College for their show* Treasures from Trunks. *She wrote the introduction and the quilt legacies in their catalog also. Her articles "Victorian Silk Template Patchwork in American Periodicals 1850-1875" appeared in* Uncoverings 1983; *"Crazy Quilts and Outline Quilts: Popular Responses to the Decorate Art/Art Needlework Movement 1876-1983" in* Uncoverings 1984; *"Quilts for Union Soldiers in the Civil War" in* Uncoverings 1985, *and "Yo-yo or Bed of Roses Quilts/19th Century Origin" in* Uncoverings 1987. *All were published by the American Quilt Study Group of which she is currently a Board member. Ginny's paper on "The Display, Care, and Conservation of Old Quilts," presented at the 1985 Bucknell symposium was published last year.*

Figure 12. *This colonial revival bedroom, selected by editor William A. Vollmer for* A Book of Distinctive Interiors *(New York: McBride, Nast & Company, 1912), features a hexagon pattern quilt on the canopied four poster bed.*

Figure 13. *The 1960s edition of the Stearns & Foster Company's* Blue Book of Quilts *features matching "grandmother's flower garden" quilts on the popular twin beds, and demonstrates the continued appeal of this hexagon pattern. Collection of Margaret Seebold.*

Jan 1st. 1845.

We shall surely meet again Dear Sister; May your slumbers be peaceful, & your waking hours cheerful and happy.

Rebekah L. Chaffin.

Concord N.H.

Mid-19th-Century Album and Friendship Quilts 1860-1920

Ricky Clark

From the time America was opened for settlement women have made quilts to keep their families warm. In the mid-19th century, however, some quilts took on a new function, as quiltmakers began adding inscriptions to their blocks. Names, addresses, dates, statements of relationships, personal messages and literary quotations were inked, stamped or embroidered on the white fabrics that only recently were being incorporated into quilt blocks. Quiltmakers called these "friendship" or "album" quilts.

The difference between friendship or album quilts and others lies not in their physical characteristics, but in their primary function: *women made friendship or album quilts to reify community*. By making them women transformed personal relationships into visible, tangible form. In this respect these quilts are textile versions of the autograph albums popular at the same time, as the term "album quilt" indicates. Because these terms are essentially synonymous, I will use them interchangeably.

The communities represented on album quilts might be family, friends, school or church. Indeed, several communities are usually involved, as the social networks of the signers overlap. As Dena Katzenberg reported in her study of mid-19th-century Baltimore album quilts, for example, many of the women whose names appear on those quilts were relatives, residents of Baltimore, Methodists and members of the same local church.

Just as a single quilt might represent several communities, it might also perform several functions for its makers or owner. Many political or fundraising quilts, for instance, were made primarily to make a social statement or raise money, although they also represent groups with common goals. In these cases a quilt's function as tangible community becomes secondary. Only those quilts whose primary function is to reify community will be discussed in this paper.

Some friendship quilts were made by one quiltmaker, who had her friends sign muslin patches, quilt blocks or a completed quilt top. Others were constructed by one or more quiltmakers from blocks designed and made by several people. Except for the inscriptions, friendship quilts resemble other quilts made in the same regions at the same time. Stylistic differences are primarily regional, temporal and cultural, as styles were established on the east coast and moved west as people migrated. Quiltmakers in the middle Atlantic and southern states preferred chintz appliqué quilts decorated with motifs cut from printed chintz fabrics and stitched to quilt blocks or borders. Since these motifs were cut along the edges of patterns, often elaborate floral wreaths or vases filled with flowers, making a chintz appliqué quilt was a time-consuming task and required considerable technical skill. Methodist quiltmakers working 1840-1855 in Baltimore developed an elaborate and spectacular variation of this style. They created realistic motifs, including specific buildings and monuments, from small fabric pieces which they appliquéd and built up in layers, much as similar stencilled designs on Hitchcock chairs were created by overlapping and layering smaller shapes. A third quilt style is made from repeated blocks identical in construction, although the fabrics may vary from one block to the next. This style is found in many areas, but was particularly favored in New England.

Most valuable to students of friendship quilts is the content of the inscriptions on them. These quilts are historic documents, and when supported by research into other sources, tell us much about the cultures that produced them. Some friendship quilts include only names; others—a joy to quilt historians—

Plate 8. Detail of quilt made by friends and relatives of Mary Pollard Tolford in Concord, Merrimack County, New Hampshire 1844-1845. Pieced print and solid-colored cottons with white back. Ink inscriptions. Back brought to front as edge treatment. 83 1/2" × 77" with 7 stitches per inch. Collection Betty Clements.

Inscribed entirely with women's names, Mary Tolford's quilt is her female "family" in tangible form. Rebekah Chaffin's ascription of sisterhood to Mary underscores the domestic nature of female friendship; these women were not natal sisters. Quilts like this, made for friends leaving a community during the period of westward expansion, allowed women to take their communities with them. Photo: Lydia Dull.

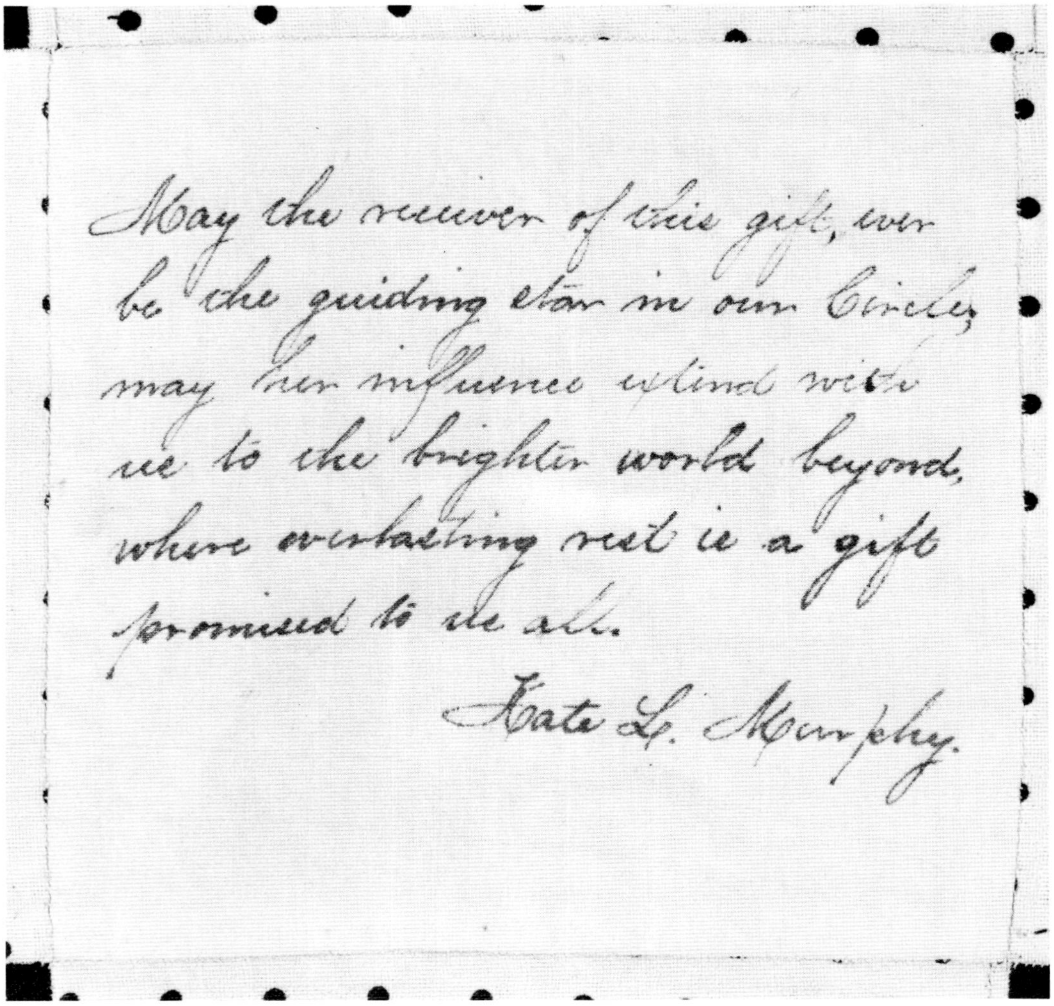

May the receiver of this gift, ever
be the guiding star in our Circle,
may her influence extend with
us to the brighter world beyond,
where everlasting rest is a gift
promised to us all.
Kate L. Murphy.

Figure 1. Detail by Kate L. Murphy of tied comfort made by friends of "I. W.H." and dated "1865." Pieced print and solid-colored cottons with print back. Ink inscriptions. Front and back folded in and buttonhole-stitched as edge treatment. 86" × 84" and tied in colored thread. Collection of the Western Reserve Historical Society.

Kate Murphy's incription includes many hallmarks of mid-nineteenth-century domestic ideology: metaphoric images of light ("guiding star," "brighter world"), references to a women's group ("Circle"), to acting through "influence," and to optimistic anticipation of a rewarding life after death. Photo: Lydia Dull.

Figure 2. Detail of quilt made by Isabell Hall Hurxthal, Baltimore, Batimore County, Maryland, 1846-1847. Pieced and applied chintzes and solid-colored cottons on white top with white back. Ink and embroidered inscriptions. Applied binding. 96" × 92" with 12 stitches per inch. Collection of the Massillon Museum. Photo: Margy Vogt.

names, dates and locations. A collection of identical quilt blocks found in Clinton County, Ohio, for instance, bears inscriptions on papers basted to each that provide valuable clues to the communities they represent. "Helen M. Graham/New Paris, Ohio/January 1st, 1864" is one that led researchers to identify the signers as a community of Quakers in Preble County, Ohio, and Wayne County, Indiana.

The most informative friendship quilts include texts as well as names, dates and locations. Some inscriptions are personal and delightful, such as "Mrs. Elsey D. Wheeler/Aged 57 years Feb. 8th 1854/I quilted this without spectacles." Others report personal tragedies, often in great detail. Messages to friends, Bible verses, poems by Shakespeare and doggerel from *Godey's* are written on many. Some signers even recorded riddles: "Why is a railroad like a quilt?/Because it rests on sleepers."

Although not original, quotations are always informative, since they were selected by the signer for a particular purpose. When all the inscriptions on a friendship quilt are studied, moreover, patterns emerge that provide valuable clues to the intended function of the quilt or the nature of the group it represents. One such quilt, probably made in Pepperell, Massachusetts c. 1860, is inscribed with quotations, all Biblical. Most refer to "affliction," "burden" and "pain," suggesting that the quilt was made to offer support to a woman who was very ill. References to friendship ("Friendship's offering" is a frequently used phrase) and appliquéd albums clearly identify the social function of many made as records of friendships; often both words are found on a single quilt. "Presented to Capt. George W. Russell," "For Ellenor A. Gorsuch" and "Merry Christmas" indicate commemorative functions, as does the comforting inscription written to a bereaved mother: "Sweet heavenborn Spirits are not to earth confined."

Friendship quilts reflect both the nature of quiltmaking communities and the concerns of their members. By studying large numbers of such quilts we learn that mid-19th-century women valued religion, the family and female communality, sentimentalized friendship, commemorated events, and dreaded separation. Why did they feel it was so important to create tangible records of their friendships at this particular time?

To answer this we must look at the world of mid-19th-century American women. Three aspects of American culture, I believe, account most convincingly for the popularity of album quilts at this time: the separation of American society along gender lines, America's westward expansion, and the rise of evangelical Protestantism.

Between 1800 and 1850 the structure of American society changed rapidly. In colonial America, family, church and community worked together as basic units of a stable society. The early 19th century, however, saw a rapid expansion of population and concommitant growth of cities, increased specialization in the workplace and its separation from the home, and the opening of the West to settlement, all of which led to the breakdown of traditional society.

A major effect of the industrial revolution was the change in workplace from the home to the factory. As men, the primary wage earners, increasingly left their homes to earn a living, child-rearing and home management fell naturally to women. Americans thus saw their society divided along gender lines and assigned to each gender-based "sphere" distinct and different characteristics. Men were considerd strong, rational, stern, sensuous, intellectually discerning and hence eminently fitted to rule the worlds of commerce and politics. Women, likened by an association of clergy to "the vine, whose strength and beauty is to lean upon the trellis-work," were nonetheless considered superior in matters of "the heart:" tenderness, compassion, piety, morality.

These two "spheres" complemented each other: "What a forlorn, what a savage creature would man be," wrote one potential savage, "without the meliorating offices of the gentle sex!" Men exercised power, women ruled by influence, which "steals in upon our hearts, gets hold of the springs of action, and leads us into its own ways," as Professor J.H. Agnew informed the readers of *Harper's New Monthly Magazine* in October 1851 (fig. 1). Home and the family were revered as the salvation of American society and became the model for other communal groups.

For women these groups were primarily female, since they spent most of their time with other women, with whom they shared common domestic roles. They developed a strong female sub-culture, a relationship of peers based on the familial model but broadened to include friends, schoolmates and members of churches and voluntary societies. Friendship was romanticised and sisterhood, the family bond that uniquely incorporated those highly valued qualities of kinship, female affection and social equality, became the paradigm of 19th-century female friendship. Women bestowed the term "sister" not only on siblings, but on friends as well, thus defining them as fictive kin.

A second factor that accounts for the development of the friendship quilt was America's westward expansion. Between 1840 and 1870 a quarter of a million Americans, buoyed by a spirit of self-reliance and optimism, crossed the continent to Oregon and California. Although some women undoubtedly set out on such treks in a spirit of adventure, for most it was a somber occasion, since it meant long-term and often permanent separation from loved ones. Because women had relied on their female relatives and friends to provide continuity and stability in their rapidly changing society, the disruption of community when a friend moved away was traumatic.

The growth of evangelical Protestantism was a third factor contributing to the development of friendship quilts. This was the dominant religion of the era and appealed greatly to women, since it emphasized morality, compassion and love—exactly those qualities that defined "woman's sphere." Evangelical religion's stress on the availability of God's grace to all people, regardless of gender or station in life, provided women with rationale for justifiable activity outside the home. Together with other church women they prayed, sewed and raised money to fight social evils that threatened the sacred family. Such activities, they believed, were a logical extension of their responsibilities as Christian wives and mothers. A random sampling of friendship quilts inscribed with texts readily illustrates the importance of organized religion to 19th-century women, as so many of these group-made quilts are filled with religious sentiments and Biblical quotations. Indeed, it would be difficult to find such a quilt with no Bible verses on it. Clearly women were Biblically literate, for many of the Scriptural verses cited are uniquely appropriate to the circumstances surrounding the quilt.

In light of all these factors it is only natural that women would transform these comforting, domestic textiles into tangible analogues of the communities that produced them. The creation of friendship quilts was an important ritual that underscored the significance of interpersonal bonds. Women made friendship quilts to affirm those communities that were most important to them; they made them to commemorate significant community events; they made them to counter community disruption.

Quilts made to affirm significant communities were made throughout the mid-19th century. Usually the basic social group was family. A quilt made by Isabell Hall Hurxthal of Baltimore, Maryland, now in the collection of the Massillon Museum (acc. no. 66.59), is one example. This quilt, dated "1846" and "1847", is signed by Isabell's relatives and friends in Maryland and Ohio. Except for four blocks, this quilt was made in the chintz appliqué style popular in Isabell's home state of Maryland. A study of the blocks and the names on them reveals certain family hallmarks. Rachel Brown and Eliza Brown used similar floral motifs cut from the same piece of chintz and stitched them to the ground fabric using buttonhole stitch in contrasting thread. "Aunt Andrews/age 83" and three others with her surname inscribed Bible verses on their blocks—the only signers to do so. The Giese family embroidered their names on seven of their eight blocks, in red counted-cross stitch. "Mary" and "Annie," who made the only pieced blocks on the quilt, shared identical fabrics and a preference for pieced stars.

This quilt represents several overlapping communities, including the intermarried Hall and Hurxthal families, and Isabell's friends. The most significant community is Isabell Hall Hurxthal's natal family. Not only are most of the names on the quilt from the Hall family, but in many cases those people signed not only their names but their specific relationships to Isabell as well, thus underscoring their kinship: "Father, "Your brother/Edward Hyatt Hall," "Your affectionate Mother" (fig. 2), "Your sister Margaret," "Your grandmother" accompany numerous aunts and cousins who signed simply their names.

Throughout the mid-19th century family continued to be the primary community represented on friendship quilts. In 1869 Emmaline Hulse Ayers of Pisgah, Butler County, Ohio, made an album quilt from blocks representing members of her family. Emmaline Ayers was a talented artist and inked charming drawings in each block to further represent her relatives. Like Isabell Hurxthal's quilt, Emmaline Ayers's includes both names of family members and their specific relationships to the quiltmaker: "Your mother/Ernestine Hulse," "Your father/ David Hulse," "Your little brother/Ernest E. Hulse." She made at least two, and in some cases as many as four, blocks for each member of her immediate family, including Lewis Hulse, who had died during the Civil War "from wounds received at the Battle of Stone[s] River" (fig. 3). Many mid-century album quilts include blocks representing deceased relatives. Like artists who painted portraits of family groups, quiltmakers were able to include the dead in these symbolic families in a way that was not possible otherwise.

Other communities, most notably schools and church groups, were so domestic in their structure and language that they might be considered fictive families. In 1848 Ellen Cook Stetson, a missionary at the Dwight Christian Mission in Osage Prairie, Arkansas, made a friendship quilt top of mosaic hexagons (Western Reserve Historical Society, Cleveland, Ohio, acc. no. 79.147.1). The center hexagon in each group includes a Bible verse or the name of a student at the Mission's school. Names on this quilt top indicate that the student body included several sets of sisters, underscoring the familial nature of mid-century schools. Letters from missionaries sponsored by the American Missionary Association (Amistad Research Center, Dillard University, New Orleans) indicate that missionaries, too, considered their stations as families, since they usually referred to fellow missionaries as "brother" or "sister," and to the people they served as "families."

Studying an entire body of quilts enables us to see the many overlapping networks involved. Dena Katzenberg's study of Baltimore album quilts (*Baltimore Album Quilts,* Baltimore: The Baltimore Museum of Art, 1981) is a model of research into quilts made by a group of women united in part by their religious affiliation, and the quilts of other religious groups can be studied as profitably. In 1864, for instance, members of the Hadley family affirmed

Figure 3. Detail of quilt made by Emmaline Hulse Ayers, b. 1842 Pisgah, Butler County, Ohio, d. 1893 Pisgah, Butler County, Ohio. Pieced print and solid-colored cotton with print back. Ink inscriptions. Back brought to front as edge treatment. 92 1/2" × 80" with 9 stitches per inch. Inscribed "Pictorial Quilt" and dated "1869" in several places. Collection of Patricia Stamm.

Although Lewis A. Hulse had died six years earlier, the quiltmaker still considered him a member of the family. A second block memorializing this Civil War martyr includes a more detailed obituary: "Lewis A. Hulse/ Member Co. A 59th Reg. OVI/Died Feb. 16 1863 at/ Nashville, Ten./From wounds Received at the Battle/of Stone [sic] River Aged 18 years." Photo: Lydia Dull.

Figure 4. Detail by Mary Eva Hunt of tied comfort made by friends of "I.W.H" shown also in fig. 1.

This is one of many references to Christmas, indicating that the comfort was a holiday gift. By making blocks that are structurally identical but individually inscribed, members of the "Circle" strengthened their communal identity. Photo: Lydia Dull their family and religious bonds in a series of quilts. Hadley names are found on a collection of quilt blocks and three quilts, dated 1864 and 1865, from Quaker settlements in Preble and Clinton Counties, Ohio. All are in the same *Album Block* pattern and represent four overlapping networks. The Hadleys, in addition to being relatives, were Conservative Friends and members of Springfield Friends Meeting. Those in Preble County, source of the block collection, had earlier lived in Clarksville, Clinton County, where the makers of the three quilts still lived.

A series of quilts from the same period and community, all signed and in the same pattern, indicates a fad. While we often dismiss fads as inconsequential, they affirm an individual's place within a social group. Each Hadley woman probably knew as she signed her name to a quilt block that her neighbors and relatives were also signing blocks for quilts made in the same pattern. Her identity as a Hadley, a Quaker, a member of Springfield Friends Meeting and a resident of Clarksville, was thus strengthened and reaffirmed each time she repeated this act. Historically Quakers have kept meticulous records, and it is hardly surprising that inscribed quilts representing a Friends Meeting as well as a family appealed to members of this sect. A high proportion of mid-century album quilts found in Ohio comes from Quaker communities.

Nor was this textile "album" limited only to Methodists and Friends. An 1850 silk quilt made by the mother of Mary Catherine Harger in the Moravian community at Canal Dover, Tuscarawas County, Ohio, is signed by relatives and friends from Lititz, Bethlehem, York and Nazareth, Pennsylvania, as well as Canal Dover. All signers were Moravians.

Women strengthened their community ties by making quilts to commemorate significant events in the community's life. Usually the group made a quilt to be presented to an honored member on a special occasion. Many Baltimore album quilts, for example, were made for Methodist class teachers or ministers about to leave the community. In fact, compared to other groups making friendship quilts, the ladies of Baltimore made an unusually large number of quilts for men in leadership positions.

A pieced and tied summer comfort inscribed and dated "1865," now in the collection of the Western Reserve Historical Society (acc. no. 47.431), was apparently a Christmas gift, since it includes a painting of holly berries and a charming inked picture of Santa Claus about to descend the chimney, as well as numerous "December 25" inscriptions and other references to Christmas (fig. 4). This bedcover makes the point that a single quilt might perform multiple functions for its makers and owners. Thirty-nine of its forty-three signed blocks include quotations, many of them Shakespearean, and eighty percent of these refer to sleep, rest, dreams, or night. Clearly its makers intended it to be utilitarian. Yet they also intended it as a holiday presentation to an honored member, described as "a guiding star in our Circle" (fig. 1). For the recipient the comfort's primary function was probably its status as a gift or as a representation of her "Circle," since it was apparently never used as a bedcover and has survived for 128 years in superb condition.

A third function of mid-century friendship quilts was to counteract the disruption of community. Most friendship quilts with this as their primary function date from the early part of this period, when so many Americans sought new homes in the West. Specific migratory routes can sometimes be traced on such quilts. Isabell Hurxthal's, inscribed with locations in Annapolis and Baltimore, Maryland, and Canton and Massillon, Ohio, is one example. Another, also in the chintz appliqué style, is inscribed with names of relatives in Franklin, Ohio; Edinburgh, Indiana; and Paris, Illinois. These communities lie in a latitudinal band, a common migratory pattern. Such quilts were clearly cherished, for many in remarkably good condition are still with descendants or in museums hundreds of miles west of their points of origin. One, now with descendants in Kansas, was made for Mary Pollard Tolford in Concord, New Hampshire, in 1845, when Mary moved with her husband and children to Ohio. This quilt, like so many similar ones, is signed only by women, and half of its readable messages refer to friendship and separation. Signers include both relatives and friends, and one block in particular illustrates the familial nature of female friendship (plate 8). Although Rebekah Chaffin, who signed this block, called Mary "Sister," she was not a relative. Another block is inscribed "Mizpah Gen. 31.49 [' . . . The Lord watch between me and thee, when we are absent one from another,' KJV]." An identical citation appears on Isabell Hurxthal's quilt, made a year later (fig. 5). Although in context this passage is a hostile warning rather than a blessing, the "Mizpah Benediction" is still recited at the end of many church gatherings, as members disperse. For quiltmakers in the 1840s as well it functioned as a ritual of separation.

Phrases like "In rememberance of" and "Remember me" inked on Mary Tolford's quilt and so many others are also found in autograph books and on mourning paintings and tombstones. When a community was broken by the departure of one of its members, those left felt this disruption as keenly as death.

"Remember me" was also inked on Emmaline Ayers's quilt, made in 1869. It appears twice, on blocks representing her mother and her father, the oldest family members represented. But in the total context of this quilt, which includes charming drawings of farm equipment, household tasks, flowers, and children training family pets (fig. 6), this phrase seems unconvincing and anomalous. By the time Emmaline Ayers made her quilt the period of westward expansion was over. People as well as states were united, and distant relatives became more accessible, as transportation and postal service improved. Physical separation was no longer permanent, and hence less threatening.

Westward migration was one of many factors that threatened communities during the first half of the century. The turbulence of the period is reflected in church history as well as in family records, as differences in theology or polity brought about lasting divisions in many denominations. Several friendship quilts reflect these stresses on religious groups. One, made in the early 1840s and signed by several Hadley women in Clarksville, Ohio, and female relatives in Newport, Indiana, records the westward migration of a group of Ohio Quakers. It also reflects the Indiana women's involvement in a sectarian struggle over anti-slavery activity. These women had moved from a community of abolitionist Quakers in Ohio to one that "tenderly advise[d] our dear friends not to join in associations with those who do not profess to wait for divine direction in such important concerns" (Minutes, Indiana Yearly Meeting, 1841, 1843). In 1842 the Indiana Yearly Meeting forbade the appointment of abolitionist Friends to positions of leadership. All the Indiana women whose names are on this quilt were read out of meeting, and within months joined other abolitionist Quakers (including Levi Coffin, father of the Underground Railroad) in establishing the Indiana Yearly Meeting of Anti-slavery Friends, with headquarters at Newport.

A second major Quaker separation is recorded in an album quilt made by Lizzie Stanton of Barnesville, Ohio. Lizzie's quilt, like the Hadley quilt of the 1840s, is signed by relatives in the intermarried Bailey, Bundy, Doudna, Frame, Hodgin, Starbuck and Stanton families, all members of Stillwater Quarterly Meeting. Lizzie Stanton had particular need to affirm her religious community when she began this quilt in 1856. Only two years earlier a growing division between the followers of conservative John Wilbur and the more evangelical Joseph John Gurney came to a head in Ohio Yearly Meeting, with members aligning themselves with one or the other leader. Stillwater Quarterly Meeting centered in Barnesville was tragically divided in this controversy, and the Gurneyites withdrew from Meeting to join what would become the largest body of Friends west of the Alleghenies. Lizzie Stanton and all those who signed her quilt became Wilburites, or

Figure 5. *Detail of a quilt made by Isabell Hall Hurxthal of Baltimore shown also in fig. 2.*

Ann Belt's Biblical reference, the only inscription alluding to separation, suggests that Isabell Hurxthal left Baltimore in 1846, following her marriage a few months earlier. In fact, church records indicate that she was residing in Massillon, Ohio, by 1848. Photo: Margy Vogt.

Figure 6. Detail of quilt made by Emmaline Hulse Ayers shown also in figs. 3 and 7. Photo: Lydia Dull

Figure 7. Detail of quilt made by Emmaline Hulse Ayers shown also in figs. 3 and 6. Photo: Lydia Dull

Conservative Friends.

More final than geographic or ideological division was separation by death, and women confronted this final disruption of community by quilting metaphoric families. An album quilt made in 1850 by Sarah Mahan of Oberlin, Ohio, was constructed "from fragments of [her stepdaughter's] dresses" and left to specified female descendents. Friends who signed this quilt wrote comforting messages referring to Sarah's bereavement and to the child's continued existence in Heaven. The quilt had been begun by Laura, the dead child. Sarah completed her unfinished task, in effect joining her in a communal project in spite of her death. By creating her quilt from scraps of fabric worn by the dead child Sarah perpetuated a family relationship otherwise totally destroyed by death. Like women who maintained ties to distant relatives by making friendship quilts, Sarah Mahan symbolically preserved her shattered family on her quilt. Death was swallowed up in victory.

Including the names of deceased relatives on quilts was not uncommon. Emmaline Hulse Ayers, as mentioned above, made two obituary blocks for Lewis Hulse, killed in the Civil War. Family, for Emmaline Hulse, Sarah Mahan and many other quiltmakers, included its dead members, sometimes several generations back.

Inscribing names and messages on quilt blocks was the customary way for women to transform significant communities into tangible form. Some quiltmakers, however, went further. Emmaline Ayers included on her quilt pictures that portray the lives of those whose names are on the blocks. One of her obituary blocks for Lewis Hulse is decorated with pictures of soldiers and national emblems (fig. 3). The other includes a sketch of a soldier, presumably Lewis's Confederate assassin, hanging by his neck from a rope. A block from the same quilt honoring "David C. Hulse . . . Your Brother" includes inked pictures of farm animals and a young man—apparently David Hulse—training his dog, riding horseback, and hunting (fig. 7). For those of us seeing this quilt over a century later, these sketches recreate the lives and values of individuals who would otherwise remain simply names.

Other quiltmakers arranged their quilt blocks in family units, creating personal relationships on the surface of the quilt itself. This is difficult to do when the quilt blocks are dissimilar and strongly visual. A Baltimore quiltmaker presented by her friends with twenty-six blocks appliquéd with floral chintz cutouts and four depicting local buildings, for instance, could hardly ignore the power of the architecture. Those four blocks are visually outstanding because they are atypical and few in number. They demand symmetrical placement, and most quiltmakers arranged them on four sides of a center block or in the corners of the quilt. Makers of commemorative album quilts sometimes placed the block bearing the name of the quilt's honored recipient in the center of the quilt, the focal point of both the quilt and the community it represents.

Quiltmakers working in the repeated block format, however, had much greater flexibility in arranging blocks, since in terms of design and often color, these blocks are virtually identical. Lizzie Stanton, for example, alternated her signed "Ohio Star" blocks with plain white blocks, but broke her system at one point by signing a plain block "Lizzie Stanton/ Barnesville/Ohio/1865." Thus the "Lizzie Stanton" block was automatically surrounded by four other pieced and signed blocks. Those she selected were signed by four significant couples: her parents, her sister and brother-in-law, and two brothers and their wives. On her quilt, as in her life, Lizzie surrounded herself with family.

Makers of a red and white "Birds in the Air" quilt now in the collection of Historic Deerfield, Inc. (acc. no. V-77), used a similar device. This quilt, made in the Hartford, Connecticut, area probably during the second quarter of the nineteenth century, includes approximately 800 names of relatives in Groton, Watertown and Weston, Massachusetts, and Francistown, New Hampshire. The large white triangle in each block is stamped "In Memoriam" and signed with a name. The smaller white triangles are signed as well, and many of the surnames within each block are the same as that of the deceased. It appears that on this quilt the "honored dead" are surrounded by their survivors.

Sarah Mahan's quilt bears names only of the living. But she arranged her quilt blocks in kinship groups, with married and engaged couples, sisters, mothers and daughters, and even missionary colleagues side by side.

It is rewarding, when studying friendship and album quilts, to diagram the locations of names on the inscribed blocks. These names can be identified with the help of census records, church records or other written documents, as well as other incriptions on the quilt. When the signers of the quilt and their relationships to each other have been determined, these diagrams should be studied again to see whether the quiltmaker has deliberately arranged her blocks in groups that parallel the social networks represented by the quilt. Such study can greatly enrich our understanding of the quiltmakers and their cultures, and put us in touch with individuals and societies long gone.

Suggested Reading:

Ahlstrom, Sydney E. *A Religious History of the American People.* New Haven: Yale University Press, 1972.

Clark, Ricky. "Fragile Families: Quilts as Kinship Bonds." *The Quilt Digest 5* (1987).

Cott, Nancy F. *The Bonds of Womanhood: "Woman's Sphere" in New England, 1780-1835."* New Haven: Yale University Press, 1977.

Dayton, Donald W. *Discovering an Evangelical Heritage.* New York: Harper & Row, 1976.

Douglas, Ann. *The Feminization of American Culture.* New York: Avon Books, 1977.

Elliott, Errol T. *Quakers and the American Frontier: A History of the Westward Migrations, Settlements, and Developments of Friends on the American Continent.* Richmond, IN: The Friends United Press, 1969.

Ice, Joyce and Judith A. Shulimson. "Beyond the Domestic: Women's Traditional Arts and the Creation of Community. *Southwest Folklore* 3.4 (1979): 37-44.

Katzenberg, Dena S. *Baltimore Album Quilts.* Baltimore: The Baltimore Museum of Art, 1981.

Kolter, Jane Bentley. *Forget Me Not: a Gallery of Friendship and Album Quilts.* Pittstown, NJ: The Main Street Press, 1985.

Lasser, Carol. " 'Let Us Be Sisters Forever': Antoinette Brown Blackwell, Lucy Stone and the Sororial Model of Nineteenth-Century Female Friendship." *Signs: Journal of Women in Culture and Society 13* (1988).

Lipsett, Linda Otto. *Remember Me: Women & Their Friendship Quilts.* San Francisco: The Quilt Digest Press, 1985.

Motz, Marilyn Ferris. *True Sisterhood: Michigan Women and Their Kin 1820-1920.* Albany, NY: State University of New York, 1983.

Nicoll, Jessica F. *Quilted for Friends: Delaware Valley Signature Quilts, 1840-1855.* Winterthur, DE: The Henry Francis Du Pont Winterthur Museum, 1986.

Smith-Rosenberg, Carroll. "The Female World of Love and Ritual: Relations Between Women in Nineteenth-Century America." *Signs: Journal of Women in Culture and Society* 1.1 (1975): 1-29.

Welter, Barbara. "The Cult of True Womanhood: 1800-1860. *American Quarterly* 18 (1966): 151-174.

The author is indebted to the following, who generously shared their quilts, knowledge and expertise: Bernita Bundy, Betty Clements, Kathleen Doerner, Ray Featherstone, Betsey Hartley, Jane Zollar Schooff, Wilene Smith, Patricia Stamm, Donald R. Friary of Historic Deerfield, Inc., John Klassen and Margy Vogt of the Massillon Museum, Dean M. Zimmerman and Phyllis Modic of the Western Reserve Historical Society.

Ricky Clark, an Affiliate Scholar at Oberlin College, is a quilt researcher particularly interested in quilts as cultural documents. In addition to lecturing and curating quilt exhibitions, she is the author of Quilts and Carousels: Folk Art in the Firelands, *a catalog accompanying an exhibition she organized in 1984 in Oberlin, Ohio, and co-author (with Stanley A. Kaufman) of* Germanic Folk Culture in Eastern Ohio, *(1986) a publication of the German Culture Museum. Funded primarily by the Ohio Arts Council/Ohio Humanities Council Joint Program in Folk Art and Culture, both publications deal with regional history and the ways in which material culture embodies and reflects regional, social, religious and personal concerns. Other articles have appeared in exhibition catalogs from Bowling Green State University, DeAnza College, and The College of Wooster, as well as in* The Hayes Historical Journal, Timeline, The Quilt Digest 5, Western Reserve Studies *and* In The Heart of Pennsylvania: Symposium Papers. *Her concern for standardized quilt documentation procedures led her and Katy Christopherson to organize a conference on the subject in 1984, and her article "Quilt Documentation: a Case Study" is included in* Making The American Home: Middle Class Women and Domestic Material Culture, 1840-1940. *She has served as a Humanities Consultant to Pat Ferrero for her film "Heart and Hands," is a member of the Traditional and Ethnic Arts Panel of the Ohio Arts Council, and is a founding member of the Ohio Quilt Research Project, which documents Ohio's quilts, quiltmakers and quiltmaking traditions.*

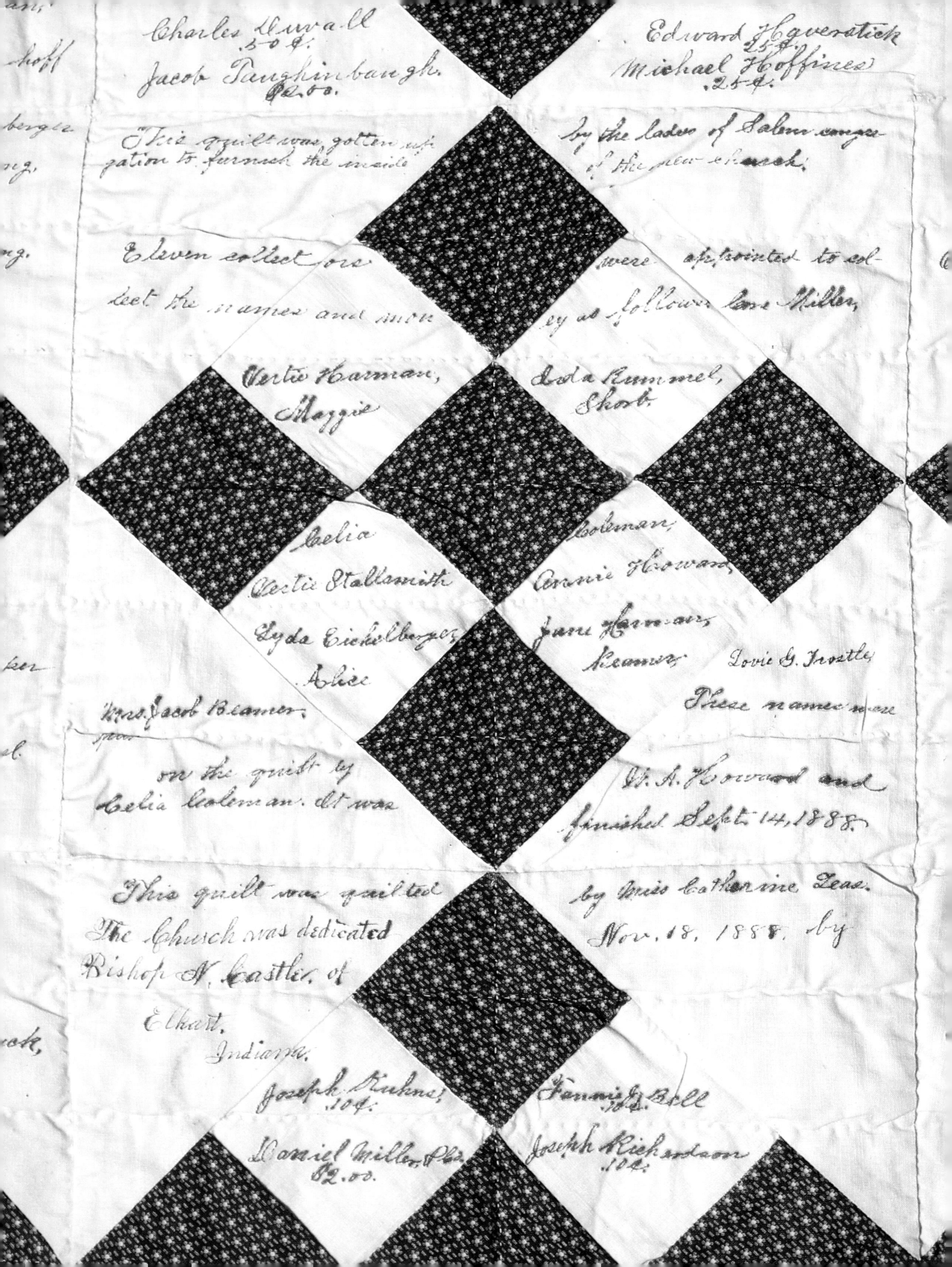

Charles Duvall
50¢.
Jacob Taughinbaugh.
$2.00.

Edward Hgverstick
25¢.
Michael Hoffines
25¢.

This quilt was gotten up
by the ladies of Salem congregation to furnish the inside
of the new church.

Eleven collectors
were appointed to col-
lect the names and mon-
ey as follows: Anne Miller,

Vertie Harman,
Ada Rummel,
Maggie
Shorb.

Celia
Coleman,
Vertie Stallsmith
Annie Howard,

Lyda Eickelberger,
Jane Harman,
Alice
Beamer,
Dovie G. Trostle,

Mrs. Jacob Beamer.
These names were
put
on the quilt by
W. A. Howard and
Celia Coleman. It was
finished Sept. 14, 1888.

This quilt was quilted
by Miss Catherine Zeas.
The Church was dedicated
Nov. 18, 1888, by
Bishop N. Castle, of
Elkhart,
Indiana.

Joseph Kuhns,
10¢.
Fannie S. Bell
10¢.
Daniel Miller Sr.
$2.00.
Joseph Richardson
10¢.

The Role and Look of Fundraising Quilts 1850-1930

Dorothy Cozart

Fundraising quilts were important sources of income for women interested in charitable work from the mid-19th century through the first quarter of the 20th century. For the purpose of this discussion, fundraising quilts are being defined as those quilts which were used to provide funds for some specified benevolent cause. The major focus will be an examination of the causes which were espoused. Three kinds of quilts will be included: 1) those that were especially designed to be fundraisers and that used signatures on the quilt to raise part of the money; 2) those made for fundraisers which were not signature quilts; and 3) those that were not primarily made to be fundraisers but were later used in this way. An excellent example of the latter is one of the Baltimore album quilts which Dena Katzenburg cites in *Baltimore Album Quilts* (Baltimore: The Baltimore Museum of Art, 1981), as having been donated to the Carmelite Monastery in Baltimore to be "chanced off" by this group.

"Ladies' Fairs" could have been very important in the development of fundraising quilts. These fairs, organized and executed by women of a community, became popular in the 1830s (see Beverly Gordon's "Playing at Being Powerless: New England Ladies' Fairs 1830-1930," in *The Massachusetts Review,* 1985). The women were usually members of a local church who banded together to form an organization devoted to raising money for some benevolent cause. They called their groups by various names such as: "sewing societies," "mission societies," or "aid societies." Since the purpose of the fairs was to raise money for charitable purposes, the women could work in public in ways that otherwise would have been censured. Men not only attended the fairs but also approved of them, even though their attitudes toward the events were very condescending. Most of the items made to be sold were small, including objects like needlebooks, cushions, aprons and baby clothes. A fundraiser made specifically for a ladies' fair was documented in *The Liberator* on January 2, 1837. It is included in a detailed account of an annual Anti-Slavery Fair held in Boston. The article states: "A cradle-quilt was made of patchwork in small stars." On the central star is a verse written in indelible ink which asks the mother who holds her baby in her arms to remember the Negro mother whose child is taken from her and sold. This quilt is in the collection of the Society for the Preservation of New England Antiquities.

A popular and, to this author significant, sale item was the autograph. Usually selling for a dime (a significant sum), autographs of the famous, or of local community leaders sold readily. Just as album verses were being transferred from paper to cloth, autographs had already begun appearing on quilts, and surely the idea of charging a dime for autographs on quilts must have occurred to the enterprising promoters of ladies' fairs.

It is quite possible that the earliest signature fundraising quilts were made in Pennsylvania, perhaps in the 1850s. When Nancy Roan questioned Sadie Kriebel about a *Rolling Stone* quilt that was from Hereford, Berks County, dated "1862," Sadie said, "It's called a Friendship quilt; everybody whose name was on it gave a dime," (see Nancy Roan's article in *In The Heart of Pennsylvania/Symposium Papers.* Lewisburg, PA: Oral Traditions Project, 1986). The people of that community called these quilts "beddelman," which means "beggar," quilts. This is what friendship quilts are called in the Pennsylvania German dialect. A similar quilt with signatures inked in the same fractur-style letters is dated "1853," (see Jonathan Holstein's *The Pieced Quilt/An American Design Tradition* Boston: New York Graphic Society:

Plate 9. *Detail of an entire block and a portion of others—all slightly to the right of the center of the quilt shown in fig. 1. Most of the writing is in indelible ink and was done after the top was completed, an unusual feature, as most fundraisers were written on one block at a time. Note the amounts of money beneath the signatures. Nine hundred and twenty-one names appear on this quilt.*

Figure 1. Quilt made by women of the Salem Evangelical United Brethren Church, Adams County, Pennsylvania, dated "November 18, 1888." Pieced calico and white cottons. 83" × 75". Collection of Annette Gero.

On the quilt are inscribed the purpose for which the money was raised, the date the church was finished and then dedicated, the amount of money paid by each person beneath the signatures but omitted was the location of "Salem Congregation." Research by the author resulted in the discovery of an article written in The Religious Telescope, *a national weekly newspaper for the Evangelical United Brethren Church. Written December 5, 1888, shortly after the dedication, the article includes the names of a number of people whose names appear on the quilt, two of which are the minister of the church, D. W. Sollenberger, and Bishop N. Castle of Elkhart, Indiana, who dedicated the new church. The article also mentions the quilt: "The ladies of the congregation with their autograph-quilt project realized the handsome sum of $300, which was appropriated to the furnishing of the new church."*

Little, Brown and Company, 1973).

It is evident that by the time of the Civil War fundraising quilts were being made. Soon Northern women were converting their sewing groups to soldiers' aid societies. As Virginia Gunn notes in "Quilts for Union Soldiers in the Civil War" in *Uncoverings 5* (Mill Valley, CA: American Quilt Study Group, 1985), many of these groups became auxiliaries of the U. S. Sanitary Commisssion, the largest private national agency sending supplies to soldiers. By 1863 Sanitary Fairs were being held throughout the North. Quilts were among the large items made to be sold at these events. As an example, General Sherman was presented a red, white and blue *Streak of Lightning* quilt made of silk. He in turn donated it to the 1863 Sanitary Commission Bazaar in St. Louis. The quilt is in the Missouri Historical Society's collection in St. Louis.

Autographs also were popular money makers at the Sanitary Fairs or Bazaars, and, although no signature quilt has been found that can be identified as having been made at that time, it is reasonable to believe that some were made then. Aid societies were also formed in the South as well, and a Confederacy's Soldiers' Relief Society was organized. However, although local groups were very successful in raising funds, their efforts were not well coordinated. In part, this was due to the lack of cooperation among the separate states. Fairs, bazaars, and raffles were planned and managed by local women, and contributions included priceless family heirlooms that very likely included quilts. Less than a month before Sherman marched into Columbia, South Carolina, a bazaar was held in that city. A signature quilt which might have been sold at a fair or bazaar is illustrated and documented in *Quilts in Tennessee* by Bets Ramsey and Merikay Waldvogel (Nashville: Rutledge Hill Press, 1986). It was one of several known to have been made and raffled by the ladies of the Raus community in Bedford County, Tennessee. Each block, in a basket design, contains names of people in the Raus community. Many names were of "Tennessee Volunteers" in the Seventeenth Tennessee Infantry Regiment.

Following the Civil War, fundraising quilts continued to be made to benefit soldiers and their families from both sides of the conflict. For example, in about 1866 a *Straight Furrows* Log Cabin, was made in St. Louis to aid the needy families of ex-Confederate soldiers. "Feed the Hungry" is embroidered in the center of this quilt, now owned by the Missouri Historical Society, and about 1880 Sarah F. Gallop of Leominster, Massachusetts, made a quilt to raise money for GAR veterans. The veterans were not forgotten by following generations either, so in 1928 a fundraising quilt made by a Kansas GAR Circle was designed as a memorial to those veterans, and one made in Oklahoma during the same decade raised funds to decorate GAR graves on Decoration, now called Memorial Day.

Many of the fundraisers made in the two decades following the Civil War were not signature quilts. An Odd Fellows quilt now in the Shelburne Museum collection is an album quilt, and many of the blocks contain IOOF symbols. Another quilt made by Mrs. Robert E. Lee to be auctioned as a fundraiser for a memorial chapel being built in her husband's honor on the campus of Virginia Military Institute has a central diamond. It is quite possible that other non-signature quilts still in existence were made to be fundraisers, but that information has been lost.

However, signature quilts were by far the most popular fundraisers from the 1860s through the 1930s. During the 1880s and 1890s, and again during World War I and throughout the 1920s, these quilts were a common source of income for all kinds of charitable causes.

One organization which made particularly good use of the fundraiser quilt was the Women's Christian Temperance Union. In its early formative years 3000 Ohio women contributed a dime apiece to have their names embroidered on what was known as the "Crusader Quilt." The quilt was given to Eliza Thompson at one of the first national meetings of the WCTU. Thompson was the leader of a group of women that succeeded in reducing the number of saloons in Hillsboro, Ohio, from thirteen to four in a matter of weeks. This inital crusade sparked others, and within two months during the winter of 1873 the Crusade spirit spread throughout the East and Midwest. In reality, the Crusade spawned the movement that became known as the WCTU which was organized in 1874.

It is important to note that the women who flocked to join the WCTU were women who believed that they, as women, were responsible for the welfare of their homes, and that saloons were an ominous threat to those homes. As good housemakers, they were also good needlewomen, so making WCTU fundraising quilts followed as a natural consequence at the time fundraising quilts were popular. Another important fact to recall is that symbols were most important to all Americans during the 19th century. Frances Willard and the WCTU used symbols continually and masterfully. In fact, the 1877 national convention platform decorations, planned by Frances Willard, used so much symbolism that, according to a recent author, "symbolism was rampant." So it is not surprising to find in WCTU and other fundraising quilts made between 1875 and 1900 much evidence of what may well be WCTU symbolism. The *Drunkard's Path* pattern became very popular, as did the *T* quilts, "T" standing for "temperance," and both were used as fundraising quilt designs. A Crazy quilt used as a church fundraiser by a group of Victoria, Illinois, women reflects the influence of the WCTU on quilts made by groups other than the WCTU. The quilt contains an embroidered water glass,

Figure 2. *Quilt made by Class #9 of the Port Royal Methodist Sunday School, Juniata County, Pennsylvania, prior to October 1929. White whole cloth with embroidery. 68" × 82" with 6 stitches per inch. Collection of Mr. and Mrs. Robert Fogelman. Photographed at the Mifflintown, Juniata County quilt documentation day by Jeannette Lasansky.*

The wheel design was the one used most frequently for embroidered fundraisers. Prices usually paid for a signature on the spoke was a dime and on the hub from 25¢-50¢. In this case, each child paid a dime and then additional money was raised when it was purchased by Jonas Fogelman.

another WCTU symbol, and one of the contributors was Frances Willard.

The WCTU also carried on a broad program of charity and social action in addition to the temperance cause. Fundraisers reflect this diversity. One quilt, made by the Chattanooga Chapter of the WCTU (now in the Tennessee State Museum, Nashville), raised funds for the Frances Willard Home for Girls in that city. And in Carrie Hall's scrapbook, (now in the Spencer Museum, Lawrence, Kansas) characteristically undated and with no source given, is the following:

> An embroidered quilt containing nearly 2,000 names will be given to the Carry A. Nation Union of the W.C.T.U. to the member who obtains the largest contributions for the old ladies' home conducted by the organization at 738 Broadview avenue [sic] Kansas City, Kansas. Space in the quilt for the names has been sold all over the state by different unions of the W.C.T.U. The women of the organization did the work.

The next paragraph states that approximately $160 was earned from the selling of names, but the obtaining of contributions by the members, in a contest to determine the eventual owner of the quilt, brought in additional funds.

By the 1890s the WCTU has begun openly to support women's suffrage, although Frances Willard and many of the organization's other leaders had always espoused that cause. The 1894 national convention adopted a resolution on suffrage that stated ". . . women are wronged who are governed without their consent." Protestant churches had liberalized their support of suffrage largely because of the Union's influence. A fundraising quilt (now in the Minnesota Historical Society Museum, St. Paul, Minnesota) made by a church in St. Paul, Minnesota, seems to verify that church attitudes were changing. Each woman responsible for a block just did her own thing, and the quilt resembles, more than anything else, a red, white and blue wall of graffiti. Some blocks contain the names of dime contributors, while others, at a cost of fifty cents each, were filled with any sentiment the buyer (and/or the maker) wished to express. Included is a message celebrating the death of the Tammany Tiger in New York City, and another rejoices in the rise of Ohio's Senator William McKinley to national importance. The sentiments expressed may or may not have been held by the congregation's members, but the women put them on the quilt!

The design of the St. Paul quilt is rather exceptional. In general, fundraising quilts adhered to the designs that were popular at any given time the quilts were made and signatures were applied in the prevailing fashion. Early quilts were appliquéd, with designs such as oak leaves being the outstanding features. Signatures, when used, were secondary. Log Cabins and Crazy quilts followed. By 1900 and thereafter, through 1920s, the primary focus of the quilts was on the signatures, and in the majority of quilts the embroidered signature's placement created the design. The embroidered circular shape, usually in a wheel design, was used most often (fig. 2) and almost without exception, as was red embroidery thread. Pieced fundraisers can be found that date from the 1850s through the 1920s, the years that this survey covers.

A truly outstanding fundraiser was seen recently at a Kansas quilt Discovery Day. Using the *Hands All Around* pattern in a beautiful blue on a white ground, the names were written in the four corners of each block. Written with the same Spencerian "hand" and embroidered in the exact same shade of blue, the total effect was breathtaking.

The method of raising money from the signatures was fairly standard, consisting of charging a small amount, almost universally a dime, for most of the names used. Names placed in prominent positions cost more, perhaps twenty-five or fifty cents. At the same time, there were also some very creative fundraising methods used. The GAR quilt mentioned previously made by Mrs. Gallop, was constructed using two-inch square blocks in the pieced design. These squares were sent to 100 people with instructions to sign their names on the fabric and to return the square with their business cards. Eighty-eight people responded, and Mrs. Gallop used part of the squares to construct the fundraiser. The money raised, however, did not come from famous people, but from local people who paid fifteen cents to guess the answer to a riddle. The person who answered the riddle correctly was to win the quilt. Mrs. Gallop finished the quilt for the raffle and intended to use the remaining blocks in a quilt for herself. But she did not ever get it finished. This delightful story was recorded in Pat Flynn Kyser's column "Pieces and Patches" in the July/August 1985 *Quilt World* (see Virginia Gunn's, "Template Quilt Construction and Its Offshoots/ From Godey's Book to Mountain Mist" in the present collection of papers for more about this method of securing signatures).

When Crazy quilts were the rage, the women of the Presbyterian Church of Victoria, Illinois, mentioned previously, used a method of collecting scraps that was quite fashionable. They requested pieces of fabric from famous people and the scraps were incorporated into a quilt which took five yearts to complete. Only two contributors' names appear on the quilt, "Grant" and "Mrs. Cleveland." All other contributed fabrics were numbered on the quilt, and the numbers and names were carefully recorded in a book, along with the circumstances under which the quilt was made. On the back of the book is the date,"March 25, 1881." The book and the quilt are still together and are owned by the grandson of the man who paid the nearest amount to $1000, the goal the women set to raise on the quilt.

The benevolent causes supported by money raised on quilts are many and varied. One of the oldest signature quilts is known as a "tithing quilt," since following each parishioner's name is an amount of money, five, ten, or at most twenty-five cents. A project to raise money for a Baptist Orphan's Home in Kentucky produced the amazing sum of almost $5,000. In

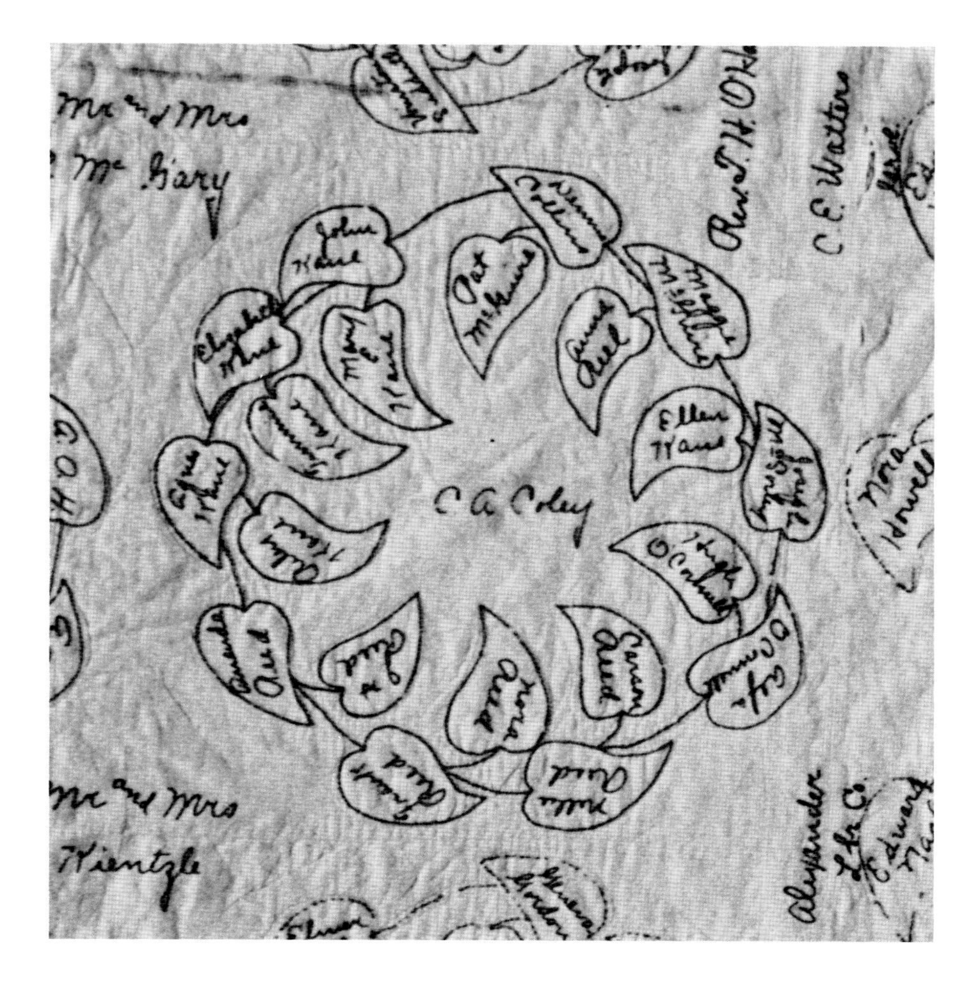

Figure 3. Detail of quilt made by members of the Western Catholic Union, the Young Ladies Sodality of the Ancient Order of Hibernia and the Ladies Auxiliary of AOH of the Immaculate Conception Church in Pittsfield, Illinois and dated "December 3 and 4, 1913." 91½" × 92" and machine quilted. The designer's name is identified and there are many advertisements such as "Take a Chance on Rafferty's Clocks." Collection of Dorothy Cozart.

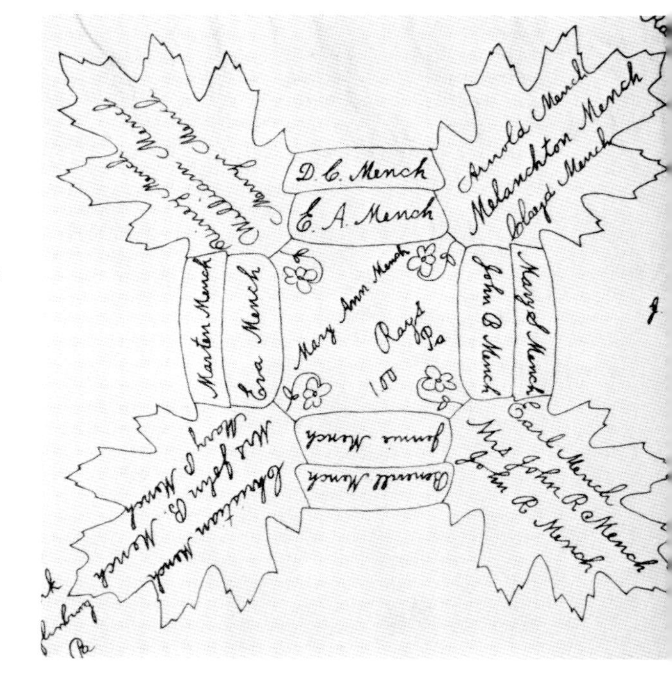

Figure 4. Detail of quilt top made by the members of St. Peter's Aid and the Missionary Society of the Ray's Lutheran Church, Hartley Township, Union County, Pennsylvania and dated "1897." White whole cloth with embroidery. 83" square. Collection of Helen Ruhl Kerstetter.

Five hundred and fifty-one names, most of which were at one dollar each, are represented on this fundraiser but some people paid as much as five dollars for theirs to be included. When completed, the piece was auctioned off and bought for one hundred dollars by Jeanne Reish Frederick, a quilter and the grandmother of the present owner.

Wartime Activities of Significance to Women

ONE THOUSAND DOLLARS FOR THE RED CROSS CAN BE RAISED ON A MEMORIAL QUILT

An army ambulance costs $1000. $1000 will buy 280 pounds of yarn. A Red Cross Nurse's equipment costs $55; it costs $990 to equip 18 nurses. A Red Cross bed must have two sheets at 75 cents each, two pillow-cases at 12 cents each, and a pair of blankets at $6.00; $1000 will furnish bedding for 129 beds. It requires $180 to furnish Red Cross assistance to one family. Within one short year of service 170,000 families of men in the Army and Navy will be needing such help; $1000 would help several families. This Red Cross quilt can be made to yield the $1000 needed for ambulance, yarn, or any Red Cross service.

In starting a quilt campaign or any money-raising campaign it must be remembered that —

"The Red Cross has an absolute rule about parties and entertainments given for its benefit. No Red Cross emblem or name can be used in announcements or advertisements of such affairs unless the *entire proceeds* are to be *devoted to the Red Cross.* The *entire* proceeds, not net or half. Red Cross uniforms at such entertainments must not be worn except by those members of the Red Cross who are also authorized members of one of the regular uniformed Red Cross corps."

A Quilt Campaign is especially adapted to church auxiliaries, women's clubs, and organized groups of women in small towns. The idea is not complicated at all, and consists simply in selling squares or space to be inscribed with the name of the contributor. The names can be written in water-proof ink or embroidered in red outline or chain-stitch. The pattern of the quilt can be like the one illustrated or planned according to more original ideas.

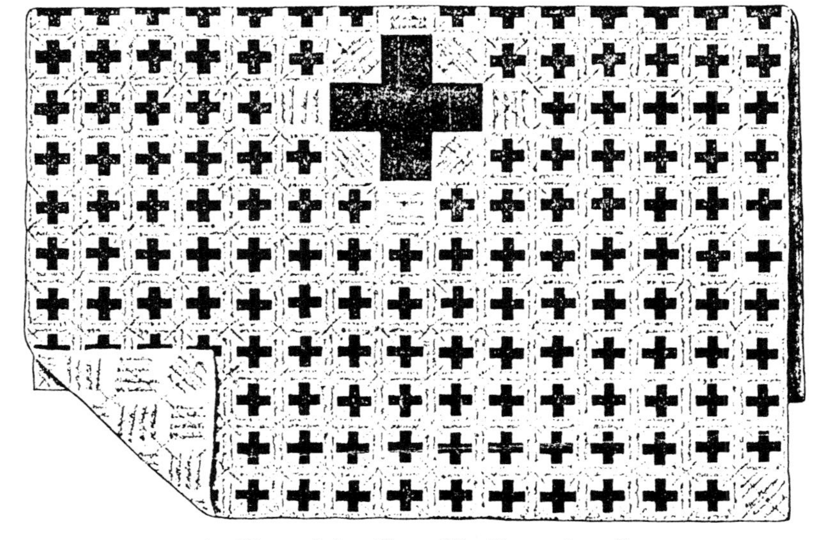

As Planned by Clara Washburn Angell

Any job printer will get out the necessary blanks (see illustration below). These are most conveniently handled if made up with a binding at the left-hand end to hold the stubs which are retained by the one who sells the space or square. The right-hand end is filled in and given as a receipt to the purchaser of the squares, and the centre is to be handed to the treasurer with money collected.

All of the names are best written or embroidered by one person, but the cutting and making of squares can be done by many.

The white squares are cut 6 inches and may be of cotton sheeting. The crosses are cut 4½ inches; cut a 4½-inch square of stiff paper and then cut out at each corner a perfect 1½-inch square. This pattern can be arranged to interlace the crosses and save as much material as possible. The large cross is made of five 6-inch squares and all of the crosses are made of Turkey red.

The quilting should be done by some one who understands the work, and when completed the quilt can be sold at auction, thus increasing the fund or making up for any deficiency. Such a quilt would prove an interesting heirloom.

About 6 yards of bleached cotton sheeting, 90 inches wide, will be needed for the white squares, and 6 yards of 27-inch Turkey red will furnish an ample amount of material for the crosses.

This Quilt Consists of

253	squares of white with Red Cross applied thereon, sold at 25 cents a space, 4 names to a square,	$253.00
266	white squares on other side of quilt, each square divided into four parts, making spaces for 4 names at 25 cents each,	266.00
8	memorial blocks around centre cross, sold at $25.00 each,	200.00
4	corner blocks on each side sold at $5.00 each (8 in all),	40.00
5	red blocks in centre forming large Red Cross sold at $50.00 each to people who do not wish their names used,	250.00
	Making a total of	$1009.00

Tips for Red Cross Workers

For Knitters. — Beware of the "split" stitch. A split stitch means a quickly broken one and a broken stitch "runs" and speedily ruins the whole garment. Wool is wasted, time is wasted, and a much needed garment is lost. Drop the offending stitch from the needle, or if discovered farther back, drop a stitch purposely to get it. Use a bone crochet-hook to pick up the dropped stitches. Picking up stitches is just like crocheting in chain-stitch and every one knows how to do that. When a stitch is dropped in the "purl" turn the work the other side out and do the same thing.

Sweater Necks. — Nothing is more individual than the work of different knitters, even when the same needles and identical wool are used. Some work is loose and some is tight. Consequently it follows that different sweaters made by exactly the same directions will vary greatly in the neck size, and some judgment must be used.

No.
Marshfield, Mass.
_______________ 1917
Name _______________
Pays for _______________ Red Cross
Squares at $ _______________ a square.
____

No.
For $ _______ paid to-day I have ordered _______
Square at $ _______ cts. _______ to be made up in the
RED CROSS QUILT
My name to be on the square.
The proceeds from this Quilt are for the Red Cross Society
Name _______________

No.
Marshfield, Mass.
Received from
$ _______ cts. _______ Square

Form (one-half size) for Selling Blanks Used in Red Cross Quilt Drive Described Above

The Friendly Bodkin. — When joining the sides of a sweater be careful to catch the *whole* stitch every time. If a stitch is split the elasticity is lost and when a joining stitch on the side gives way the whole seam will come apart. A bodkin is the best instrument for joining sweater seams and for the famous "Kitchener toe."

Junior Red Cross Auxiliaries. — Organization of the Junior Red Cross among public school children has been warmly approved by President Wilson, and, starting first, some months ago, in Chicago the work is developing rapidly throughout the country. Schools are recruited in units with membership fee of twenty-five cents for each pupil. There are many things the children can do and the work is educational as well as helpful. Miss Cook, Supervisor of the Junior Red Cross work in Chicago, strongly recommends the knitting of five-inch squares of odds and ends of colored yarns. The work interests the children, and when squares are joined together, five one way and six the other, a much needed comfort for the infant welfare work in France has been made. The filling of scrap-books for the soldiers is another work that interests children, and the books are much appreciated by the boys at the front. The Committee on Comforts urge the making of heaters — old newspapers rolled tightly, pasted to hold, and boiled in paraffin — for the use of soldiers in localities where coal cannot be sent. Children make them rapidly and well and enjoy the work.

Supplies that Juniors Can Make. *Ages* 5-8. Gun wipes, face protectors, glass covers, filling "housewives." *Ages* 8-12. Beginners in knitting — wash-cloths; handkerchiefs; 18-inch squares; help fill comfort bags; hem scrub-cloths, dust-cloths, dish-cloths, glass-towels, bath-towels. Make hot-water bag covers and rest pillows. *Ages* 12-16. — Knit scarfs, socks, sweaters, wristlets, sleeveless jackets, bath mits, helmets. *Boys* can make knitting-needles and splints.

Christmas in Home Camps. — No matter how generous a supply of gifts some of our men may receive from families and friends, we must see to it that no man goes unremembered. To fill Christmas packets, the following suggestions are made: 1. *Send nothing that will not keep.* 2. Pack dried fruits and all food products in tin. 3. For sweets, *hard* candies and chocolate in tinfoil. 4. Variety rather than quantity in dainties and confections. 5. *No liquids or articles packed in glass.* 6. Wrap gifts in khaki-colored handkerchief, 27 inches square, forming base of package by placing on centre of handkerchief a 7 x 10 writing-pad. 7. Select articles from list (or according to individual taste) to an amount not exceeding $1.50, and arrange on pad so that package shall be width of pad and 5 or 6 inches high. 8. Wrap and tie with ribbon and place card under bow. 9. Wrap again in Manila paper, tie, and ornament with Christmas labels.

List of Gifts. — *Khaki-colored handkerchief, 27 inches square, for container; *Writing-paper pad, about 7 by 10 inches; Envelopes; Pencil; Postals; Book (in paper covers); Home-made Scrap-book, containing a good short story, some jokes, etc.; Knife such as boy scouts use; Steel Mirror; Khaki-colored Handkerchiefs; Neckties; Mouth Organ; Katch the Kaiser (puzzle); Mechanical Puzzles (an assorted lot of twelve small mechanical puzzles can be bought at the rate of twelve for 50 cents); *Red Cross Checkerboard (this is a combination set of checkerboard, checkers, chessmen, and dominoes made of heavy cardboard especially for the Red Cross and can be purchased for 5 cents apiece); Electric Torch; Compass; Playing cards and other games; Tobacco; Pipe and pipe cleaners; Cigarette papers; Water-tight match-box; Chewing gum; Anola chocolate confections; Fruited Educator crackers; Fruit cake; Preserved ginger; Salted nuts; Prunes; Figs, Dates; Raisins; Chiclets (listerated); hard candy; chocolate in tinfoil; licorice.
Articles marked * can be bought from Red Cross Chapters.

1911 a New York chapter of the DAR raised funds to help pay the debt on the Memorial Continental Hall in Washington D.C. (see the author's article "A Century of Fundraising Quilts 1860 to 1960" in *Uncoverings 1984* for the locations of these and other fundraisers referred to in this article). Probably the most unusual use of funds was done by a group of citizens in McMinnville, Oregon, who made the quilt to benefit the defendants in a murder case. It, of course, is now known as the "Murder Quilt." As the 20th century progressed, the "benevolent causes" became more self-serving, and it is not uncommon to find a fundraiser made in the teens or twenties to produce funds for a class trip of a school's senior class.

Churches, however, had always been the most frequent users of the quilt fundraising device, and that fact continued to be true until the middle of the 20th century. Almost universally, the funds were used to support some local church need: the building of a new church, repairs on an existing one. Since by far the largest number of fundraising quilts made by churches were done by Methodist women, an attempt to ascertain why this was true has been made. Although a number of possible reasons have been found, the present conclusion of this author is that most of the reasons might also apply to the making of fundraising quilts by women of other denominations.

Nevertheless, in some respects Methodist women were different. They were important in the church structure from the beginning. In England, John Wesley, the founder, encouraged women to become lay leaders and to form "support groups" so that housebound women would always have someone to talk with about their fears, weaknesses, aspirations. Anti-feminist prejudice became prevalent during the decades following Wesley's death, and in the United States 19th-century Methodism was far less liberal than Mr. Wesley had been. The major reason for the change in attitude was society's insistence that women were meant to be homemakers and child rearers. Church was the only place women could go to escape endless household duties, and there they were again reminded that "woman's place is in the home." Beginning in 1830 Methodist evangelism under Charles G. Finney began encouraging women's active church participation. He even espoused the almost-heretical idea that women should pray in public.

These circumstances, combined with the experience Methodist women had gained in conducting ladies' fairs, found many of them ready and eager to take care of the soldiers' needs at the outbreak of the Civil War. Many Methodist women became a vital part of the Northern Sanitary Commission, and Southern women also insisted on participating in the war relief efforts. An Alabama woman wrote to her bishop during the war. "Bishop, give us work! We can do it, not at once, perhaps, but let us begin." In 1844, because of the temper of the times, the Methodist Episcopal Church in the United States split into two separate denominations, the Methodist Episcopal Church and the Methodist Episcopal Church, South. The two denominations did not re-unite until 1949. However, since there was little difference in the churchwomen's relationship to their churches, and in their desire to raise money for their churches, distinction has been made between them only when differences occurred.

Shortly after the Civil War the Women's Foreign Missionary Society of the Methodist Episcopal Church (North), was founded, and similar organizations in other denominations, including the M.E. Church, South, were founded shortly thereafter. It was in the decades of the 1870s through the 1890s that churchwomen found an important way to use their needlework skills and make money as well. Fundraising quilts became popular. These women had the needle skills, they had the organization, they loved their churches, and they could produce fundraising quilts so quickly that their husbands had no time to protest until it was too late. In addition, very little cash outlay was required for these projects.

Although the money raised by most fundraisers seems small—rarely more than $300 for the signatures—that money had far more purchasing power than the same amount of money would have today. A simple frame church could be built in the 1890s for $700. Almost half that amount could be earned through one fundraising quilt!

The relationship of Methodist women and the WCTU is also important. Many of the national leaders, including Frances Willard, were Methodists, and Methodist women comprised a large segment of the membership. The reason for this is understandable. The aims and goals of the WCTU were compatible with the beliefs of Methodist women. The influence of the WCTU on Methodist churches was also important. Two such influences deserve mention,

Figure 5. *Instructions for making a Red Cross fundraiser appeared in* The Modern Priscilla, *December 1917. It suggested that signatures could be placed on the back as well as the front of the quilt and showed a model for the ticket form to be used in selling the signatures.*

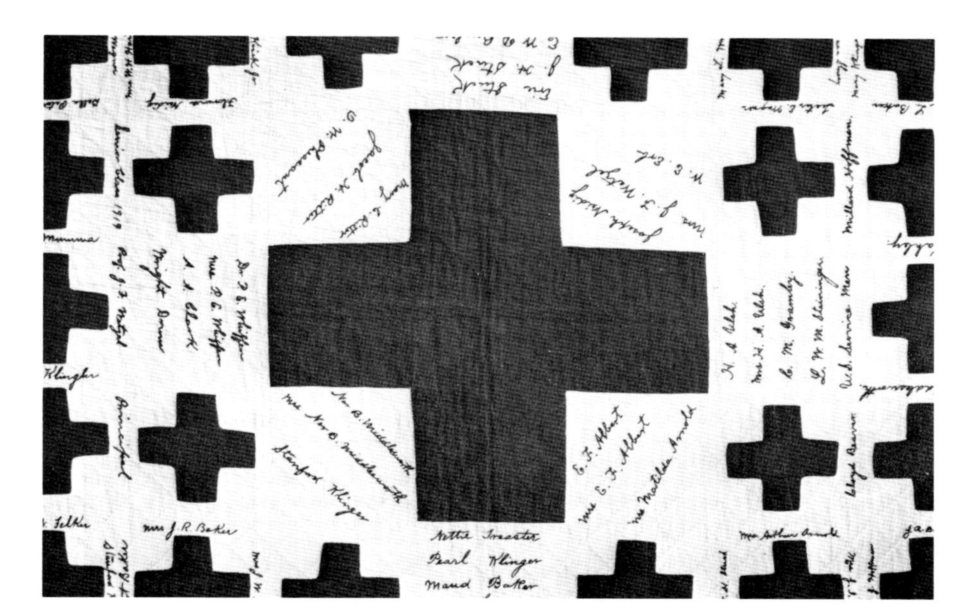

Figure 6. *Detail of quilt made in Snyder County, Pennsylvania between August 1918 and April 1919. Appliquéd solid-colored cotton on white top with white back. Applied white binding. 83" × 82" with 8-10 stitches per inch. Collection of Jean W. Haines.*

This quilt was made following the instructions from The Modern Priscilla.

one as an example and one because it relates directly to fundraising quilts. By 1880 grape juice had replaced the use of wine at communion tables in almost all Methodist churches (as well as in Baptist, Congregational, and some Presbyterian churches). Although other forces were involved, it is surprising that this happened only six years after the WCTU was organized. Because gambling was considered by the WCTU to be closely related to the use of alcohol in destroying the home, by 1900 the Methodist Episcopal Discipline clearly stated that "playing at games of chance" could lead to an offender's being expelled from the church. Prior to 1890 the majority of fundraising quilts had been raffled, because that in itself was a far more lucrative way of collecting money than the sale of the signatures. However, during the 1890s quilts began to be auctioned off or disposed of in some other way, such as being given to a minister or some other person involved in the project. This continued to be the trend in Methodist and other denominations such as the Baptist, Presbyterian, Lutheran. Strife sometimes arose between the ministers and the women about this matter, and, in one instance at least, as noted in Ricky Clark's paper, "The Needlework of an American Lady/Social History in Quilts" in *In the Heart of Pennsylvania/Symposium Papers* (Lewisburg, PA: Oral Traditions Project, 1986), the Salem Ladies Aid of a Methodist church in Ohio raffled a quilt in 1919. One member refused to participate because raffling was a form of gambling.

Another organization which benefited from the revenues raised by fundraising quilts was the Red Cross, particularly during World War I. Numerous Red Cross quilts, featuring red crosses and using red and white fabric in their construction, were made between 1915 and 1920. Some included the names of soldiers serving from one community, some featured blue stars for living combatants, and a few contained gold stars symbolizing those men who had lost their lives. Almost all were signature quilts, and the idea of obtaining autographs of famous people remained a popular feature. Many of these quilts were made by individuals, rather than groups, and in December, 1917, an article appeared in *The Modern Priscilla* titled "One Thousand Dollars for the Red Cross Can Be Raised on a Memorial Quilt" (fig. 5). Instructions included prices to charge for signatures, the placement of the red crosses, and even a model for the ticket form to be used for selling signatures. These, the only written directions for fundraising quilts that have been found so far by this author, were most explicit.

For three-quarters of a century the news of a sure-fire way to raise money had been passed by word of mouth throughout the United States. Undoubtedly the news was told in the many letters that were written from the older settled areas in the East to the pioneering women in the West. It is not impossible that such a letter will come to light some day.

Suggested Readings:

Bordin, Ruth. *Woman and Temperance: the Quest for Power and Liberty* 1873-1900. Philadelphia: Temple University Press, 1981.

Clark, Ricky. "The Needlework of an American Lady/Social History in Quilts," *In the Heart of Pennsylvania/Symposium Papers* Lewisburg, PA: Oral Traditions Project (1986): 65-75.

Cozart, Dorothy. "A Century of Fundraising Quilts 1860-1960." *Uncoverings 4* Mill Valley, CA: The American Quilt Study Group (1984):41-53.

Garrison, William Lloyd, ed. *The Liberator* (Boston) vol. 7, no. 1, January 2, 1837.

Gordon Beverly. "Playing at Being Powerless: New England Ladies' Fairs, 1830-1930. *The Massachusetts Review* (1985):144-160.

Gunn, Virginia. "Quilts for Union Soldiers in the Civil War." *Uncoverings* 5 Mill Valley, CA: The American Quilt Study Group (1985):95-121.

Holstein, Jonathan. *The Pieced Quilt/An American Design Tradition.* Boston: New York Graphic Society; Little, Brown and Company, 1973.

Katzenburg, Dena S. *Baltimore Album Quilts.* Baltimore: The Baltimore Museum of Art, 1981.

Kyser, Pat Flynn. "Pieces and Patches," *Quilt World* (July/August 1985): 46-48.

Lasansky, Jeannette. *Pieced by Mother/Over One Hundred Years of Quiltmaking Traditions.* Lewisburg, PA: Oral Traditions Project, 1987.

"One Thousand Dollars for the Red Cross Can Be Raised on a Memorial Quilt," *The Modern Priscilla* (December, 1917): 2.

Ramsey, Bets and Waldvogel, Merikay. *The Quilts of Tennessee.* Nashville: Rutledge Hill Press, 1986.

Roan, Nancy, "Quilting in Goschenhoppen.: *In the Heart of Pennsylvania/Symposium Papers* Lewisburg, PA: Oral Traditions Project (1986):48-55.

____ and Gehret, Ellen J. *Just a Quilt or Juscht en Deppich.* Green Lane, Pennsylvania: Goschenhoppen Historians, Inc. 1984.

Rowley, Nancy J. "Red Cross Quilts for the Great War." *Uncoverings 3* (1982):43-51.

Thomas, Hilah T. and Jeller, Rosemary Skinner. *Women in New Worlds.* Nashville: Abingdon Press, 1981.

Dorothy Thomas Cozart is a native Oklahoman who received her B.A. from Phillips University and her M.A. from Oklahoma State University. For twenty years she taught at public schools in Kansas and Oklahoma before teaching ten more at Phillips University. In addition to teaching English and American folklore class there, each year she supervised a folklife festival that her students planned and executed — a quilt exhibit always being a featured event. These led to an interest in quilt history and to her lecturing frequently on the subject including a series of talks in Sweden in 1980 at a time when worldwide interest in American quilts was burgeoning. Since her retirement in 1983, Dorothy has been able to pursue her research in quilt history fulltime. Her papers "Women and Their Quilts as Portrayed by Some American Authors" in Uncoverings 1983, *"A Century of Fundraising Quilts, 1860 to 1960" in* Uncoverings 1984, *and "An Early 19th Century Quiltmaker and Her Quilts," in* Uncoverings 1986 *attest to this research as does her article on tobacco-related fabrics in quilts in* The Quilt Digest *(1987). Dorothy is on the Board of Directors of the American Quilt Study Group and has recently served as a consultant to the Kansas Quilt Project. She and her husband, Hugh, live on a livestock and wheat farm in Waukomis, Oklahoma.*

***Figure** 7. Quilt made by the Salem Church Ladies Aid Society, Blair Mills, Juniata County, Pennsylvania and dated "1931/32." Pieced velvets with chintz back. Front brought to back as an edge treatment. 75" × 72" with fancy stitches in colored threads. Collection of Rosie Goss.*

THE COLONIAL REVIVAL AND QUILTS 1864-1976

JEANNETTE LASANSKY

For over 100 years we have seen quilts treated first as antiquarian then as historical objects, more recently as consciously-designed textiles as worthy of aesthetic consideration as are the fine arts, as integral parts of women's lives, as indices of economic and technological change, as mirrors of ethnic diversity and also of acculturation, and here as objects not isolated from but reflective of historical times and attitudes. This paper will examine quilts and the role of quiltmaking within the complex and continuing cultural phenomenon called the colonial revival.

Fifers and drummers marched about. Craftsmen and women in period costumes plied 18th century trades. People ate from outdoor stalls and flocked to the Liberty Bell. They cheered as costumed riders on magnificent Morgan horses rode up to Independence Hall in groups, state by state. . . . "

The colonial revival, instead of being just an aesthetic movement in the decorative and fine arts, in architecture, and in literature, and one which occurred within a narrow time frame (c. 1880-1920), rather is a complex and constantly resurfacing phenomenon, one which has waxed and waned for over 120 years and which is represented in many guises and in many forms. This latest example, described in *The New York Times* on May 24, 1987, was the kickoff of our Constitution's bicentennial. The same description, albeit with slight modifications, might have been used for numerous centennial, sesquicentennial, and bicentennial celebrations, fairs, and assorted happenings. Quilts and quiltmaking traditions have often played a part in such celebrations.

What comes to mind when thinking of colonial revival?: Sturbridge Village, Greenfield Village and particularly Colonial Williamsburg; home furnishings by Ethan Allan Furniture, Pennsylvania House or earlier, Wallace Nutting; colonial tract housing and those endless ramifications on the Mt. Vernon theme; restoration and reproduction hearths both strictly decorative as well as functioning; magazines such as *Early American Life, Country Living,* and *Americana;* tricornered hats and mobcaps; fifes and drums; those ubiquitous Paul Revere pierced tin lanterns, and reenactments, 4th of July celebrations, or festivals complete with their requisite spinning and weaving demonstrations, candlemaking and quiltmaking areas.

What do all these disparate elements—objects, tasks, sights, smells, sounds, and images—have in common? All are meant to evoke an earlier time in America repeatedly, though inaccurately, grouped together as the colonial experience: the pilgrim era through the Federal period which is represented as more in touch with the earth—bucolic, simple, direct, thereby more virtuous, honest, humane, and stable—a time in which the base of our political system was created, and our political and genealogical pedigrees were established (George Washington, Thomas Jefferson, Benjamin Franklin, James Madison, et al).

The colonial revival is almost always very New England, white and Anglo-Saxon. Objects from this broad time period, dubbed "colonial," and recently hybridized into "country," evoke a past which is presented by the naive, the highly manipulative, and the scholar alike. This past—a usable past—has been carefully maintained to educate us, to console us, to distract us, and to lend credibility to a wide range of issues and people. Whether we are the children of recent immigrants or Daughters of the American Revolution, we have been told there is (and we actually seem to find) great comfort in the American colonial experience.

Let us examine how quilts and quiltmaking

Plate 10. *Detail of quilt made by Mary Ellen Pursley Fessenden Crouse, Union County, Pennsylvania, c. 1890. Pieced wools with cotton print back. 80" square with 5-6 stitches per inch. Collection of Mr. and Mrs. Philip Snyder.*

The quilts and comforts (haps) made during the colonial revival period encompass a broad range of types: traditional pieced and appliquéd patterns, Log Cabin variations, newly "designed" quilts — primarily appliqués, many string quilts, and variations on the country Crazy type as illustrated here.

Figure 1. Sampler quilt made by Rebecca Graham, Northumberland, Northumberland County, Pennsylvania, c. 1890. Pieced and appliquéd calico and print cottons. Back brought to the front as edge treatment. 82" × 81¾" with 7 stitches per inch. Collection of Country Squire Antiques, Selinsgrove.

played important roles in not one or two but the *repeated* and ongoing colonial revivals which our country has gone through. We must be mindful that forms will vary, accuracy to the past might be secondary, but it is the idea—the concept of colonial—that will remain preeminent.

The Civil War was a wrenching experience. Essayists and cartoonists used images of George Washington and Columbia, then our mother earth, in their call for reason and unity while the colonial kitchen became the center piece of the great fundraisers for the Union's Sanitary Commission—the Sanitary Fairs.

Starting first in Brooklyn in 1864 (opening on George Washington's birthday) and then going on to New York, Philadelphia, Indianapolis, St. Louis, and Poughkeepsie "New England Kitchens," a "Knickerbocker Kitchen," and a "Pennsylvania Kitchen" raised ever increasing funds for supplying the Union army. These kitchens, with their regional variations (most strongly felt in Pennsylvania), all had certain elements: the large and central fireplace, a gun over the mantel and candlesticks on it, a nearby string of dried apples, a tall clock and a spinning wheel. The women always wore mobcaps and a quilting bee was often part of the tableau (and one of the eight stereo views one could purchase of the Brooklyn Kitchen).

Figure 2. *Sampler quilt made by Mary Jane Bennett Sill b. 1832 d. 1922. Picture Rocks, Lycoming County, ca. 1910. Pieced calico and print cottons with sugar sack back and applied binding. 81" × 74" with 7-8 stitches per inch. Collection of Mary E. Artley.*

The few sampler quilts seen were made of fabrics from the 1880s-1920s, a time when catalogs, such as The Ladies Art Company's *(see inside cover), were very popular and distributed widely. Such catalogs had hundreds of single block pattern designs illustrated and available for purchase. It may be that such catalog pages served as the inspiration for some of these sampler quilts.*

Figure 3. An "Old Time Kitchen"—complete with Windsor chair, wool wheel and quilt in cradle—on parade c. 1910 at location unknown (card purchased in Lewisburg, Pennsylvania). Collection of Oral Traditions Project.

Quilts were also among the needlework objects displayed in the fairs' other exhibits and sold there through raffles. Locally, J. H. Harmon, a lawyer and agent for the Catawissa Railroad, solicited contributions and consignments in the Bloomsburg newspaper, hoping that "the people of Columbia [County] and all others desirous to aid in the noble enterprise, for the benefit of our suffering soldiers, will avail themselves of the offer [to have them transported to Philadelphia gratis]."

These first colonial kitchens proved to be popular attractions with the general public. One was constructed for the Centennial exhibition of 1876, followed by one at the permanent exhibition in Philadelphia, and then yet another at Chicago's Columbian Exposition of 1893—there, "old-tyme" meals were served by Wellesley and Vassar coeds (directed by Emma Southwick Brinton of "Centennial Kitchen" fame).

As Rodris Roth notes in his article "The New England, or 'Old Tyme' Kitchen Exhibit at Nineteenth-Century Fairs," (*The Colonial Revival in America,* New York: W. W. Norton, 1985), "A reflection of interest in the American past, these rooms had popular appeal. They reinforced colonial virtues as codes for the modern citizen to follow even as they showed how far the country had progressed. . . . [they] are early instances of the collecting and study of artifacts for private pleasure as well as public edification (p. 183)," and in effect they were the precursors of the first early American period rooms in museum settings [of Charles Wilcomb's at the Golden Gate Park Museum in 1896 and at the Oakland Museum in 1910, of George Francis Dow's at the Essex Institute in 1907, of the American Wing at the Metropolitan Museum of Art in 1924]."

The Centennial of 1876 and the White City of the Columbian Exposition of 1893 fostered state pride, national unity, and Americanization as mirrored in the latter's display of George Washington's relics, the Liberty Bell, the state of Virginia's copy of Mount Vernon, and Pennsylvania's of Independence Hall. Millions of lives were touched in the six months that the 1893 Exposition was open. As Susan Prendergast Schoelwar notes in her article "Curious Relics and Quaint Scenes: The Colonial Revival at Chicago's Great Fair," (*The Colonial Revival in America,* New York: W. W. Norton, 1985). "it was. . . . an unprecedented amount of colonial material gathered in a proto-museum atmosphere at a time when few established museums collected American art and artifacts (p. 214). (A directive of the fair said it was desirable that all exhibits relating to the Civil War be *excluded,* supporting the contention that those things relating to the colonial experience were, in contrast, meant to be not only instructive but reassuring.)

Following the Civil War, many parts of the country reflected our becoming a rapidly changing, highly urbanized and industrialized society. There were those reformers who felt the need for a counterbalance. For some that was represented by a new aesthetic and an attitude that glorified the handmade, the homemade, and the past. The arts and crafts movement, started earlier in England (c. 1834-1896) by John Ruskin and William Morris, was embraced here by arbiters of taste such as Candice Wheeler, Charles Lock Eastlake, Elbert Hubbard, Gustav Stickley, and Clarence Cook. In his *House Beautiful* (1878) Cook called for those with taste to selectively embrace objects from the past that would give beauty and meaning to their lives. Not only would these old furnishings inspire but he maintained that they were available and often inexpensive. In a treatise published twenty years after Cook's, Thorstein Veblen in his *Theory of the Leisure Class/ An Economic Study of Institution* (1899) observed how members of the new leisure class, the very creatures of the industrial revolution, looked back with nostalgia to a more archaic scheme of life. Such historical revivalism embraced the colonial period with its wholesome simplicities.

At this time Sybil Lanigen wrote a lengthy article on pieced quilt designs called "Revival of the Patchwork Quilt" in *The Ladies Home Journal* (October 1894). As she noted, "The vagaries of fashion are unaccountable and no one can tell in what direction they will lead next. Of late months everything which could be recognized as old-fashioned is the new fashion. . . . The decree has gone forth that a revival of patchwork quilts is at hand, and dainty fingers whose owners have known only patches and patchworks from family description are busy placing the blocks together in new and artistic patterns, as well as in the real old-time order." Indeed, since the late 1880s, there had been occasional mention of "grandmother's" patchwork, as contrasted to the silk and velvet Crazy quilt phenomenon, but it was Lanigen who first coined the return to "mosaics of calico" as a revival. The patterns she presented in 1894 were a *Nine Patch* variation, the *Bethlehem Star,* a Central Medallion pattern, and *Flying Geese,* all in contrast to ". . . . the rock of ugliness and the whirlpool of intricacy," or the Crazy quilt. Only two years later, periodicals like *The National Stockman and Farmer, Hearthstone, Hearth and Home,* and *The American Agriculturalist* joined *The Ladies Home Journal* in praising the use of woolen and cotton scraps, in advocating the purchase of good, dye-fast materials in quiltmaking, in telling of old-fashioned quilting bees as well as in publishing dozens of quilting patterns and patches. Simultaneously a series of popular books extolling the colonial experience appeared.

Alice Morse Earle drew exclusively upon the American colonial past when she issued her influential *Home Life in Colonial Days* in 1898. It was one of twelve books she researched and wrote from 1891 to 1903, all dealing with different aspects of colonial life. Though she found the piecing that was required to make a quilt, "almost painful to regard," she did place quiltmaking solidly within this colonial tradition.

Others, like Helen Blair in an article, "Dower Chest Treasures," in *House Beautiful* (February 1904) felt that "if, however one has not preserved the work of some piecing and quilting ancestress, she may, 'an' it please her, 'fall herself apiecing." As she noted "The old quilts which are reappearing under such interesting circumstances are, many of them, quite worthy of their recall consequence. The colors are often old hand-dyes, the patterns marvels of design, and the quilting intricately beautiful. One of these old quilts, into which a woman of long ago put so much creative and adaptive skill, will give an air to even the most commonplace beds. It will glorify a beautiful old bed." And on such an affirmative note, the revival of quiltmaking as done by one's grandmother—real or imagined—was well on its way.

Helen Blair's call, to make a traditional quilt if you were not fortunate enough to have inherited one, can be seen as another example of the then current cultural phenomenon of "ancestor worship." The D.A.R., Colonial Dames and the S.A.R. were formed at this time. As Celia Betsky notes in her article "In the Past: The Interior and the Colonial Revival in American Art and Literature 1860-1914," (*The Colonial Revival in America,* New York: W. W. Norton, 1985) p. 261, "The colonial revival interior came to present physical and social exclusivity." It was, she maintains, "A kind of nobility of native origins evolved as the fear of foreign immigration grew (p. 266)," and indeed immigration at the turn of the century was at a new high point. Between 1880-1930 our foreign born population doubled from 6.7 to 14.2 million. Their Americanization was a required and intense ex-

Figure 4. *Colonial tea scene from an amateur theatrical in Tecumseh, Michigan. Collection of Virginia Gunn.*

perience illustrated by Henry Ford's campaign to assimilate his foreign-born workers (1914), later by his Wayside Inn Boys School (1928) where by living with 18th-century furnishings "the boys" were expected to absorb early American values.

What comprised this idealized past was well represented in the period's literature and art: the written works of Nathaniel Hawthorne, Oliver Wendell Holmes, John Greenleaf Whittier, and Henry Wadsworth Longfellow, and paintings such as Francis Millet's *Cozy Corner* (1884). Articles, such as the series published by *The Designer* called "Beautiful Colonial Interiors/Full of Points for the Average Home-Maker" were illustrated exhortations on the subject:

> There is, at the present time, a great rage for interior decoration that represents a distinct period of life. And perhaps, among Americans, there is no more popular style of furnishings than that which reproduces in every minutest detail the house of the first inhabitants of the United States. Picturesque, indeed, is the atmosphere of legend and story which surrounds the home of those early settlers. Simplicity is the keynote—and good taste in every particular carried out the Colonial scheme.
>
> Much of the furniture that was used by our Colonial ancestors has been preserved in one way or another. There are antique shops where it may be purchased for fabulous sums. But, on the other hand, many families have harbored and saved this furniture until now it has become a substantial and a most valuable part of their possessions. All of the cabinet work accomplished in those early days was done in the most thorough and workmanlike manner. The wood used was of the finest quality, the finishing and polishing were attended to with the greatest care—so that even the smallest bit of Colonial furniture is bound to be worth cherishing until it has crumbled to pieces.
>
> The beauty and the utility of this furniture has lately been fully recognized to the end that all of the good examples have been faithfully copied. They may be had at any furniture store. A few good Colonial pieces will make a much more satisfactory room than a multitude of furnishings of varied patterns and designs.
>
> New England is generally regarded as the most fertile field for finding authentic Colonial specimens, and indeed, throughout those states there are homes completely filled with the furniture which was put there in Colonial days. Philadelphia and vicinity is also the home of much Colonial architecture and furniture. Many of the homes in this locality have been preserved with their original decorations almost intact.

Pictured was a hallway, "pure in character and beautiful in design," a reception hall" decorated with the arms of ancestors, "the dining room with a spacious and hospitable fireplace" and an old spinning wheel, and the bedroom with "a chest which doubtless holds treasures unnumbered (November 1915, p.18)."

Hazel Boardman's articles were followed by like-minded ones by Frances Garside "Patchwork Romance/Century-Old Quilts Found in Small Weather-Beaten Log Cabin in Tennessee, *House Beautiful,* January 1919; Ada Stoddard's "A Story of Patchwork, Old and New," *Needlecraft Magazine,* 1929; and Jessie Farrall Peck's "The Bed of Yesterday In The House of Today," *Good Housekeeping* April 1933, pp. 54, 55, and 122.

Figure 5. The back of a Mountain Mist batting wrapper with instructions—in this instance for The Double Wedding Ring. *Collection of Margaret Seebold.*

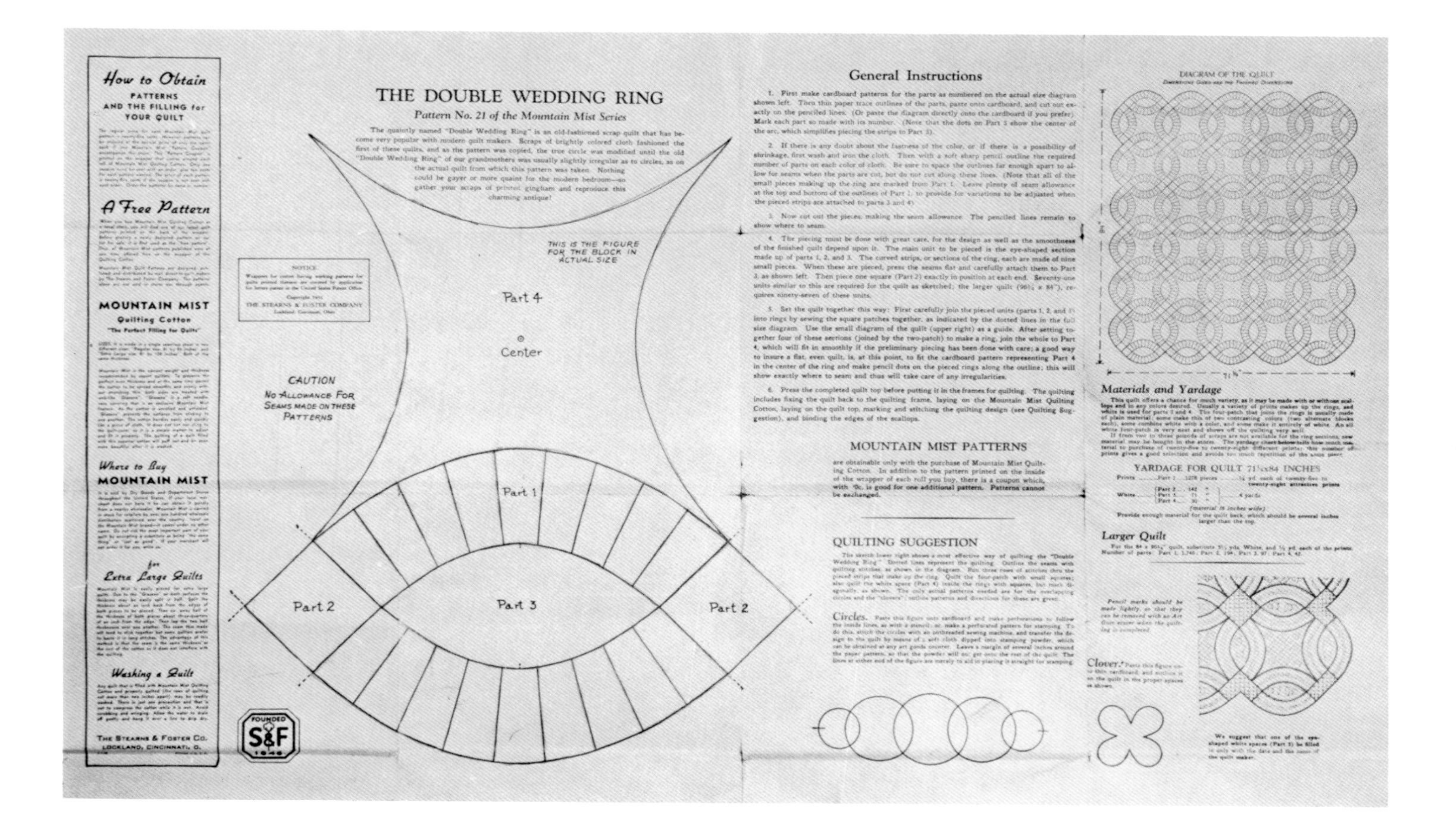

Again, if you did not own an ancestor's quilt nor had learned how to quilt from a mother or grandmother, there was not a lack of instruction. Just as entrepreneurs had begun to commercialize Christmas in the 1870s-1880s (see Nada Gray's *Holidays/Victorian Women Celebrate,* Lewisburg, Pennsylvania: Oral Traditions Project, 1983, pp. 4-6) so too they stepped into quiltmaking traditions with great force.

Starting in the late 1880s with the Ladies Art Company of St. Louis, Missouri, firms and individuals were accumulating and selling hundreds of pieced and appliquéd designs and quilting motifs. Some drew upon the dialogue and pattern exchange between rural readers of periodicals such as *Farmer's Fireside, Hearth and Home, The National Stockman and Farmer, The Rural New Yorker,* and *The Progressive Farmer.* Clara Stone published 186 such patterns in her *Practical Needlework - Quilt Patterns* (1919). Joseph Doyle Company had earlier presented "The Patchwork Companion (1911)," Artamo Thread its "Colonial Patchwork (1916)," along with *The Household Journal's* "Aunt Jane's Prize-Winning Quilt Designs (1916)," and Martha Washington's "Patchwork Book (1916)." Aunt Martha, Virginia Snow, and Grandmother Clark, all were commercial ventures established after World War I to meet the insatiable needs of quiltmakers. Similarly, quilt batting manufacturers like Mountain Mist and Lockport Batting were quick to respond with new and old patterns printed on their batting wrappers.

Others, like Anne Orr and Ruby Short McKim, who started as art/needlework editors for *Good Housekeeping* and *Better Homes and Garden* respectively, at first presented traditional patterns but soon went on to design their own and to market them. The Anne Orr Studio located in Nashville, Tennessee published over seventy needlework books and pamphlets which included quilt patterns like the popular *Jonquil* and *Iris,* while the McKim Studio in Independence, Missouri, produced patterns for the *Kansas City Star* before concentrating on their mail order business. Quilt projects like Ruby McKim's *Johnny-Jump-Up* were originals and she was an early advocate for "apartment" or lap quilting. Her book *One Hundred and One Patchwork Patterns* was well received in 1931.

While neither woman was a quilter but rather an artistically-trained designer, their influence was extensive and well publicized amongst traditional quilters. Their aesthetic changed the look of quilts with the use of modulated pastel colors, undulating borders, large central motifs, different sized pieced blocks, and a decline in intricate quilting.

It is during this same time period—the first and second decade of the 20th century—that we see quilts become objects of serious study. Though still exhibited by their makers at local fairs they were also displayed in university galleries and decorative arts museums. Trendsetters were the Newark Museum in 1914 and the University of Kansas in 1920. Quilts also began to be the subject of researched articles by Fanny Bergen, Charlotte Boltman, Frances Garside, Mrs. Leopold Simon, and Elizabeth Daingerfield from 1908-1911 and then in books by Marie Webster, *Quilts: Their Story and How to Make Them* (New York: Doubleday, Page and Company, 1915), by Carlie Sexton, *Early American Quilts* (Southampton, New York: Crackerbarrel Press, 1924) and by Ruth Finley, *Old Patchwork Quilts and The Women Who Made Them.* (Philadelphia: J. B. Lippincott & Co., 1929).

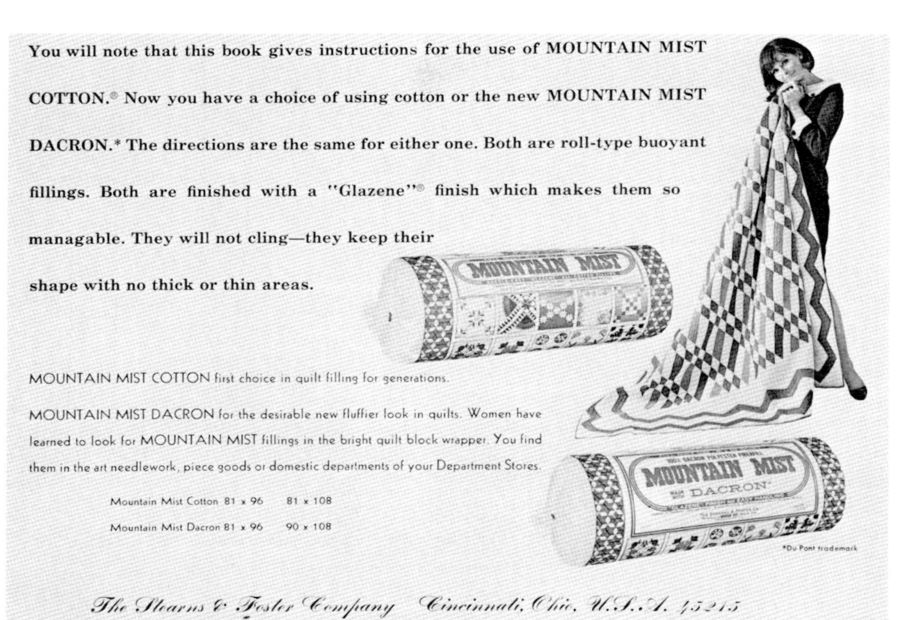

Figure 6. An advertisement for Mountain Mist batting. Collection of Margaret Seebold.

So, when the 1930s arrived quilts were valued for their romantic and historical associations—with grandma and the colonial past, they were placed in period rooms and hung on museum walls, they were objects of serious study, and their patterns were being redefined by fine artists and designers. Quilts were being done by families that had never stopped quiltmaking as well as those who newly introduced to the phenomenon.

Sears, Roebuck's national quilt competition, announced in 1933, came at a crucial juncture in the nation's psyche. The Great Depression was in its fourth year and did not appear to be of transient nature and 1932's bicentennial celebration of George Washington's birthday established by the United States George Washington Bicentennial Commission (four years earlier), had taken some curious turns. Its chairman, Representative Sol Bloom of New York, decided it was time to meet the *real* George. Although Bloom saw to it that school children would all study under Gilbert Stuart's portrait of the great white father as they licked his likeness on their one and two cent (there are 12 issues in the series, ranging in value from 1/2¢ to 10¢, each with a different portrait stamps), he relished this campaign which separated myth from reality. His was the first in a series of efforts to debunk standard colonial mythology such as Parson Weems's tale of young George and the cherry tree. Others, like Grant Wood, who grounded their work in popular culture, were also making wry visual comments about Washington, Weems, and the D.A.R.—subjects previously sacrosanct. (See Wood's *The Midnight Ride of Paul Revere* (1931), *Daughters of Revolution* (1932), and *Parson Weems' Fable* (1939).)

While the colonial exhibits at Chicago's Columbian Exposition (1893) had provided comfort and nationalistic pride, the Sears quilt contest held at Chicago's "Century of Progress" Exposition (1933) temporarily distracted the public from the country's massive social and economic problems. It also provided traditional quiltmakers, as well as those with a "moderne" impulse, something to respond to as would the New York World's Fair later (in 1939) with its larger than life George Washington and its futuristic Trylon and Perisphere. Sears 1934 catalog asks the question, "Were You There?":

> About 5,000,000 persons visited Sears national prize winning quilt exposition at A Century of Progress, probably the most priceless collection of hand-made quilts ever gathered under one roof. If you were among the 5,000,000 this book will recall vividly your breath-taking admiration of the most exquisite, perfect examples of the handicraft of quilt-making.
>
> You will live again the happy hours spent in comparing, memorizing, exclaiming over the beauty of color, originality of pattern, fine stitches and elegance of the quilting designs. They seem like living, breathing things; certainly they were works of art to be prized for generations to come.
>
> If you are one of the millions who stayed close to 'the home shore' and did not 'do the fair' . . . never mind, here are some of the prize winning patterns, some of the most famous and sought-after quilting designs.
>
> Choose an 'original'; choose a new interpretation of a history-old pattern. . . . but whatever you do, MAKE A QUILT. It's the fashion, expresses your own individuality in glorious colors and the finest of fine stitches.

The contest had inspired 24,878 quilts to be submitted in old patterns, adaptations such as the "Ohio Rose," and entirely new designs like "Philadelphia to Pittsburgh in Twenty Days" by Mrs. George R. Leitzel of Northumberland. When the prizewinning quilts were selected, some of their patterns and instructions were published and promoted by this merchandising giant so that thousands of other women could similarly make prizewinning quilts: *Martha's Vineyard, Colonial Rose,* and *Delectable Mountains* among others. Sears concluded:

> In the last few years quilt-making has revived, not as a necessity, but again taking its place among the fine arts. Everywhere one sees groups of women making quilts, joyous old time neighborliness is again binding our women together. Patterns are exchanged, notes compared and materials traded. And so to this growing neighborliness we dedicate this book . . . MAKE A QUILT!!!

Perhaps inspired by, and certainly coming on the heels of the Sears competition, was the Works Progress Administration's publication of thirty colored quilt designs in poster format which, along with a manual, were given to home economics teachers for classroom instruction. The series of traditional designs (including a Crazy quilt) were gathered along with the quilts' oral histories: *Baskets of Tulips,* Philadelphia 1839; *Lotus Flower* 1867; *Dutchman's Puzzle* Staten Island 1820; *Rocky Glen,* Southern States; *The Love Apple* New England; or *Star and Crescent,* Pennsylvania Dutch origin.

***Figure** 7. Cover of Sears Roebuck's catalog* The Quilt Fair Comes To You, *c. 1933. Collection of Jean Creznic.*

The Sears quilt contest in 1934, the publication of Carrie A. Hall and Rose G. Kretsinger's *The Romance of the Patchwork Quilt in American* in 1935, and the W.P.A. series in the late 1930s/early 1940s were followed by a dormant period punctuated by the appearance of Margaret Ickis' *The Standard Book of Quiltmaking and Collecting* in 1949 as well as books and articles by Florence Peto in the late 1930s through late 1940s. Not until the late 1960s and early 1970s does the colonial revival—as mirrored in quilts—come full force again, inspired in part by the 1960s back to earth movement and the looming Bicentennial celebration. This time around in fact quiltmaking usurps spinning and weaving as the "colonial" craft.

Throughout all these 120 years the form that quiltmaking took was exceptionally diverse, in large part due to the fact that there were two distinct then merged traditions: the maintenance of an ongoing oral tradition, often rural, and the numerous introductions of new quiltmaking ideas—primarily through periodicals, books, and then kits—to that audience as well as a new one, often urban.

Figure 8. *Quilt top possibly made by Marie Spahr Landis, b. 1896, d. 1977, Boiling Springs, Cumberland County c. 1917. Applied calico, print, and solid-colored cottons and solid-colored wools on white cotton with embroidery. 54½" × 52¾". Collection of Clara Zawadski.*

Suggested Reading:

"Ann Orr—She Captured Beauty." *Quilters Newsletter Magazine.* June 1973, p. 12-16, 27

Axelrod, Alan ed. *The Colonial Revival in America,* New York: W. W. Norton, 1985.

Benberry, Cuesta. "The 20th Century's First Quilt Revival." *Quilters Newsletter Magazine.* July/August 1979, pp. 20-22; September 1979, pp. 25, 26, 29; October 1979, pp. 10-11.

Brackman, Barbara. "Quilts at Chicago's World's Fair." *Uncoverings 1981.* Mill Valley, California: American Quilt Study Group, 1982

Earle, Alice Morse. *Home Life in Colonial Days.* New York: Macmillan Company, 1898.

Finley, Ruth E. *Old Patchwork Quilts and the Women Who Made Them.* Philadelphia: J. B. Lippincott & Co., 1929.

"Ruby Short McKim." *Quilters Newsletter Magazine.* December, 1976, pp. 14-15.

Sears Century of Progress in Quiltmaking. Chicago: Sears, Roebuck & Co., 1934.

Sexton, Carlie. *Yesterday's Quilts in Houses of Today.* Des Moines, Iowa: Meredith Publishing Company, 1930.

Townsend, Louise O. "Eveline Foland, Quilt Pattern Illustrator." *Quilters Newsletter Magazine.* April 1985, pp. 20-22.

Jeannette Lasansky is the director of the Oral Traditions Project and a lecturer at Bucknell University. She has conceived of, researched, and authored a series of monographs on Pennsylvania craft traditions: stoneware pottery, basketry, redware pottery, forged iron work, plain tin, and quiltmaking. Her work over the past fourteen years has been supported by grants from the Pennsylvania Council on the Arts, the Early American Industries Association, and the National Endowment for the Arts and has received state and national awards from the American Association for State and Local History, the Historical Foundation of Pennsylvania, the Pennsylvania Federation of Historical Societies, the American Institute of Graphic Arts, and the Communication Arts. She has guest curated major exhibitions of this material culture at the State Museum in Harrisburg, the Hershey Museum of American Life, the Heritage Center of Lancaster County, and Bucknell University, and lectured at places such as the Smithsonian, Winterthur and the Pennsylvania Farm Museum. In 1985 she organized and executed a large fieldwork project on contemporary traditional quiltmaking in New Mexico for the Museum of International Folk Art, and she has just completed quilt consultancies in Oregon and Ohio. Jeannette has also published extensively in The Magazine Antiques *and also in the European folk life magazine* Volkskunst *among others. She has served on the crafts panel of the Pennsylvania Council on the Arts, on numerous grant review committees, and on the Pennsylvania Folklife Advisory Committee which she chaired.*

Morning Star
Premium Star
Miss Jo Basket
The Rolling Stone

What's In A Name?

Quilt patterns from 1830 to the Present

Barbara Brackman

It is a rare quilt pattern that goes unnamed today. Quilters and quilt owners recite names like *Dresden Plate, Drunkard's Path,* and *Grandmother's Flower Garden* with assurance. Pattern names are so well-known that editors of quilt magazines can construct crossword puzzles and write poetry using quilt names, confident their readership will instantly recognize the references.

There is a certainty that every patchwork pattern has a name. Some people, refusing to accept a pattern as unnamed, spend years corresponding with experts in the hopes of finding the name. Those who sponsor state and regional quilt surveys report that the desire to learn a pattern name is one of the prime motivations for families to bring old quilts to be registered.

The person on the trail of a quilt name has a number of resources, including the authority of an experienced quilter, many of whom can recall scores of pattern names. The quilter may have learned her repertoire through the oral tradition, hearing names from her family or other quilters; but today it is far more likely she acquired her knowledge by reading published sources, such as quilt magazines, books, catalogs, and indexes that cross-reference the other published sources.

Most of us think of quilt names as folklore with all the implications of the word, charming traditions that have somehow lingered in the midst of an industrial world. Although we know that most quilters today learn their pattern names from published sources, we somehow believe that the names are just a step removed from the 19th century (or earlier). The names seem to be derived from oral tradition, collected by folklorists doing field work in Tennessee hollows and on Pennsylvania farms. In some cases this perception is accurate. But, unlike the names for other types of folklore such as weaving patterns or the words to Appalachian ballads, the majority of our information about quilt patterns was not collected by folklorists, amateur or scholarly, but comes to us through a commercial network of magazine editors, professional designers and mail-order entrepreneurs.

Because the commercial network has been motivated by concerns other than an accurate recording of folklore, anyone viewing quilt pattern names should consider the source and its limitations. The commercial network for American quilt pattern names goes back to January, 1835 when *Godey's Lady's Book* printed a pattern and gave it three names: "the hexagon," "six-sided," or "honeycomb patchwork." Between 1835 and 1880 quilt patterns occasionally appeared in magazines. Some were given names (*Peterson's Magazine* in April, 1859 offered "the Chinese Pattern"), but the unnamed design was more common. A typical pattern included a drawing of a design or two under the general title "Patchwork" or "Patterns For Patchwork."

During the mid-19th century, American patchwork developed the style and diversity of design that make it unique, but when one compares quilts made during these decades to the patterns in print, it is evident that printed sources were rarely an inspiration to the quiltmakers or a reflection of their art. The magazines printed patterns for piecework, although appliqué was also popular with quiltmakers; they printed patterns for mosaic-style construction rather than the block-style designs favored by American seamstresses, and they often recommended silk fabric rather than the popular cottons. The editors, by ignoring vernacular design characteristics, seem to have attempted to elevate the taste of their readers—without much success, if the quilts we have left from the era are any evidence.

Plate 11. *Detail of quilt top made by M. Hettinger, Pine Grove Mills, Centre County, Pennsylvania. Signed and dated "M. Hettinger March the 18th 1897." Pieced and appliquéd, printed and plain cottons, 81½" × 66½". Collection of Gloria Braun.*

Old Time Patchwork Quilts

Treasured beyond the wildest dreams of our grandmothers, are the patterns, styles and combinations used in the making of their old patchwork quilts. Today, of course, we have improved methods, and opportunities to purchase a larger variety of materials, thereby making the modern quilts more artistic. However, if we would duplicate in beauty the quilts of our grandmothers, the handiwork must, first of all, be of the finest. Poorly made quilts were not to be found in the early days. Also, the best materials obtainable should be used; time is too precious to waste in piecing material that will not wear.

Never have quilts been so popular as at the present time. Families fortunate enough to have quilts stored in their treasure chests display them proudly. However, there are many who have not fallen heir to even one old-time quilt, and these are eagerly searching for patterns typical of colonial days. The two quilts illustrated below are copies of early-day patterns.

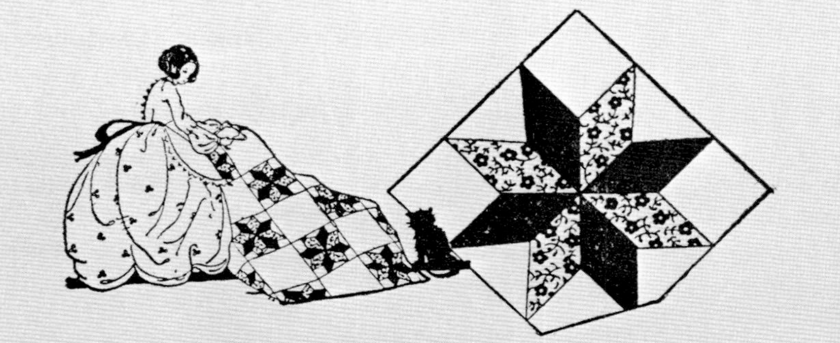

THE PURITAN STAR QUILT

Figure 1. The Joseph Doyle and Company catalog, Patchwork and Quiltmaking, *added several centuries to the history of this quilt pattern with a name recalling 16th-century New England colonists. The name, probably generated by this company, did not catch on.*

"Guam" Quilt-Block

Use three colors, red, white and blue, or any remnants of dark, medium and light, or white, you happen to have. The quilt may be entirely of pieced blocks, or the latter may be joined by means of plain strips, squares, or half squares, to give the zigzag effect; the latter being an especially attractive "setting." Mrs. M. B. Tuthill.

Apple-Leaf Lace

Cast on 32 stitches, knit across plain.
1. Knit 2, purl 1, knit 5, (over, narrow) twice, over, knit 1, (over, narrow) twice, over, knit 5, purl 1, knit 1, fagot (that is,

"GUAM" QUILT-BLOCK

Figure 2. Mrs. M. B. Tuthill sent the quilt pattern block "Guam" to Hearth and Home *magazine for their early-20th-century series of blocks named for states, capitals and U.S. possessions. Readers unable to draft the design could buy a full-size drawing by mail.*

A reader looking for pattern names in mid-century periodicals is generally disappointed. For example: a design which has, since the turn of the century, appeared in print under the descriptive names *Twist Patchwork, Twisted Rope, Plaited Block,* and *Round the Twist* was first published in *Godey's* in December 1851 under the general caption of "Patchwork: Combination Designs." One might conclude that the quiltmakers of the era did not give their designs the fanciful names found in later literature, but we have some evidence to refute this conclusion: an occasional quiltmaker has left us a pattern name stitched into her quilt. In 1847, Parnel R. Grumley wrote "The Peony and Prairie Flower No 6" on the back of her quilt.[1] In 1855 Jane Shelby inscribed the name "Mississippi Beauty" on the back of her appliqué quilt.[2] We also find mention of imaginative names in mid-century written records. Elizabeth Range Miller left a "Rose of Sharon" quilt in her 1857 will[3] and Elizabeth Myer wrote a letter about her "Flowering Almond" quilt in 1859.[4] We realize that the mid-19th century needlework columns were a poor reflection of the actual quilts being made; we can guess that they were also a poor reflection of the use of names.

In the 1880s magazines increased references to quilts, advocating patterns like the Fan, the Crazy quilt and outline embroidered designs, and in the 1890s the number of quilt patterns appearing in print increased significantly. Quilt designs were a feature in the needlework and reader's exchange columns of women's and farm magazines, and they began to reflect the vernacular patchwork quilts, in that they were block designs to be made in cotton, sometimes appliqué but more often pieced, using the American running stitch method. The quilt design did not include full-size pattern pieces, but rather a sketch or photograph representing the finished block.

During these decades names became an increasingly important component of the quilt feature. Typical of the magazines directed at farm families was the *Ohio Farmer,* which during 1894 printed patterns for eleven designs. Five were unnamed patterns, but six were given names like *Bird's Nest, Ocean Wave, Kaleidoscope,* and *Hour Glass* by their reader/contributors who signed themselves Doris, Olga, and Clara Merwin. Contributors to *Orange Judd Farmer* in 1899 offered patterns named after contemporary events. L.M.A. sent a *Dewey Dream* quilt and Allie L. Nay sent *Manila* quilt design.

By the turn of the century, the use of specific pattern names became the standard. In a February, 1912 article in *Ladies Home Journal* Elizabeth Daingerfield captioned patterns with names like *Lady-Finger, Tulip Wreath,* and *Sunflower;* names such as "Pretty Patchwork" or "Unnamed" are uncommon in the 20th-century literature.

The increasing importance of pattern names is illustrated by *Hearth and Home's* request for blocks named after states, capital cities and U.S. territories. In 1907 readers were asked to design new blocks or rename old favorites. Over the next decade the magazine printed patterns with names as far-fetched as *Porto Rico* [sic] and *Guam* for blocks that surely never graced a tropical bed.

It is difficult to know the sources for the names in the periodicals. Reader/contributors like Allie Nay did not often say whether they recorded old patterns and their names, or originated their designs. That readers did both is evident in *Hearth and Home.* Viola E. Hahn said she designed *Hawaii* "especially as a representative of the 'Island Possessions' formerly my home," and Mrs. L.W. of Mt. Vernon, Indiana sent in a design copied from a quilt her Kentucky grandmother had pieced. "We always called it the 'Kentucky quilt' so I think it may well represent the state."

Professional writers like Marie Webster and Elizabeth Daingerfield of the *Ladies Home Journal* often mentioned that they collected the patterns (and possibly the names) in their travels, and thus they were acting as folklorists, doing field work in rural communities. Daingerfield's 1912 article was titled "Kentucky Mountain Quilts" but close reading indicates that at least one of the designs came from an Illinois reader.

Whatever the sources, these turn-of-the-century periodicals are a valuable collection of pattern names, but because they were disposable, the magazines and the information on quilt names had a short life span. We today can identify the *Guam* or *Dewey Dream* quilts because they were indexed in the early 1980s, but it is probable that dozens of other regional magazines with small circulations have not been indexed and may never be.

In the early 20th century many magazines began selling patterns through the mail. *Hearth and Home* offered full-size paper pattern blocks of their state patterns to readers who sent five cents. The combination of the pictured design and a mail-order pattern became the standard periodical format for decades (although there were exceptions, most notably the *Kansas City Star* which printed a full-size pattern weekly for over thirty years).

The magazine mail-order departments competed with companies exclusively devoted to selling quilt patterns by mail. During the last decades of the 19th century when Montgomery Ward and Sears, Roebuck and Company were taking advantage of rural free delivery to sell American women quilt fabric, batting, and frames through the mail-order catalog, another entrepreneur sold them patchwork patterns. H. M. Brockstedt and his Ladies Art Company are credited with the first mail-order pattern catalog in 1889. The pamphlet underwent many revisions that featured small drawings of about 300 to 600 patterns, each with a single name.

The Ladies Art Company has been an important influence on the transmission of patterns and their names. Because catalogs are often revised and reprinted, and because quilters save them for decades, the catalog names seem to be more durable than those recorded only in a magazine. Reprints of the copyright-free 1928 LAC catalog are common in contemporary quilters' libraries (The House of White Birches in Seabrook, New Hampshire, currently sells a copy in a booklet called *700 Old Time Needlecraft Designs and Patterns*).

The Ladies Art Company's sources for patterns and pattern names were most likely midwestern magazines. A *Farm and Fireside* article from June, 1884 features twelve designs that appeared in the LAC five years later with many of the same names. The question of which came first—the magazine article or the Ladies Art Company listing—is not often so clear. The *American Farmer* printed "A Basket Quilt" on April 1, 1895; it is in an early LAC catalog in *Flower Basket*. Another basket design was listed as "Unnamed" in *Farm and Home* in 1889; the same design was called "Some Pretty Patchwork" in the LAC. After Jackson represented the Mississippi capitol in *Hearth and Home* magazine, it became a LAC listing as "'Miss Jackson."

Soon after the Ladies Art Company developed the mail-order pattern format others followed. Magazines advertised full-size patterns through the mail for a price (usually a nickel or a dime) and, after the turn of the century, companies like Joseph Doyle and Co., which printed a catalog in 1911, joined in the market. Like other companies in the teens and later, Doyle sold patterns copied directly from the Ladies Art Company.

Doyle's names sometimes differed from the LAC entries but some were direct copies down to the artwork. *White Day Lily* was identical in every respect to the LAC's example, but the LAC design *Flagstones* was sold by Doyle as *Snowball*, and the LAC's *Eight-Point Star* was Doyle's *Puritan Star*. Such copying was the usual practice. Pattern catalogs were not often copyrighted; copyrights seem never to have been enforced, and everyone was undoubtedly confused as to what was in the public domain as a true folk pattern.

Pattern names served several purposes. Customers could order by name. The names also distinguished one company from another, and names added to the patterns' appeal. It would

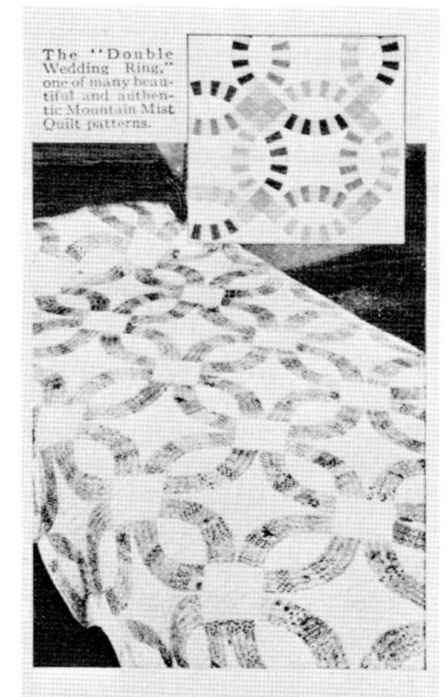

"I copied that quilt from one my grandmother made before the Civil War"

"PERHAPS, because I made it myself, that quilt has even more significance to me than the original. It has all the sentiment of the old, plus the added charm of my having made it."

You can make an old-time quilt, anyone can with Mountain Mist Quilt Patterns and Mountain Mist Quilting Cotton.

With Mountain Mist Quilt Patterns quilt-making is easy, one of the easiest forms of sewing. These patterns, the most complete of all quilt patterns, give you not only full size cutting blocks, but also show you how to lay them out, how many pieces to cut, how much cloth to buy, and suggest an appropriate design for the quilting.

But whatever make of pattern you use, be sure to fill your quilt with Mountain Mist Quilting Cotton, made only from all new cotton, washed with

***Figure 3.** The Stearns and Foster Company gave patterns as premiums with their Mountain Mist batting. The* Double Wedding Ring *has no 19th century history, but long pedigrees sold patterns—and batting.*

PORTRAY THE PRIMROSE PATH.

DRUNKARDS PATH PATTERN 480

Drunkard's Path—sometimes known as Wonder of the World—is a quilt that has been a favorite since the earliest days of quiltmaking To the quiltmaker it is indeed a world wonder for it is formed of but two pattern pieces. These interchange in the light and dark materials forming a simple block which, when joined, makes a seemingly intricate pattern. And that certainly sounds like something to wonder at!

Pattern No. 480 comes to you with complete, simple instructions for cutting, sewing and finishing, together with yardage chart, diagram of quilt to help arrange the blocks for single and double bed size, and a diagram of block which serves as a guide for placing the patches and suggests contrasting materials.

Give pattern number, and allow ten days for delivery. Patterns by mail only. Send 10 cents for the pattern to The Kansas City Star, Needlecraft Dept., Kansas City, Mo.

***Figure 4.** Syndicated quilt columns like this one from the Needlecraft Company, which also used the names Laura Wheeler and Alice Brooks, sold mail order patterns for both traditional and original designs.*

Figure 5. *Quilt top made by an unknown quiltmaker in the first quarter of the 20th century. Pieced and appliquéd, printed and plain cottons 85 1/2" × 76 3/4". Collection of Paulette Peters.*
Stitched to the back of many of the top's blocks are paper labels with pattern names. One of the blocks called Happy Home *appeared in a 1910 booklet,* Practical Needlework: Quilt Patterns *by Clara Stone who often contributed patterns to* Hearth and Home *and* Comfort *magazines. Of the 21 names remaining on the quilt, seven do not appear in the literature.*

Figure 6. *Schematic of block patterns of quilt top shown also in fig. 5.*

WANDERING JEW 1	DIAMOND POINT 2	BEAR'S PAW 3	4	SNOW FLAKE* 5
RED CROSS 6	7	RED BIRD IN THE CORNER* 8	CHICAGO PAVEMENT* 9	FARMER'S DAUGHTER 10
HAPPY HOME 11	KITTY CORNER* 12	13	BLAZING ARROW-POINT* 14	SWING IN THE CENTER 15
16	17	THIS AND THAT* 18	19	JACK IN THE PULPIT 20
SNOW BALL 21	NEW ALBUM 22	23	WANDERING LOVER* 24	THE HOME QUEEN* 25
CUT THE CORNER* 26	IRISH CHAIN 27	PRAIRIE QUEEN 28	29	YOUNG MAN'S FANCY 30

*Patterns with an asterisk do not appear in the literature.

seem that early competition encouraged variation in pattern names. In October, 1899, the Ladies Art Company advertised their catalog in the *Home Needlework Magazine,* "Every quilter should have our book of 400 designs, containing the prettiest, queerest, scarcest, most grotesque patterns from old log cabin to stars and puzzle designs." Whether it was the design or the name that made a pattern grotesque is unclear, but the advertising copywriter may have had in mind *Spider's Den, Bat's Wing,* or *Hearts and Gizzards,* patterns innocuous in appearance if queer in name.

During the late 1920s a new format, the syndicated pattern column, evolved, combining the periodical pattern feature with the mail-order company. Although some periodicals continued to run an exclusive pattern column after 1930, most printed columns syndicated by companies such as Colonial Pattern, Nancy Page, Home Art, and Laura Wheeler. Advertisements in thin disguise, they usually included a sketch of a pattern with its name, a short description of the history of the design (although the accuracy of that history is often questionable) and a few shading or fabric suggestions. The reader who desired a full-size pattern sent a coin to her local paper, which forwarded the request to the syndicate office in New York or Des Moines. Some syndicates sold single patterns; others sold a booklet of several.

Most columns included both original designs and antique patterns, but, as with the earlier reader contributions, true sources are not easy to determine. The columnists, who did not realize they would be serving as folklorists to future generations, casually sold new designs by fabricating a "Colonial" past, and often changed old designs or gave them new names to distinguish their offerings from another company's and to avoid copyright problems (although copyright continued to worry few).

It would seem that mail-order pattern companies and periodicals that sold patterns through the mail were influenced by marketing strategies in choosing and naming their designs. Periodicals dating back to the mid-19th century that did not offer mail-order patterns must have also considered commercial factors, since the inclusion of quilt patterns and their variety was part of subscriber sales appeal. In addition, some writers hoped to sell a style of patchwork they considered more genteel or artistic than the vernacular. These triple commercial motivations—selling full-size patterns, increasing subscriptions, and uplifting American needlecraft—undoubtedly influenced the decisions made about including patterns and their names.

We can imagine that names deemed offensive might never make it into print. Although many political names were printed, few that recorded a losing side or an unpopular idea are in the literature. *Union,* and *Underground Railroad* represent the victorious side in the Civil War but *Rose of Dixie, Confederate Rose* and *Ku Klux* are names that were never paired with a pattern in the commercial literature. In recent years we find no published references to any type of swastika designs although many were printed before the mid-thirties when the Nazis gave new and menacing meaning to the symbol.

Ungenteel or indelicate names may have been screened out. We hear of designs called *Pig Pen, Tobacco Worm,* and *Ham Shank* but we find no records in the commercial literature. Did they speak too much of the backwoods for the middle-class magazine and pattern-buying public?

String quilts have been a common design since the 1880s, but very few of the string quilt designs and their names (if they ever had them) were recorded. Was it the primitiveness of the design that caused their exclusion or the fact that one really didn't need to buy a pattern to make a string quilt?

Although the commercial sources dominate the published information on quilt names, there are other types of popular publications which mention the names of quilt designs. Quilt names occasionally appeared in fiction and memoirs from mid-19th century and later authors. The majority of the names like *Irish Chain* and *Job's Troubles* often appear in the commercial network (with accompanying designs) but occasionally one like *Nine Diamond* from George Washington Harris's 1856 story "Mrs. Yardley's Quilting Party" has gone unrecorded by the periodicals and pattern companies.[5]

In 1915 a new and durable source for pattern names appeared—the quilt book. The first was *Quilts: Their Story and How To Make Them*[6], by Marie D. Webster, who was part of the commercial network as needlework editor at *Ladies Home Journal* where she occasionally wrote about old quilts and pictured her own original designs. In her book Webster recorded many names and included some folklore about a few, such as the story of the *Radical Rose* (a tale told in dialect about the inclusion of black fabric to represent the slaves in a Civil War pattern). In the chapter called "Quilt Names" she grouped them according to subject matter but like the fiction writers she gave no illustrations, to the enduring frustration of pattern collectors who wonder what a *Bounding Betty* design might look like. Most of the names in Webster's lists can be traced to earlier sources, particularly the Ladies Art Company catalog.

Webster has been followed by dozens of other authors who have written about quilts. They have, for the most part, followed her pattern which in turn repeats the earlier dominant mix of sources in the periodicals and mail-order catalogs. Some of the names are derived from folklore (possibly through family traditions, through interviews or through correspondence with periodical readers). Others are original designs with new names, and some of the information is compiled from previous sources.

A few of the early 20th century authors emphasized the traditional pattern information collected from quiltmakers, and their sources seem to be clear. Ruth Finley[7] and Ruby McKim[8] are two whose books are still in print. Finley collected patterns and names in Ohio and the East; McKim near her Independence, Missouri home. They most nearly approximate our contemporary view of a folklorist conducting field work, but both came from the commercial network. McKim owned a mail-order pattern company; Finley was a journalist who had been women's page editor for several newspapers.

At the time Finley and McKim were writing (around 1930), there was little scholarly interest in quilt pattern names. A rare example was an article by Vance Randolph and Isabel Spradley who recorded "Quilt Names in the Ozarks" for the journal *American Speech* (Vol. VIII, No. 1, February 1933). After stating they knew nothing of the literature, they listed scores of quilt names they had heard with no illustrations. Most of the names like *Road to Oklahoma, Radical Rose,* and *Churn Dash* were patterns that had appeared in earlier sources, but others like *Burgoo Trollop, Ham Shank,* and *Sooner's Delight* are an intriguing mystery.

Randolph and Spradley were scholarly folklorists, but dilettantes and members of learned societies provided much folklore in the first decades of interest in American folklore: Randolph and Spradley's attitude reflected the field in the 1930s when the language, myths and songs of ethnic groups and rural people were of more interest than the actual objects they produced. Today's folklorists also study material folk culture (objects like quilts), and thus today we see more scholars interested in patterns as well as their names. The methods of today's folklorists in the field are different from those of earlier generations, so although articles such as "Quilt Names in the Ozarks" were not written for the popular press, they cannot be assumed to be more accurate.

The few early folklore articles seem to have had little influence on the quilt columnists, pattern companies and authors of the mid-20th century. On the other hand, the commercial network undoubtedly influenced the fieldwork of the folklorists. Randolph and Spradley probably had no idea how many Ozark quilters owned a copy of the Ladies Art Company's catalog or Webster's book.

In recent years we begin to see a more careful collecting of quilt pattern names. We also see a more analytical approach to our knowledge about patterns and names. Many historians now view the published information with a good deal of skepticism, treating every published story as myth until corroborated by evidence such as primary written accounts. On the other hand, authors including Suellen Meyer[9] and Cuesta Benberry[10] have suggested that current skepticism might go too far. Since many of the tales can be corroborated, we should view those we cannot with a little more faith.

The dilemma of the quilt historians of the 1980s is that we realize in viewing the past through the mirror of the commercial publications, our information is limited, but we do not know in what ways. We also fear that it is too late to find more accurate information about the names earlier generations called their quilts. Has the printed word totally corrupted oral tradition? But those who do ask quilters and quilt owners the question: "What do you call this quilt pattern?" find enough fresh answers to encourage us that it is not too late.

At a quilt day in Missouri, a family brought a quilt in the pattern commonly known as *New York Beauty.* When asked what they called it, the sisters brought forth a note written by their mother with the date (1849) and three names: *Rocky Mountain, White House,* and *Poke Dallis* [sic] *Texas. Rocky Mountain* is common in early 20th-century periodicals, before the Stearns and Foster Company sold the design as *New York Beauty* in their Mountain Mist catalog and established that name as the nationwide standard. Neither of the other names has been found in the literature. *White House* is a political reference that is also attached to other patterns; the obscure *Poke Dallis Texas* may refer to the election of President James K. Polk and Vice President George Dallas in 1846. (Dallas, Texas was named for the Vice President who supported Texas statehood.)

Other encouraging examples: a *Feathered Star* quilt that looked to be from around 1840-1860 was displayed in Wyandotte County, Kansas with a family story printed on the label saying it was made by slaves and called *Tabacco* [sic] *Worm.* The *Nine Diamond* design mentioned by George Washington Harris in his tale of mid-19th century mountain quilting is still a common name in the southeastern United States, although it is not found in our contemporary pattern indexes, because it was missed by the commercial network.

These anecdotes give us a glimpse into the richness of the folklore that still exists to be collected, as well as evidence of its enduring quality. The fact that for generations a family will call a quilt *Tobacco Worm* despite the "experts" calling it *Feathered Star* encourages one to believe that it is not too late to collect pattern names and clarify our knowledge about them.

There are three directions in which we should direct our research. First, we should be looking for more diversity in names. There is a tendency to standardize names, for instance, using *New York Beauty* as the only name for a design that has many. Second, we should be looking at how names vary from region to region. Tracking such regional differences in a mobile society is difficult, but variations in names have recently been documented with relatively isolated ethnic groups such as Afro-American quiltmakers living in rural communities and the Amish. We do see some mainstream regionalisms (*Sunbonnet Sue* in Kansas is *The*

WHITE HOUSE STEP 1	BOX PATTERN 2	LIVONIA CHOICE* 3	BASKIT M. HETTINGER/ MARCH THE 18 - 1897 4	MOLIE'S CHOIS 5	COFFEN* 6
ALBUM QUILT FEBRUARY THE 22 1897 7	ROLING STAR 8	TREE OF PARADISE 9	STAR FEBRUARY/ 27 1897 10	FRIENDSHIP PATCH 11	NEW DOBLE FOUR/ PATCH 12
SUGAR BOLE* 13	DOUBLE T 14	MORNING STAR* 15	PREMIUM/ STAR 16	TRIANGULAR TRIANGLE 17	STEPS TO THE ALTAR 18
BARISTER BLOCK 19	THE FOXES PUZZLE 20	MISS IDA BASKET* 21	THE FOLING STONE 22	WANDERING/ LOVER* 23	MRS. CLEVELAND/ CHOIS 24
MORNING STAR 25	STEP TO THE ALTER/ F 23 1897 26	OCEAN WAVE 27	DOVE AT THE WINDOW 28	ROAD TO AND/ CALIFORNIA AND BACK* 29	KANSAS TROUBLE 30

*Patterns with an asterisk do not appear in the literature.

***Figure 7.** Quilt by M. Hettinger shown also in Plate 1.*

M. Hettinger inked the names of 29 different blocks on her sampler top in 1897. Many of the 19 published names are found in the Ladies Art Company catalog, in print at that time. However, Wandering Lover *(the name for the small block in a striped frame–4th row down, 2nd from the right) is not in the literature but the same name was given to a similar block in the top of Paulette Peter's top (see fig. 5) indicating the one-time popularity of a name that has now fallen out of use.*

***Figure 8.** Schematic of block patterns of quilt top shown also in fig. 7.*

Little Dutch Girl in Tennessee) but the extent to which women living in Massachusetts or Illinois call patterns by different names has not been documented. And whether they called them by different names fifty or 100 years ago, although harder to prove, may be a question that the current regional quilt surveys will do much to answer. Volunteers in the North Carolina Project alone have asked variations of the question, "What do you call this quilt pattern?" 10,000 times. A comparison of the responses to both the published literature and the findings in other states will give us new insights into regional variations.

Third, we should be looking at changes across time. Some feel that early quiltmakers did not use poetic, specific names and the written records support this theory to an extent. Sarah Robert Lawton's 1832 will lists generic names such as "eagle quilt," "hexagon quilt," and "new patchwork quilt,"[11] but by the 1850s and 60s when Ellen Reed wrote her sister that she was piecing a pattern called *Boneapart's [sic] Retreat*[12] specific names seem common. Ellen's letter breaks the heart of every pattern collector who wishes she had included a sketch of the pattern; today we have no record of a *Bonepart's Retreat.* It may be that we have completely lost a design called *Bonepart's Retreat* but it is more likely that we have only lost that name for a familiar pattern.

A similar story with a happier ending is told in Elizabeth Myer's unpublished 1859 letter in which she writes of her *Flowering Almond* quilt. *Flowering Almond* is not in our indexes either, but Elizabeth left a quilt as well as a letter, and its pattern has been published often as *Coxcombs and Currents, Poinsettia,* or *Oak Leaf and Acorns.* The name *Flowering Almond* also persists in the oral tradition in Tennessee, as found during the state search there.

The anecdotes illustrate where we are going to find the information. We can look to the oral tradition, which has been haphazardly collected, but still seems to have the potential to offer us much information. There is also the written word, the diaries, wills, and letters of earlier generations of women who occasionally mentioned a quilt name. And there are the quilts themselves, those quilts which have names on notes pinned to the back, or even more reliable, actually inscribed on them (fig. 5-8, and plate 11). There are not many, but those I have found tell us surprising things.

We believe we know a good deal about quilt pattern names (I have counted nearly 6000 names for pieced designs published between 1835 and 1980) but a comparison of those names to a single very small body of information—19th-century or early 20th-century quilts with pattern names sewn or inked on them—tells us how little we know. In these six quilts, half of which were samplers, there were 89 patterns with names. Fifty-two of the names had appeared in print for that design, but 37 names are not indexed and thus were the maker's own names, names that never were recorded in the commercial network, or that were published in a rather obscure periodical or catalog, and are now essentially lost. The discrepancy between the names in print and the names on these quilts should make us think more than twice about presuming to know what earlier quiltmakers called their patterns.

[1]Quilt # 10.398, Shelburne Museum, Shelburne, Vermont.

[2]Bresenhan, Karoline Patterson and Nancy O'Bryant Puentes, *Lone Stars: A Legacy of Texas Quilts, 1836-1936.* University of Texas Press, 1986. Quilt, page 40.

[3]Ramsey, Bets and Merikay Waldvogel, *The Quilts of Tennessee: Images of Domestic Life Prior to 1930.* Rutledge Hill Press, 1986. Page 9.

[4]Unpublished letter to the author March 3, 1987.

[5]Harris, George Washington. "Mrs. Yardley's Quilting" in Cleanth Brook, R.W.B. Lewis and Robert Penn Warren's (eds). *American Literature: The Maker and the Making. Volume 1,* St. Martin's Press, 1973.

[6]Webster, Marie D. *Quilts: Their Story and How To Make Them.* Tudor Publishing Co., 1915.

[7]Finley, Ruth. *Old Patchwork Quilts and The Women Who Made Them.* Lippincott, 1929.

[8]McKim, Ruby Short. *101 Patchwork Patterns,* McKim Studios. N.D.

[9]Meyer, Suellen. "Pine Tree Quilts", *The Quilt Digest 4,* Quilt Digest Press, 1986.

[10]Benberry, Cuesta. "A Quilt for Queen Victoria", *Quilters' Newsletter Magazine.* # 189, February, 1987, pp 24-25.

[11]Berry, Michael W. "Documenting the 19th Century Quilt", *American Craft,* Feb/Mar 1985, pp 23-27.

[12]Lipsett, Linda, "A Piece of Ellen's Dress", *Quilt Digest 2,* Quilt Digest Press, 1984.

Barbara Brackman is a quilt historian, a quilt teacher and a quilter. She has been writing regularly about the history of American quilts and about design in contemporary quilts for popular magazines since 1977. She is a contributing editor of Quilters Newsletter Magazine *where her articles on traditional patterns, dating old quilts, and contemporary design are frequent features. She has a chapter "Out of Control in* Quilt Digest 3 *which reflects her particular interest in pattern names and bizarre quilts. Along with Marie Shirer, Barbara wrote* Creature Comforts: A Quilter's Animal Alphabet Book *(1986) and she has written and published* An Encyclopedia of Pieced Quilt Patterns, *eight volumes used as a standard index of patterns on such state quilt documentation projects as Kentucky's, Tennessee's and North Carolina's. She has curated a number of quilt shows featuring antique and contemporary quilts. With Chris Wolf Edmonds she co-edited* Influences: Traditional and Contemporary Quilts, *a catalog of an exhibit at the Spencer Museum of Art at the Universtiy of Kansas, and her* American Patchwork at the Spencer Museum *is just published. She is co-organizer with Laurie Metzinger of the infamous "The Sun Sets on Sunbonnet Sue" and her own quilts reflect her sense of humor. Barbara is on the Board of Directors of the American Quilt Study Group, and Kansas Quilt Project, and was secretary of the Quilt Conservancy. She has taught quiltmaking and design in adult education centers since 1976 and has a Master Degree from the University of Kansas. Barbara has lectured and taught workshops at many national meetings and was featured in the PBS-TV series* Quilting II.

New Thoughts On Care and Conservation

Virginia Gunn

Quilts, like people, age. Aging cannot always be measured in chronological years. If exposed to increased stress, quilts, like people, age faster. The initial stages of aging are sometimes invisible, but eventually we recognize alterations in hand and appearance that we describe as stiffness, dryness, brittleness, yellowness, or fading. We say the textile is weak or fragile. Scientists would say the textile has suffered changes in mechanical properties of strength, elongation and elasticity due to fatigue, tensile distortion, and abrasion from handling and cleaning. They would note changes in chemical properties like molecular weight, solubility, oxidation, and crystallinity due to exposure to heat, light or radiation, chemical reagents and enzymes. Moisture, dirt, dust, insects, and bacteria also cause deterioration.

The various aspects of quilt conservation and care call for a wide variety of skills. No one can be an expert in every aspect of the field: scientific, artistic, historical, technological, and sociological. "Curatorial experience" or observation of similar situations informed most conservation decisions in the past. Today, scientific research is helping conservators understand what they are up against, even if it cannot provide magic solutions to all problems. Applied research on the conservation of irreplaceable antique textiles is still inadequate and underfunded. The useful research being done is usually reported at professional conferences or published in technical journals where it is not widely or rapidly available. Industry is understandably more concerned with funding research on new fibers used for commercial applications. We must remember we are still in the pioneering days of quilt and textile conservation. While research and observations have raised as many questions as they have answered, they have helped us reassess some of our old glibly rationalized rules and suggestions.

Trying to select a sampling of the research and writing that has been helpful to my current thinking on the conservation and care of quilts reminded me of the story of the family "expert," who soon after finishing graduate school published a book for parents entitled "Rules for Raising Children." The book proved to be quite popular and the author updated a second edition at the end of five years. In the interim, he and his wife had several children and he decided to retitle his work "Suggestions for Raising Children." This volume also enjoyed success calling for a new edition in five years. Much more experienced with family problems and complexities, the author entitled this third edition, "Hints for Raising Children." When the publisher next approached him about revising and updating his work, his own children were in their teenage years and he decided to let his work go out of print.

Exhibiting Quilts

Starting with a success story, I believe that the quality of quilt exhibits has increased aesthetically, educationally, and from a conservation point of view. While decorating magazines unfortunately continue to feature quilts displayed in precarious manners, formal showings have begun to pay attention to techniques that are conservationally sound as well as visually pleasing. The "American Doll Quilts 1840-1940" show held in the Seibu Department store in Tokyo, Japan from December 20-28, 1985 is an example of a well conceived exhibition with some worthwhile ideas to study. Roderick Kiracofe of San Francisco designed and organized this show. He arranged display racks which allow viewers to walk completely around quilts, satisfying the urge to see both sides without touching. The plexiglas shields around the center displays let viewers press closely to investigate small details without damaging the quilts. The railings and low platforms against the wall unobtrusively but firmly keep quilts beyond reach in a pleasing manner—a big improvement over the ropes that move and impede vision at the same time. The show included dolls, accessories and photographs that helped one interpret these small quilts' role in the lives of children. The use of lighting and the length of the show also reflected concern for quilt conservation.

Textile fibers are remarkably strong. They do not break easily. They have visco-elastic properties. They can be stretched to a point and recover. However, if the force is great enough, textile fibers will elongate to the breaking point. Old or weakened fibers show the effects of tensile stress more quickly than new fibers. Research by A. J. de Graaf of Holland and Bresee, Chandrashekar and Jones at Kansas State University helps us begin to understand the complexities of creep, or change in fiber length. Their studies show how fibers under pressure elongate or creep, causing an invisible distortion of bond angles and bond length. If the force is not too great, the fibers will not stretch past their yield point and they will recover or regain their original length when the stress is removed. However, if the force is too great, the fiber will stretch past its yield point and the chain segments that make up each fiber will slip or reorient their position, leaving permanent stretching or deformation even when the force is removed. The higher the load has been, the greater is the permanent distortion. Perhaps you have noticed that a textile embroidery tightly stretched over a backing in a frame often noticeably relaxes in the frame after hanging on the wall for a period of time. The fibers of the fabric have actually stretched to reduce stress.

When a heavy quilt hangs for a prolonged period, its fibers can stretch under the force of the quilt's own weight. Distributing the weight evenly helps alleviate stress problems, but the top of the quilt is still under more force than the lower part. If fibers stretch past their yield point, irreversible structural changes take place in the arrangement of chain-molecules of the fibers. The same phenomenon takes place when quilts are folded. Sharp folds actually provide very high enforced elongations of some fibers and can eventually cause permanent distortion or even breaking of these fibers which are under stress.

Fading of Natural Dyes

The damaging effects of light must also be considered when quilts or textiles are on display for any length of time. Many believe that ultraviolet filters remove the need to worry about light. In his research, Michael Bogle framed Pre-Columbian Peruvian textiles in mountings which incorporated thin-film ultraviolet light barriers between layers of matting. He then exposed the samples to window light for 195 days. Results demonstrated that UV-filtering materials offer only degrees of protection against color change, not total protection.

Patricia Crews at the University of Nebraska—Lincoln studies the effectiveness of ultraviolet absorbers on reducing fading of natural dyes. In recent research Crews tested the effectiveness of clear or amber tinted ultraviolet filtering sleeves recommended for use on fluorescent lamps in exhibition and storage areas. The amber tinted sleeves distort color but filter out some visible regions of the light spectrum as well as ultraviolet rays. She used wool fabrics dyed according to 19th century procedures, selecting six red, yellow, and blue natural dyes most commonly used in European and American textiles—cochineal, madder, fustic, turmeric, weld, and indigo. Crews' study showed that natural dyes were not as well protected from fading as the synthetic dyes on which most previous studies have been done. In addition, some of the natural dyes faded as much behind clear sleeves as they did without any sleeves at all. The amber sleeves offered better protection, but none prevented fading altogether. Installing clear plexiglas filters on all windows does not remove the danger of light damage to historic quilts.

A. R. de Torres, N. B. Fair, and J. J. Howard have explored a method to analyze the quantitative changes in lightness, chroma, and hue of natural dyes used on wool and silk fabrics. Their experiments with indigo, logwood, cochineal, madder, fustic and turmeric show that dyes fade in different manners. Some lighten and dull. Some darken and dull. Some darken before getting progressively lighter. They are attempting to establish the pattern of fading for particular dyes. This could be used to ascertain the stage of the fading process for dyed historic textiles and would also help establish the probable original color.

Conservation of Cotton Fabrics

Fading is one visible symptom of chemical aging or deterioration. The yellowing of white cotton fabrics is another visual sign of aging. Chemical aging not only makes visible changes but also makes or breaks covalent bonds and is largely irreversible. Cellulose decomposition by oxidation, which we recognize in visual forms such as yellowing, is a highly complex chemical process in which cellulose breaks down to form unstable peroxide radicals upon exposure to oxygen. A reliable test to determine how far an individual textile has aged or deteriorated in storage, display, or during treatment would be helpful in assessing the risk of further treatment as well as the effectiveness of conservation procedures such as deacidification or the use of antioxidants.

Jeanette Cardamone and Peter Brown at Ohio State University have worked on a method to monitor degradation in cotton cloth by comparing the yarn tensile or tearing strength of a historic sample to points on a half-life decay curve that starts at the new point and ends with deteriorated fabric. The concept of half life assumes textiles decay steadily until they deteriorate if acted upon by a normal environment. Textiles complete the curve faster if exposed to above normal chemical and mechanical stresses. As they decay their strength decreases. Thus a test of yarn strength could indicate how deteriorated they were already. This reported method uses more yarns per test than many conservators find acceptable, but it is a worthwhile attempt to determine degradation of specific cotton textiles.

Wet washing can clean and improve the appearance of historic cotton textiles but it is not a reversible process and does involve some risk. Manfred Wentz at the University of Wisconsin compared washing and drycleaning and noted more changes in textile properties with washing. Hersh, Hutchins, Kerr, and Tucker at North Carolina State University have analyzed the soluble components of degraded cellulose. Wet washing removes degraded cellulose as well as dirt. When the wash water looks yellow or brown it is likely to be soluble degraded cellulose rather than dirt. If the textile is sufficiently oxidized or degraded, swelling of fibers in washing may cause more damage and generate more extractable material. Extraction of degraded cellulose causes weight loss and may leave a higher crystalline fraction in the remaining fabric. The fabric may look better, but be weaker. Many questions surrounding wet washing remain unanswered at this time. If the individual quilt really needs to be cleaned, wet washing should be cautiously and carefully done following the best procedures known.

Silk Fracturing

Silk fabric deterioration is also a complex subject. Silk is very sensitive to light and heat. It will eventually deteriorate even in dark storage. Deterioration is faster with the use of particular dyes or when silks have been weighted with metallic salts, a very common practice in the late 19th and early 20th centuries. Research on historic silks is difficult for each fabric has been subjected to different chemical and physical stresses.

Randall Bresee and Gail Goodyear analysed fractured fiber ends from historic silk textiles and modern silk fabrics artificially aged by exposure to heat or light. They compared photographed silk fiber fractures to the ten types classified by Hearle, Lomas, and Clark and identified an additional type of silk fracture. Bresee and Goodyear's study demonstrated that artificially aged fabrics do not react in the same manner as naturally aged fabrics. Short term stresses of large magnitude seemed less damaging than large numbers of mild stresses over a fairly long period of time. The artificially aged modern silks showed fewer types of breaks, usually the kind attributed to surface flaws. The naturally aged older silks displayed a greater diversity of fracture types including those indicating a loss of interfibrillar cohesion. Seeing photographs of silk fractures helps us understand why there is no cure for shattered silk and why it must be treated gingerly even if protected by a net overlay.

The scanning electron microscope has become a valuable tool for helping diagnose causes of fabric or fiber wear. It allows researchers to see structural details of fibers in great magnification. Developed in the 1950s, it became available commercially in the 1960s. A very small sample (.5x.5cm) of the fabric to be scanned is coated with gold under vacuum. After being placed in the microscope, the sample is bombarded with a beam of electrons, under controlled voltage. As the sample is scanned, the image is viewed on a Cathode Ray Tube screen and can be photographed for later study. Researchers at the University of California—Davis have used the scanning electron microcope to study fiber damage caused by tensile, twist, and flex stresses that would appear after wear or use in a variety of natural and synthetic fabrics. While most quilt lovers will never use a scanning electron microscope, the study of published micrographs can aid their understanding of the conservation process.

Chemical Stains

In today's world, we must be increasingly concerned about chemical stains, by-products of our modern industrial society. More than fifty common household products contain chemical substances which can permanently stain, spot, or discolor textiles used or on display in a home. For example, acne medications and age creams contain benzoyl peroxide, a strong oxidizing or bleaching agent difficult to wash off and easy to transfer to a quilt. It is not too hard to imagine how small drops of disinfectants, plant foods and insecticides, swimming pool chemicals, furniture cleaners and polishes, or cosmetics could carelessly or accidentally come into contact with quilts.

Chemical stains are more insidious than ordinary stains, for as the American Textile Manufacturers Institute points out "the time between contact and appearance of the stain could be days or months." By the time the spot is noticed, no one remembers who spilled what and they wonder how someone could have let the spill go unattended. The chemicals actually lie unnoticed and dormant until the right changes in humidity, temperature, or light occur to activate the chemical reaction. Then a spot or stain seems to appear almost spontaneously. Once the chemical reaction takes place, it cannot be corrected. Since dyes rarely resist chemical attack, the only solution is prevention. Be very careful in the use of household chemicals.

Insect Control

Wool quilts or quilts with wool batting have always required special efforts to prevent moth or insect damage. It is interesting that Swiss chemist Dr. Paul Muller discovered the insecticidal properties of DDT while looking for a new mothproofing agent for fabrics in 1939. The side effects of DDT made it too dangerous for general use. Today other mothproofing products are proving hazardous to health also. The chemical products formerly recommended for dealing with moth and carpet beetle problems now appear to be toxic to humans and animals. The risk of using these products is probably not worth taking. Alternative methods of killing moths and carpet beetles, like microwaving and freezing, still need further research. Even drycleaning is not without risk and cannot be guaranteed to eradicate moth problems.

Cleaning is an important key to controlling insect problems. Vacuuming quilts will help get rid of moth eggs before they hatch into hungry larvae. However, in a three-layered quilt or comforter, vacuuming may not pick up all moth eggs and larvae. It is probably safest to isolate wool textiles for a year or two before introducing them into a collection. Check regularly to be sure they remain free of moth and insect infestation. Keeping storage areas very clean also helps prevent the dry-litter conditions these pests love.

George Ordish, an entomologist specializing in the control of crop pests, has written a charming and helpful book entitled *The Living American House*. It explores the 350 year history of a New England house from the time it was built in 1633 until 1980 focusing on the ecology and biology of living forms, both human and insect. This book is particularly useful in helping us understand the complexities of the dry-litter community of insects. The Tineidae family of insects has 130 species in North America including the clothes moth, the webbing cloths moth, and tapestry moths. These insects are scavengers that thrive on oxygen and water from dampish air and digest fibrous proteins like keratin and fibroin found in wool, hair, leather, fur and feathers. Originally making their homes in bird's nests and bat dung, they quickly adapted to man's fur and wool clothing, often dirty and full of sweat, food, and excrement these insects prefer. However, being adaptable in order to survive, moths will eat clean fabric if dirty material is unavailable. If food and moisture conditions are not ideal, they can vary the length of the larval stage and develop more slowly or into a smaller adult that can still reproduce.

The Dermestidae family which includes the carpet beetle or woolly bear also belongs to the dry-litter community. Carpet beetle larvae feed on high protein fibers. They bore a passage to the surface when ready to pupate and can penetrate inedible substances like wood and lead covered electric cable. Originally more active in the summer and fall, dry-litter insects now reproduce rapidly year around with centrally heated environments. Regardless of precautions, a home can be easily reinfected if birds are near and animals and/or children run in and out. Bringing antique stuffed furniture and quilts into a house can also introduce the insects as well as provide their favorite dry-litter habitats. The best prevention seems to be cleanliness. One is always reminded of the biblical admonition "do not lay up for yourselves treasures on earth, where moth and rust consume. . . . (Matthew 6:19)."

Documentation and Records

However, our natural inclination is to value and keep objects that have meaning for us. Our interest in material culture often leads us to explore other historical avenues. The value we place on quilts has led us to preserve not only the items themselves, but the family stories surrounding them. All across the country dedicated volunteers in state quilt projects are collecting pages of information on quilts and quiltmakers, building up a valuable research base that is beginning to allow us to recognize regional variations of design themes and to sort out the typical from the unusual in terms of design. Historical research on quilts and quiltmakers is becoming more widely shared through publications like *The Quilter's Journal*, the American Quilt Study Group's *Uncoverings*, and the symposium papers of the Oral Traditions Project.

Sometimes new thoughts include reiterating the continued value of old ideas. I am in charge of a costume and textile collection where each item is properly labeled with a number keyed to match all filed records about it, including student research projects and conservation reports. In spite of the usefulness of these archival records, I find simple messages about a textile's background basted unobtrusively onto the textile itself very helpful. I have begun to add conservation summaries also. They conveniently jog one's memory and actually lead back to the more extensive records on file. In 1843, Miss Leslie recommended:

> When a picture is finished it would always be well for the artist to inscribe on the back of the canvas the subject of the painting, the date of its completion, his own name and that of the person or place for which it was painted. In short a concise history of the picture....It is a practice well worthy of adoption.

In spite of the best intentions, historical artifacts can get separated from the filed records keyed to go with them, or people can fail to check records. The fabric message someone thoughtfully provided will often last longer than paper and provide a wonderful link to a family story.

Individual quilts will not last forever, so it is important to remember that we benefit from visual records of them. Slides, prints, films, and video-cassette recordings all provide valuable records for present and future study. A scrapbook with beautiful photographs of favorite quilts can provide the same shared pleasure as the old family photo album. There are many ways to preserve and enjoy quilts.

Research and observation should continue to